The Steel Drug

The Steel Drug

Cocaine and Crack in Perspective

Second Edition

Patricia G. Erickson

Edward M. Adlaf

Reginald G. Smart

Glenn F. Murray

LEXINGTON BOOKS
An Imprint of Macmillan, Inc.
NEW YORK

Maxwell Macmillan Canada
TORONTO

Maxwell Macmillan International
NEW YORK   OXFORD   SINGAPORE   SYDNEY

Any views expressed in this book are those of the authors, and do not necessarily reflect the views of the Addiction Research Foundation.

Library of Congress Cataloging-in-Publication Data
The steel drug : cocaine and crack in perspective / Patricia G.
Erickson . . . [et al.].—2nd ed.
     p. cm.
   Includes bibliographical references and index.
   ISBN 0-02-909645-6
   1. Cocaine habit. 2. Cocaine habit—Canada—Longitudinal studies.
3. Drug abuse surveys—Canada. I. Erickson. Patricia G.
II. Title: Cocaine and crack in perspective.
HV5810.S84   1994
362.29'8—dc20   94-20173
                                                                        CIP

Copyright © 1994 by Patricia G. Erickson
Copyright © 1987 by Patricia G. Erickson

Lexington Books
An Imprint of Macmillan, Inc.
866 Third Avenue, New York, N. Y. 10022

Maxwell Macmillan Canada, Inc.
1200 Eglinton Avenue East
Suite 200
Don Mills, Ontario M3C 3N1

Macmillan, Inc. is part of the Maxwell Communication Group of Companies.

Printed in the United States of America

printing number
1 2 3 4 5 6 7 8 9 10

To Oriana Josseau Kalant,
a pioneer in the study of stimulant use

"I have tested this effect of coca, which wards off hunger, sleep and fatigue and steels oneself to intellectual effort . . ."

—*Sigmund Freud, "Uber Coca", 1884*

"The middle class users of steel drugs like cocaine and heroin . . . who dismiss ganja as 'soft' enter the ghetto with their devilish concoction . . . for the sake of making a fortune."

—*Jah Bones*
Letter to the Editor
Manchester Guardian Weekly
1985

Contents

Foreword

During the seven years since the first edition of *The Steel Drug*, the cocaine problem continued to evolve. In the United States the issue skyrocketed. This rise of "crack" use in the United States spurred two great expansions of the battle against drugs: the Anti-Drug Abuse Acts of 1986 and 1988 were passed, and the United States Congress created much longer prison sentences and larger fines for crack possession than those established for less threatening forms of cocaine.

The authors trace the powerful influence of the American media upon Canadians' perception of their own cocaine problem. They argue persuasively that the Canadian problem was exaggerated and that the media did a disservice to their control efforts by portraying a dire situation that did not, in fact, exist. Comparisons between cocaine use in Ontario and in the United States suggest that the wave of cocaine use occurred at about the same time in both countries, but in Canada the degree of cocaine use was much less. Cocaine use in Canada appears to be diminishing, and similar claims have been made about American cocaine use.

Why the decline? The first response might naturally be that new severe laws have had a powerful effect in discouraging use. Although we cannot measure the number of nonusers who have been kept from experimentation because of these laws, the authors have in their second study located 100 regular users whose initiation and, in many cases, their cessation of cocaine use was rarely affected by legal constraints. The authors seriously question media depictions of cocaine as inevitably addicting or as curable only through treatment by professionals. The experience of cocaine can lead the user to quit, a vital factor when trying to explain the self-limiting nature of drug use for many experimenters.

The intriguing question raised is, does a particular drug affect all societies similarly? Although this study excluded Canada's worst cases of cocaine misuse in order to concentrate on more typical users, the cocaine problem—taken as a whole—does appear to be substantially less than in the United States. A useful analysis of what is called the "mechanistic" theory of drug addiction—that the same drug will cause the same social problems in any society—leads to the important conclusion that we cannot neatly extrapolate from one nation or culture to another when analyzing the drug problem. In explaining differing reactions to cocaine in the two nations, the authors hypothesize that social welfare and racial conditions in Canada have ameliorated the effect of cocaine.

Could the epidemics of cocaine or other drug use follow their own pattern of rise, culmination, and decline regardless of society's formal attack on interdiction, dealing and possession? In my own work I have been fascinated by the patterns that emerge from studies of drug use over many decades.* This book contributes a kind of study essential to evaluating the internal control measures inherent in a wave of drug use. Because so often the prohibitive laws come after the peak of drug use (the Harrison Act of 1914 in the United States being a classic example), teasing out what decline is due to law and what to perceived risk of harm—what the authors call "user rationality"—is difficult. What this current study demonstrates is that a substantial amount of decline is due to the actual negative effects of the drug on the users or the users' acquaintances, and that decline would occur in any event. This has always been true, but as we become more and more intolerant of drugs and fearful of the effects of experimentation, it is harder to see or to say.

A viable drug policy must take into account that laws have a limit in their effect, and that public compliance and public awareness of drug effects are the only guarantee that a campaign against

---

* D. F. Musto, "Cocaine's History, Especially the American Experience," *Cocaine: Scientific and Social Dimensions*, (Ciba Foundation Symposium 166) Wiley & Sons, Chichester, England, 1992, pp. 7–19. D. F. Musto, "Opium, Cocaine and Marijuana in American History," *Scientific American* 265: 40–47 (July, 1991).

drugs can be sustained and kept from degenerating into mere punishment. The authors of *The Steel Drug* conclude that a policy of "harm reduction" is preferable to present policies. Harm reduction represents a toleration of drug use in the hope that by providing clean equipment, health care and even pure drugs a user can be sustained until the wisdom of cessation occurs. This is an option that would seem unlikely to flourish in a time of growing intolerance toward drugs and drug users. It is a conflict over drug policy that we shall witness with intense interest in the coming decade. To this debate, *The Steel Drug* makes a valuable contribution.

D. F. Musto, M.D.
Yale University

Preface and Acknowledgments, Second Edition

When we submitted the first edition of *The Steel Drug* to our publisher in July 1986, the Canadian police had just reported their first seizure of crack. Now, as we complete this second edition, we are looking back on several years of the Canadian experience with crack use and problems. We have been prompted to continue our study of cocaine use and the emergence of crack, as documented in surveys, treatment statistics, criminal justice statistics, and a new community study of cocaine and crack users.

We have updated and expanded part I while leaving part II, the report of the first community study, virtually untouched. In particular, the explosion of the research literature on cocaine and crack meant that chapter 3, on recent trends in use, was completely rewritten. Part III presents the method and findings of our second study of a new sample of one hundred cocaine and crack users in Toronto who were followed up after one year. Some detailed case studies of a small number of respondents who were interviewed a third time are also included. Part IV reflects our conclusions, as originally presented in 1987 and after several more years of research and cogitation.

Thus, this new edition offers not only an update on the evolving phenomenon of cocaine use but also a current perspective on the crack experience in the context of Canadian society. Canada presents a picture of less serious drug problems than in the United States, yet with many similar aspects and insights to be learned from the comparison. As our societies worldwide continue to grapple with the dilemmas of effective and humane drug policies, we believe that a dispassionate examination of the evidence will aid in the formulation of better harm-reducing strategies for responding to cocaine and crack.

A number of people made an invaluable contribution to the second phase of this project. Valerie Watson, Tim Weber, and Tammy Landau conducted the new wave of interviews, Tim Weber also did most of the follow up interviews, and they also contributed to the analysis of data. Joan Moreau has continued to provide expert overall research assistance and help with the references, and Barbara Shimizu provided reliable secretarial support. Yuet W. Cheung joined the team as a coauthor of chapters 10 and 14. We are especially grateful to the one hundred cocaine users who shared their experiences with us.

This second empirical study was made possible by a grant from the National Health Research & Development Program, Ottawa, Canada. We deeply appreciate the extension of the grant that enabled us to prepare this major publication of the funded study, "A Longitudinal Study of Cocaine Users: The Natural History of Cocaine Use and Its Consequences Among Canadian Adults" (6606-3929-DA). We are also grateful for the ongoing support of the Addiction Research Foundation. The interpretations and conclusions in this book, as well as any errors or omissions, however, are the responsibility of the authors, and not of their affiliated or sponsoring institutions.

Preface and Acknowledgements, First Edition

Our interest in writing a book about cocaine was prompted by its reentry into the cast of popular illicit drugs in North American societies. We were interested in many aspects of cocaine—its history, cultural definitions, legal ramifications, use patterns, and the perceptions of users. Our curiosity led us to pursue these topics by gathering extensive background material on the international aspects of cocaine and developing and completing an in-depth study of users. These efforts culminated in the preparation of this manuscript which we believe is unique in its scope and thought-provoking in its conclusions.

Part I of this book places the current cocaine issue in a social and historical context. The introduction of cocaine into Europe and North America and the roots of the current harsh legislative response are described. Then the image of cocaine in popular culture is highlighted. Finally, an extensive review of the world literature on cocaine documents the recent trends in use patterns.

Part II presents the method and findings of the research study. A project was undertaken in 1983 in which 111 users of cocaine in the community were interviewed. Major areas investigated include the attraction of cocaine, positive and negative reactions to the drug, the circumstances and nature of use, the legal response to cocaine, and users' concerns with punishment. Some detailed case histories are presented to enliven the detailed but sometimes impersonal statistical results. The final chapter presents the conclusions and implications of our research and future research needs.

We would like to thank the many persons who contributed advice and expertise to this final product. Helpful commentary at early stages of formulation was provided by Addiction Research

Foundation (ARF) colleagues Judith Blackwell, Kevin Fehr, Michael Goodstadt, and Eric Single. Elsbeth Tupker facilitated access to clients of the Clinical Institute at ARF for purposes of piloting the questionnaire. Les Samuelson got the "snowball" rolling and conducted many of the interviews. Lecia Hanycz and Jean Mitchell provided us with reliable secretarial support, and Joan Moreau ably prepared and checked the references. Lise Anglin contributed her editorial expertise; Sylvia Lambert graciously and swiftly prepared the index. We owe a special debt of gratitude to the one hundred eleven persons who agreed to contribute their experiences, anonymously, to the research.

We offer to the reader what we believe to be a timely book on the topic of cocaine use. Many facets of this fascinating drug are explored. By providing an overview of the available literature on the social context, history and meaning of cocaine, with an original research study, we endeavor to dispel many myths surrounding this drug and provide a factual basis for assessing its impact on society.

Part I

Background to the Studies

1

A Historical Perspective on Coca, Cocaine, and Crack Cocaine

Cocaine hydrochloride is an odorless, white crystalline powder that is readily water soluble. Classified as a central nervous system (CNS) stimulant, cocaine increases feelings of alertness and energy, inhibits appetite and sleepiness, and produces intense euphoria (Jacobs & Fehr 1987). Its local anesthetic properties, extremely important after their discovery in the 1880s, have been duplicated by modern synthetic anesthetics. However, cocaine derivatives are still used as topical anesthetics as sprays or creams.

In the 1970s and early 1980s, the more usual form of ingestion, averaging about 25 mg per dose, was by snorting—the sniffing of finely chopped cocaine crystals into first one nostril and then the other. This powder form can also be dissolved in water and injected or drunk. More recently a smokeable or "freebase" form of cocaine has been developed, prepared by mixing powder cocaine with an alkali and boiling it with a solvent such as ether. When dried, this form can be smoked with regular tobacco or marijuana or in special pipes.

Crack cocaine is produced by mixing powder cocaine with baking soda or sodium bicarbonate and water. The mixture is boiled until all the water has evaporated, leaving a waxy substance containing cocaine and the alkali that usually appears as crystalline pebbles or small rocks. Crack is smoked in special pipes, improvised devices such as soft drink cans, or added to cigarettes. The name *crack* is of unknown origin. However, some claim that it comes from the cracking sound made when the rocks are smashed (Mofenson, Copeland & Carraccio 1987). Others suggest that it refers to the cracking of glass pipes when smoked (Kirsch 1986).

Crack cocaine when smoked produces a respirable aerosol of cocaine base (Snyder et al. 1988). Cocaine base smoke, found to have 93.5 percent cocaine particles with the remainder as cocaine vapor, is a very potent form of cocaine with a high bioavailability compared to cocaine sniffing. When cocaine products are taken intranasally, peak blood levels are obtained in 15 to 60 minutes, and the maximum heart rate increases are seen in 15 to 25 minutes (Javaid et al. 1978). When taken intravenously or by smoking, effects are apparent within seconds and wear off in 15–30 minutes.

After the appearance of crack in the mid-1980s, the debate as to the addictive liability of cocaine intensified. Some users and commentators claimed that crack was immediately addictive after only one session. Others were less certain; one television reporter claimed to have smoked crack without any addiction or craving resulting. Still other users also reported that crack was not always addictive. An early study by Inciardi (1988) showed that only 54.7 percent of crack users were taking it daily. Nevertheless, smoking crack cocaine may be more likely than snorting to lead to compulsive use patterns, but this has not been clearly established. It is, however, the route of administration and not any difference in psychoactive ingredients that is crucial in distinguishing powder cocaine from crack.

The question of cocaine tolerance—that is, the need for more and more of a drug in order to achieve the desired effect—is complex and has not been fully resolved. It does appear, however, that the user becomes progressively less sensitive to the mood-enhancing properties of the drug over the course of several rapid administrations. Expert opinion also continues to be at odds as to whether physical dependence, indicated by a pronounced set of withdrawal symptoms, occurs (Fischman & Foltin 1992). After prolonged heavy use, termination of cocaine use is usually followed by a "crash" characterized by depression, exhaustion, restless sleep patterns, and intense hunger on awakening. It is not disputed that intense craving for cocaine can develop in some individuals to the point of obsession with the drug and exclusion of all other interests.[1]

Origins of Coca Use

The chewing of coca leaves by the native peoples of South America dates back at least to 2500 B.C.[2] Early explorers of this continent, such as Vespucci and de Leon, described the practice of chewing coca leaves and the Indians' reasons for doing it: to stave off hunger and thirst and provide vigor and strength. The coca bush grew prolifically on the high slopes of the Andes Mountains, in the western part of the continent. The "divine leaves" were a focal point of the religion and social organization of the Inca civilization. The Spanish conquerors at first forbade coca use, then rescinded their ban when coca's work-prolonging powers in their native laborers were realized. Thus, the practice of coca leaf chewing by the indigenous peoples was sustained after the discovery of the New World by Europeans.

Despite early accounts of coca's medicinal uses by natives (as a topical application for sores and broken bones) and its invigorating properties, coca attracted little attention in Europe for the next 300 years. Perhaps a deterioration of the leaves in transit, an association of the practice with natives, and the early stage of modern medicine and pharmacology combined to produce this indifference. Botanists did grapple with classification of coca specimens, labeling the plant *Erythroxylon coca* in 1786. Eventually enough accounts of coca's virtues surfaced for the medical and scientific community to take notice; an example is provided by an Italian physician in 1859: "Borne on the wings of two coca leaves, I flew about in the spaces of 77,438 worlds, each one more splendid than the others. . . . I prefer a life of ten years with coca to one of a hundred thousand without it."[3] With the isolation of the cocaine alkaloid in 1860 by Albert Niemann, experimentation with a readily obtainable, pure form of the drug could begin.

Discovery by Europeans and North Americans: Medical Applications and a Growing Popularity, 1880–1911

Cocaine Use at the Turn of the Century

"[It] is now getting more into vogue in Canada."
"[It's] the 'new craze'."
"The use of cocaine is becoming so widespread."

"[I]t has grown to alarming proportions."

"[T]he profits made . . . are stupendous."

"This curse of cocaine has existed for a short time [but] it goes on spreading so fearfully that it is time for society to take a marked notice."[4]

Remarks like these can be found in contemporary expositions of cocaine, yet these particular statements refer to a problem that plagued Canada between 1900 and 1910. They have been culled from the popular press, House of Commons Debates, and health profession journals in Canada between 1906 and 1910. At that time, concern about the use of cocaine was voiced by politicians, church leaders, health professionals, criminal justice system personnel, and various moral crusaders. Cocaine was perceived as a problem that was "rapidly developing into a danger spot of threatening proportions" (*Canadian Pharmaceutical Journal* [*CPJ*] 1908c:404).

Although cocaine use was considered a social problem in the early 1900s, contemporary writers tend to describe it as a new phenomenon. One reason, no doubt, is that the 1960s and 1970s are viewed as the time when drug use first became a widespread social problem, and *marijuana, hashish, LSD, MDA, speed, PCP* ("angel dust"), and *cocaine* entered the everyday vocabulary of a drug-conscious era. Prior to this, illicit nonmedical drug use was linked with particular, usually small, segments of the population—typically Chinese opium smokers and marijuana-using bohemians. Yet the accuracy of this perspective on drug use is called into question by historical records.

At the turn of the century, drug users could be found in most segments of the population because of the widespread and legal availability of patent medicines, beverages, and powders containing opiates and cocaine. The problem of the "cocaine habit" was raised in Canada's House of Commons on November 25, 1910, when a member of Parliament, citing a newspaper report, claimed that there were "thousands of men and women, many of them in respectable families, who are victims of the [cocaine] habit" (House of Commons Debates [HCD] 1910–11a:261). W. L. Mackenzie King, the Minister of Labour, subsequently described the problem of cocaine to the House, quoting a letter from Montreal's chief of police indicating that the police had made over 125 arrests for selling or using the drug in the previous six months. King also referred to an article, "The Cocaine Habit Has a Grip on Ottawa," that reported on the local cocaine traffic. Furthermore, a probation officer was quoted as having met "as many as fifty or sixty little girls and boys within the same day, in the city of Montreal, all of whom had acquired the cocaine habit to some degree" (HCD 1910–11b:2524, 2526).

King noted as well correspondence from various church officials who indicated their concern about cocaine. One, a minister, wrote that "the use of cocaine is becoming so widespread, among young people as well as seniors, among foreign races . . . as well as Canadians, and the effects are so disastrous, that it is becoming a grave social peril." Another church spokesman wrote that "the use of drugs is not confined to so-called poorer classes. It obtains amongst the people who should and do know better" (HCD 1910–11b: 2527–28). Apparently cocaine use was widespread.

A parallel exists between the nature and degree of the problem that appeared nearly a century ago and the one society confronts today. A recent account indicated that "cocaine is now second . . . in popularity [to cannabis] as far as illicit drugs are concerned" (*The Journal* 1982a:1); a 1906 report suggested that "with the speed at which the cocaine habit seems to be growing, [it] stands a good chance of soon becoming a close second [to morphine]" (*Sessional Papers* 1906:16). In the earlier period, cocaine's euphoric effects were first praised by a few and ultimately echoed and enjoyed by many. Within a few years, however, reports of cocaine's adverse consequences began to appear. A recent article closed with the following statement: "Today the confessions of addicted celebrities and athletes and the advent of cocaine hot lines and detoxification centers are signs that the cocaine user is once again wising up—for the second time in a century of abuse" (*Life* 1984:68).

Medical Discovery and Experimentation

Albert Niemann named cocaine when he isolated the alkaloid in 1860. His discovery was followed by various studies on cocaine's physiological and psychoactive effects (Ashley 1975). About a century ago, researchers became intrigued with cocaine's medicinal potential and began to experiment with it. Sigmund Freud played a significant role in spreading the findings of these early studies. In 1884, he examined the effects of cocaine, using himself and several other physicians as subjects. In "Uber Coca" he reported cocaine's exhilarating and euphoric effects and recommended it for medicinal use to alleviate various ailments, including depression, fatigue, and opiate addiction (1884). Freud referred to his paper as a "song of praise to this magical substance" (Musto 1968:128).

Within a few years of the first published reports, medicinal and recreational use of cocaine became popular practices. Freud observed that "at present there seems to be some promise of widespread recognition and use of coca preparations in North America" (Freud 1884:63). Indeed, one account in an 1880 American medical journal suggested that "since the publication in these columns of Professor Palmer's article on coca as an antidote to opium eating, the demand all over the country for the coca has been so great as to put the drughouses to their best efforts to fill orders" (*Therapeutic Gazette* 1880:215).

Therapeutic Gazette 2(2):79, 1881

COCA IN THE OPIUM–HABIT

Several months ago I noticed an article by Dr. Palmer recommending "coca as a possible cure for the opium-habit": and as I had under treatment at that time a case which had resisted ordinary treatment, I determined to give the coca a trial. I did so, with the following results:

R.T.P. had for several years taken large doses of laudanum several times a day for what he called "disease of the stomach." Was always complaining, and was low-spirited, sallow, poor, and a dejected, lifeless-looking creature generally. He often took as much as a pint of the tincture of opium per week, and suffered intensely when without it even for a short time. As he said, his disease returned as soon as the laudanum gave out. I told him I at last had found a cure for his "stomach disease," and ordered the coca to be taken in drachm doses as often as he felt the disease returning, or whenever he felt that he could no longer do without the laudanum. He used it frequently for two or three days, but gradually lessened the dose and frequency until cured. Since his cure he has rapidly improved in health and strength, both mental and physical; in short, he is a new man.

Dr. P. R. Henderson, in Louisville Medical News

The publicity given to cocaine's therapeutic effects, and particularly the demonstration of its value as a local anesthetic by Freud's friend and colleague, Carl Koller, made the drug known to

> virtually every doctor in Europe and America and to most of the educated public as well. Newspapers and magazines heralded the new wonder drug, and medical journals carried accounts which came close to advocating an unlimited intake of cocaine. . . . In America, the former surgeon general of the Army, William Hammond, proudly informed the public he used cocaine as a tonic and stimulant on a daily basis, found it constantly refreshing, and never suffered any subsequent depression. In England, the 78-year-old president of the British Medical Association, Sir Robert Christison, wrote an enthusiastic report describing how under the stimulus of cocaine he had been able to take fifteen-mile hikes and climb mountains with 'youthful vigor' and no feelings of fatigue. (Ashley 1975:50–51)

Interest in cocaine quickly spread beyond the realm of science and medicine to popular literature.

The Golden Age of Patent Medicines

In the late nineteenth century, self-medication was the norm rather than the exception throughout the vast and largely rural continent of North America. For the patent medicine industry, the publicity given to cocaine was "better than money could buy" (Ashley 1975:55). A market for cocaine had been created, and the patent medicine industry wasted no time in taking advantage of this opportunity. Various remedies containing cocaine were soon available not only at the drugstore but through the mail and door-to-door. Assorted tonics and powders containing cocaine were sold as cures for a range of ailments, including headaches, colds, toothaches, asthma, piles, impotence, and diseases of the blood.

Cocaine was sold as a soft drink and as an alcoholic beverage as well, both promoted for their medicinal value as cures for almost every ailment, from the common cold to hysteria. Coca-Cola, which came on the market in 1886 and contained cocaine, was originally promoted for its utility as a "brain tonic and cure for all nervous affections" (Phillips & Wynne 1980:53). A *Life* magazine article concludes that "America's favorite soft drink once was, in-

Canadian Pharmaceutical Journal 7:367, 1874

PATENT MEDICINES

The trade in patent medicines may be regarded as one of the institutions of America. Of all places on this wide earth it seems best fitted for the growth and development of this species of imposition. Transatlantic countries may boast of names standing high in the annals of empiric fame, but they cannot show the mountains of wealth, the mighty influence, or the millions of subjects over which the princely potentates of quackery preside on this side of the water. To the United States must be awarded the palm; there the system flourishes in unrestrained luxuriance. Nor is Canada far behind, at least as far as devotion to the cause is concerned. The field of operation is, necessarily, much smaller, but the desire to quack and be quacked is not less ardent; and though we have, so far, been in great part dependent on the Americans for the wherewithal to foster this spirit, we are fast merging into a position of independence, and no doubt will shortly be able to claim a fair second place.

Editorial

deed, 'the real thing'" (*Life* 1984:60). A number of similar beverages, including Care-Cola, Dope Cola, Kola Ade, and Wiseola, were soon available. Apparently those who abstained from alcohol served as a ready market for these so-called soft drinks. In fact, Coca-Cola was advertised as a temperance drink. Another popular drink was coca wine. Vin Mariani, a Bordeaux containing concentrations of two ounces of coca leaves per bottle, was a popular drink touted by some of the more powerful and successful people of the era, among them, Ulysses S. Grant, Pope Leo XIII, and Sarah Bernhardt. It was even advocated as a "substitute for the cerebral excitement of pipes and cigars" (Siegel 1982a:284).

Coca cigarettes and cigars were promoted for medicinal use too. Parke, Davis and Co., for example, reprinted a physician's findings regarding coca smoking in a brochure that promoted "coca cheroots, coca cigarettes, and a cocaine inhalant" (Siegel 1982a:284). The physician, Dr. F. E. Stewart, had studied the effects of coca smoking on patients and on himself, finding that it relieved fatigue and imparted "increased vigor to the muscular system as well as to the intellect, with an indescribable feeling of satisfaction" (Parke, Davis and Co. 1885:134). He proposed that coca smoking should be applied for the therapeutic "treatment of the opium habit, as a substitute for tobacco and for the treatment of hay fever" (Siegel 1982a:284).

Catarrh powders for sinus trouble introduced the practice of snorting. One popular remedy, Dr. Nathan Tucker's Asthma Specific, was widely used to provide relief from hayfever and asthma. Each package contained as much as half a gram of pure cocaine. Apparently, there were other remedies that contained even higher amounts (Phillips & Wynne 1980:49). The use of catarrh snuffs was a major cause of the rapid growth of cocaine addiction at that time. Statistics gathered in 1903 showed that "no less than nine-tenths of the cocaine habitués have been led there by the use of proprietaries or prescriptions containing" cocaine, moreover, a 1906 report indicated that "a large number of patent medicines contain morphine or cocaine" and "these are the two drugs which form most drug habitués" (*Sessional Papers* 1906:16,17).

Concern with Effects of Cocaine: From Self-Medication to Self-Abuse

Although cocaine was gaining recognition and praise in the late nineteenth century, reports of its misuse and dependence-producing capacity also began to appear (Anglin 1985).

This adverse publicity concerning cocaine led many physicians who had once lauded the drug to withdraw their support of it, yet the number of doctors in the anticocaine ranks remained small, and the dangers of cocaine were "not generally accepted for many years" (Musto 1968:130). Ashley (1975) has argued that it was the patent medicine boom that drew physicians into the anticocaine ranks because they perceived the public's self-medication with proprietary and patent medicines as a threat to their profession. A perusal of Canadian medical journals from this period in history supports Ashley's conclusion. The medical profession seemed to be more concerned about curtailing the trade in patent medicines than with the potential dangers of the drugs contained in these preparations. Editorials denigrated patent medicines as "nostrums" and "quack medicines" and questioned the utility of such products in relieving "symptoms or supposed symptoms." Instead, these preparations were said to "create pleasant feelings. This impels the user,

---

Annual Report of the Ontario Provincial Board of Health 23 (36):113, 1904

PATENT MEDICINES AND DRUG FOODS

There seem to be several perceptible reasons for the widespread use of proprietary medicines. In the first place many people from careless-ness in diet, overwork, or worry allow themselves to run down, and, while not quite sick enough to consult a physician are attracted by the specious advertisement of some popular cure-all. The symptoms de-tailed appear wonderfully like those of the interested reader and he forthwith resolves to try a bottle or two; it might fix him up, he argues, but if not no harm would result. If he is a persevering subject he sticks to it and in the words of the advertisement gives it a "good fair trial" until either disgusted or cured. If his perseverance is rewarded, and he luckily strikes something which he thinks has cured him, or as is more likely, he has become better in spite of it, then he considers himself a clever fellow, and in his delight publishes his cure far and wide. Thus we hear of the successes only; the failures are buried in obscurity.

Then there is the large number of people who are fond of drug-ging themselves as a sort of amusement, cranks on the latest patent medicine. These people always have something new wrong with them, and not only do they take the nostrums themselves but are extremely fond of recommending them to others.

There is a third class which takes these medicines because they like them, for their stimulating, sedative or other effects. Thus in temper-ance states, in the northwest, and among Indians certain remedies are quite popular. For instance, Peruna is said to be a popular society bev-erage. Many of the bitters, tonics, malt extracts and peptone prepa-rations are taken for their alcohol content. I have been informed that old people who take Paine's Celery Compound do not seem to be able to stop using it. At New Liskeard in Northern Ontario one individual takes several dozen Radway's Pain Killer every month. At Niagara Falls the negro population use a great deal of Dr. Agnew's Catarrh Cure for the effect of the cocaine present.

Geo. G. Nasmith, M.A., Ph.D., Chemist to Provincial Board of Health

---

who is unconscious of what he is taking, to continue their use until a habit is acquired, which eventually leads to the ruin of his mental, moral and physical nature" (*Montreal Medical Journal* 1906:274). Another author wrote, "A human being appears to differ from the lower animals among other things in being an experimenter, and from babyhood on through life his greatest lessons are the sad lessons of experiment and thus of experience. Nowhere perhaps is

Journal of the American Medical Association, 28:1092, 1897

CHRONIC COCAINISM FROM CATARRH SNUFF

A woman was received recently at a *Montreal hospital* with the trembling hands, staggering gait, insomnia, dyspepsia, loss of appetite, etc., of alcoholism, also visual hallucinations, dilatation of the pupils, mental dullness and pronounced moral depravity. She had always been a person of quiet, modest tastes, and her husband asserted that she never took liquor. Asked whether she took any drug, he went home to investigate and returned with a bottle of Agnew's catarrh powder, a patent remedy which she had been using as a snuff for four or five months, consuming three bottles a week. The bottle held 80 grains and contained 1.75 per cent cocain [sic]. The therapeutic dose is 1/4 to 1 grain. [1 grain = .065 grams]

Université Medical du Canada, April

this tendency so well exhibited as in the attempts of people to experiment upon themselves with drugs" (Nasmith 1904:113).

The developing controversy over the trade in patent medicines included another group of health professionals, the pharmacists. In nineteenth-century Ontario,

druggists were caught in a veritable commercial and professional maelstrom over patent medicines. Some they perceived as injurious to the consumer's health, others as harmless, and still others as safe and effective. All of them competed with their compounding business. A few enterprising druggists attempted to convert this liability into an asset by patenting and manufacturing specially formulated products. If they were shrewd, their manufacturing business rapidly outgrew their stores and their incomes increased proportionally. . . . For druggists, in general, however, patent medicines represented not only a threat to their compounding skills, but also a commercial dilemma. An insatiable public appetite meant profits, and profits attracted relentless business competitors: in this case, chiefly general merchants and grocers. (Clark 1983:7–8)

On the federal level, it appears that concern over the possible controls on patent medicines led to the formation of the Canadian Pharmaceutical Association, which met on September 3, 1907. In

May 1907, one of the principal organizers of the association stated that "probably those who dreamed of and advocated an Association for Canada similar to the A.Ph.A. [American Pharmaceutical Association], would have kept on dreaming and advocating for many years longer without awakening any great interest, had it not been for the recent attempt at patent medicine legislation at Ottawa. This occasion pointed out, if it did not even create, an urgent need for some such organization" (*CPJ* 1907:475). When the association met in September "two important committees were appointed . . . one to prepare a constitution and bylaws and the other to study and report on [the proposed legislation to control patent medicines]" (Raison 1967:9).

Other sources from that period, such as editorials in medical and pharmaceutical journals, also suggest that health professionals were worried about the dangers of drug abuse. For example, physicians were questioning "the use of cocaine in catarrhal conditions" (*Montreal Medical Journal* 1904:656). In the *Canadian Pharmaceutical Journal*, the problem concerning cocaine abuse was referred to as the "dread evil," a conclusion buttressed by clippings from daily newspapers and correspondence from public officials in which cocaine was depicted as "the principal cause of the ruination of our young girls . . . and . . . the demoralization of young boys" (*CPJ* 1910:213–14).

In 1905 the Council of the Ontario College of Pharmacy passed a resolution stating its concern over the indiscriminate sale of cocaine (*CPJ* 1905:67). After subsequent efforts on the part of pharmacists an anticocaine bill was passed by the Ontario legislature on April 10, 1908, via an Act to Amend the Pharmacy Act, which placed restrictions on the sale of cocaine, requiring "the written prescription of a legally qualified medical practitioner" (*CPJ* 1908b:401).

Prior to the amendment, cocaine had been widely available not only as one of the ingredients in many patent medicines but also in pure form at drugstores. Although a legitimate medical need existed for some cocaine, indiscriminate sales also occurred. For example, debate over the amendment revealed some startling conditions:

> Upon authority which admits of no question as to reliability, we have it that one drugstore in the east-end of Toronto purchases cocaine by the

pound, and the intervening time between such purchase is not even measured by months, but weeks. . . . Now every reputable pharmacist in the city knows that there exists no legitimate output for such quantities of cocaine . . . and only one conclusion is permissible, the stuff is supplied to dope fiends. (*CPJ* 1908c:404)

The indiscriminate sale of cocaine was a concern for reputable pharmacists. Reports such as the following one in the *Montreal Star* fueled their concern about professional integrity and competence: "For a few dollars the druggists are exposing the families of Montreal to complete ruin, and the future of our young people to abject disgrace through the cocaine traffic." Pharmacists were depicted in the press as "assassins," and their conduct was described as "diabolical" and "evil." The medical profession did not escape this slander. One writer declared that "there are a certain number of doctors who are conspiring with the druggists to continue this traffic" (*CPJ* 1910:213).

Another concern was the nature and extent of criminality associated with the use and distribution of cocaine. Although it was not illegal to possess or use the drug, 1908 provincial legislation restricted its sale. The supply of cocaine was thus somewhat limited, with the result that "no article of merchandise carried by a wholesale drug house . . . had been the cause of so heavy loss through thieving as cocaine" (*CPJ* 1908d:456).

The purported connection between cocaine use and criminality was made by a number of reports. The Montreal chief of police said that "two thirds of the pickpockets and similar criminals were cocaine habitues" (*CPJ* 1908e:176). Cocaine "fiends" were described as the most "persistent" of criminals: "Four times since September this man [druggist] has been before the police magistrate" (*CPJ* 1911:306). The comments of a parole officer were presented in the House of Commons: "I am safe in saying that 12 to 15 percent of all the young prisoners I come in contact with credit these drugs with the cause of their downfall; . . . had I time and opportunity to make a census of prisons, I would be greatly surprised if the percentage would not reach over 25 percent" (HCD 1910–11b: 2523).

The professional interests of physicians and pharmacists and concern about the health of the population were two important factors that led to legislative action and to the eventual decline in cocaine's popularity. There was another important issue as well: concern over individual immorality. This period in history has been described as the era when personal morality became the object of formal control. Emphasis was placed on social order as a means to curtail the evils of crime, poverty, and vice. "It was an era of strong faith in the effectiveness of criminal sanctions in solving social problems" (Giffen, Endicott & Lambert 1991).

"The famous catch-phrase 'peace, order, and good government,' enshrined in the British North America Act [1867], suggested a social emphasis on order, not on liberty" (Rutherford 1982:170). The evils of excess and moral degradation were seen as posing a "threat to the leadership and lifestyle of the established Anglo-Saxon population" (Giffen, Endicott & Lambert 1991). "The daily press popularized the belief that the community was shaped by a thicket of moral and social disciplines. The overarching discipline, of course, was Christianity itself" (Rutherford 1982:171). The campaign of reform was led by fundamentalist and evangelical Protestant clergymen. The "good

---

G. Decarie, "Something Old, Something New . . .: Aspects of Prohibitionism in Ontario in the 1890's"

Many churches saw that they could no longer concern themselves solely with the salvation of the individual. They were caught up in the effort to preserve the lifestyle of which they were a part against the assaults of urban and industrial influences. . . .

[The] mundane application of the principles of Christianity was a part of what was to be known as the "social gospel." Prohibition was closely associated with that message; it preceded the social gospel and broadened to embrace it. . . .

The Woman's Christian Temperance Union was "consciously treating prohibition as one aspect of the general rehabilitation of society. . ." At the Ontario W.C.T.U. convention of 1896, for example, though alcohol held a central place in discussion, other interests had developed from it. Tobacco and opium were condemned; there was concern expressed for the morals of children, the secularization of the Sabbath and the moral and physical safety of female workers in the cities. Moreover, the tenor of the resolutions makes it clear that the W.C.T.U. was seeking to use the power of the state to assist in the maintenance of its ideal society.

In D. Swainson (ed.), *Oliver Mowat's Ontario* Macmillan, Toronto, 1972:166–8

---

news" was spread in newspapers, which in themselves were "prime instruments of reform." They were "independent in politics and sensational in tone" (Rutherford 1974:ix).

The connection between the moral reform movement and the efforts to criminalize use of cocaine is clear from the evidence: A newspaper report in 1910, for example, indicated that "the spread of the cocaine vice has become a matter of such concern to the authorities and moral reformers that they are looking around to find some means to make it impossible to secure the drug for other than legitimate purposes" (HCD 1910–11a:261). In the *Montreal Gazette* of November 26, 1910, Judge Leet of the city stated, "I also think it [cocaine] should be made a criminal offense the same as opium is" (HCD 1910-11b:261).

Mackenzie King told the House of Commons that he had been inundated with unsolicited communications concerning the problem with cocaine, and these reports indicated the importance and urgency for action to address the problem. The Reverend E. I. Hart of Montreal's Dominion Methodist Church wrote: "I hope that the House may be convinced of the need of immediate action, for every day in Montreal new victims are being claimed by this monstrous vice." The archbishop of Montreal said that "one is unable to take too severe measures against a plague which is still more terrible perhaps than that of alcohol." And the Anglican bishop of Montreal wired, "Delighted that you are giving hearty support to Cocaine Bill. Hope you will not rest until this much needed reform is accomplished" (HCD 1910–11b:2527–28). King received communications from many different organizations, including the Young Men's Christian Association, the Dominion Alliance for the total suppression of the liquor traffic, and various women's groups. Even the pharmacists presented their concerns to King in the form of a moral issue. The Quebec Pharmaceutical Association suggested that "a federal Bill should receive the support of every man who is interested in the health and morals of his fellows" (HCD 1910–11b:2529).

The Legislative Response: Repression and Successful Control, 1911–1970

Between 1908 and 1911, three different and separate legislative measures—one provincial initiative and two federal statutes—were adopted. At the provincial level, the new restrictive measures regulated the sale of cocaine, prohibiting its sale except on a physician's prescription. The provincial controls came in response to resolutions passed by provincial pharmaceutical associations. The tenor of those resolutions indicated that these interested bodies wanted to safeguard the public against cocaine's future prevalence. An editorial in the *Canadian Pharmaceutical Journal* challenged all the provincial legislatures to prohibit the sale of cocaine "without delay. Total prohibition is the requirement which will prevent future trouble" (*CPJ* 1908a:357). In a subsequent editorial in the *Canadian Pharmaceutical Journal*, the Ontario legislature was commended for its promptness in responding to "this dangerous drug on the first intimation of peril to the community." The article went on to say that "an ounce of prevention in this matter will, we are confident, obviate the necessity for the many pounds of cure required in communities where the 'habit' has secured a hold which it maintains with a tenacity defying the strenuous efforts of the authorities to break its hold" (*CPJ* 1908b:401).

Ontario's new legislation became law on April 10, 1908, via An Act to Amend the Pharmacy Act. It added five subsections to section 26 of the Pharmacy Act, restricting the retail sale of cocaine "except upon the written prescription of a legally qualified medical practitioner"; limiting the wholesale distribution "except upon the written order of a legally qualified pharmaceutical chemist, a legally qualified medical practitioner, a licensed veterinary surgeon or a licentiate of dental surgery"; and stipulating that "the prescription shall not be filled more than once" (*CPJ* 1908b:401).

On the federal level, new legislation regulated the trade in and content of patent medicines and prohibited the use of opium and other drugs, including cocaine. The regulating legislation developed first in response to the most common type of cocaine use during this period: consumption of patent medicines containing cocaine. A pharmacist who had been commissioned by the government to examine the use and trade in proprietary and patent medicines reported that "a large number of patent medicines contain morphine or cocaine [and that these are] the two drugs which form most drug habitués." Statistics gathered in 1903, he said, showed that "not less than nine-tenths of the cocaine habitués have been led there by the use of proprietaries or prescriptions containing it." He pointed to the use of certain catarrh snuffs, which he indicated were the main cause of the "rapid growth of cocaine addiction" (*Sessional Papers* 1906:16–17).

Cocaine did not appear to be given special attention in the initial debate over patent medicines in the Senate or the House, but on 3 April 1908, three months prior to the act's adoption by the House, the matter was finally addressed. The problem with cocaine in patent medicines was of such magnitude that it became the only substance absolutely prohibited by the 1908 Proprietary and Patent Medicine Act. Thus, when contemporary writers discuss the purposes of the 1908 act, the first purpose referred to is that of "prohibiting the use of cocaine" (Guest 1966:788; see also Soucy 1953). Indeed, section 7 in the act deals with prohibited medicines and reads as follows:

No proprietary or patent medicine shall be manufactured, imported, exposed, sold, or offered for sale

a. if it contains cocaine or any of its salts or preparations;

b. if it contains alcohol in excess of the amount required as a solvent or preservative, or does not contain sufficient medication to prevent its use as an alcoholic beverage;

c. if it contains any drug which is included in the schedule to this Act but the name of which is not conspicuously printed on, and an inseparable part of the label and wrapper of the bottle, box or other container.

The Opium and Drug Act of 1911 became an extension of the Opium Act, a two-paragraph statute that had been enacted in 1908 but was

so limited in its scope that it proved to be very ineffective in suppressing opium smoking. The police criticisms met with a sympathetic ear in Ottawa. In 1909, Mackenzie King attended the Shanghai Commission and was party to a resolution urging domestic control of morphine and other derivatives. After he had presented his Bill to Parliament, reformers concerned over the non-medical use of other drugs—particularly cocaine—exerted influence to extend the scope. (Giffen, Endicott & Lambert 1991)

In their discussion of the making of the 1911 act, Giffen, Endicott, and Lambert (1991) argue that the "Cocaine Scare" became one of the main forces that helped shape the legislation. Their archival research demonstrates

> considerable feeling among influential community leaders that cocaine and morphine were a menace that should be brought under control. . . . Clearly a cocaine scare existed in the Fall of 1910 and clearly King was aware of it before he presented his revised Bill in late January, 1911. . . . Given the receptivity of Parliament, the law likely would have been extended to include cocaine even if King had not become aware of the tide and placed himself in its van. . . . We can conclude, then, that the manifest public opinion that came to bear on this legislation had more to do with the perceived misuse of cocaine and morphine, as well as various popular remedies containing opiates, than with opium smoking. . . . The wave of concern among civic leaders in Montreal over what was believed to be a dangerous epidemic of cocaine use among young people served as the catalyst.

The Opium and Drug Act of 1911 provided controls on the importation, manufacture, sale, and possession (for other than medical or scientific purposes) of cocaine. The maximum penalty prescribed for each of these offenses was one year of incarceration and a $500 fine.

Some observers viewed the provisions for penalties as insignificant. The *Canadian Pharmaceutical Journal*, for example, editorialized, "Our only regret . . . is that the penalty provided is by no means adequate to the enormity of the transgression." In connection with provincial measures, the same editorial refers to the "paltry fine of $25" that was inflicted on four successive occasions to the same druggist (*CPJ* 1911:306). Another observer's view, presented in the House of Commons, was that the fines do "not help us at all. As it is now, cocaine is sold at $12 the ounce, and the profits made thereby are stupendous" (HCD 1910–11b:2525). He believed that the costs (penalties) in relation to the rewards (profit) rendered the legislation ineffective in curtailing the practices of certain unscrupulous physicians and druggists.

Problems were voiced regarding breaches of the Proprietary and Patent Medicine Act of 1908. For example, one article indicated that five years after the act had been passed, certain remedies containing cocaine continued to be imported and sold through legal channels (*Canadian Medical Association Journal* 1913:303). Apparently one product in particular, Asthma Specific, created a problem. The manufacturer had removed cocaine from the medicine when the act came into force, and consumers had protested, first to the manufacturer and then to the government: "Accordingly, members of Parliament have been inundated with letters from cocain [*sic*] users, who may also be suffering from asthma, pleading for their drug" (*Canadian Medical Association Journal* 1913:302). As a result of this pressure, the government permitted the importation and sale of the nostrum from the United States.

How cocaine was used after this legislation is difficult to determine. Although the previous widespread availability and use of cocaine was dramatically reduced, the laws likely were contravened to some extent. Over the next half-century, cocaine use was confined to medical usage and to a small segment of the population for recreational purposes. It remained a chic pastime in some circles, particularly in the entertainment industry (Ashley 1975:105–7; Phillips and Wynne 1980:101–2). This glamorization of the drug eventually helped to revive popularity in the 1970s.

A New Cycle of Popularity for Cocaine, 1970–1985

Cocaine use once again became a social problem during the 1970s. In identifying this reemergence, many of the observations to be made are now commonplace. Tales of cocaine use by Hollywood celebrities, sports heroes, rock stars, and other well-known entertainers began to emerge in the early 1970s. The glamor and expense of cocaine earned it the name "champagne of drugs." These accounts were soon followed by stories of prominent cocaine users' arrests, economic ruin, physical and mental debilitation, and even death. Recognition of a cocaine problem was forthcoming from the medical community in the form of numerous journal articles on the topic, the development of specialized treatment programs, and coroners' reports on the rise in cocaine-related deaths. The U.S. drug survey literature portrayed a trend of increasing cocaine use not only among the older and affluent but also among a broader cross-section of the population (Miller et al. 1982). And in this new cycle, the machinery of criminal prohibition, already in place, was mobilized against cocaine users and traffickers. An effort to prevent importation and distribution of cocaine from its South American sources was the focus of enforcement strategies.

The portrayal of an emerging cocaine problem in the 1970s and the 1980s bears a strong resemblance to that described at the turn of the century, yet a number of features common to both the United States and Canada appear to be unique to the new cocaine problem. Foremost among these is the change from licit to illicit sources of supply. At the turn of the century, cocaine was imported legally by the patent medicine and pharmaceutical companies and was readily available in drugstores. In the new era, a well-established and lucrative black market in cocaine has provided a relatively expensive yet readily obtainable supply (Wisotsky 1983). Additionally, the sheer volume of potential cocaine-carrying commercial airline flights and the enormous profits for high-level traffickers have made the cocaine trade quite impervious to enforcement efforts. Cutting off the legal supply in the 1910s was an effective measure of curtailing use and did not lead to a thriving black market.

Another contrast is in the sophisticated drug-using generation that was primed by widespread cannabis use to embrace cocaine. The barrier of illegality appears to be a minor inconvenience to those raised in the 1960s and 1970s, when illicit drug experimentation flourished. Here too, the very nature of most contemporary cocaine use—as a group-oriented, recreational activity—provides an easy transition from alcohol and cannabis to cocaine. No doubt some turn-of-the-century use at parties fit this description as well (Phillips & Wynne 1980), yet there was a predominant self-medicating aspect to consumption then. Perhaps the increase in disposable income and leisure time for a greater segment of the population has also shaped contemporary cocaine use patterns.

The societal response to the cocaine problem has been similar in reliance on legal repression and criminal penalties, but the sentences now are more severe. For example, in Canada, the 1911 legislation provided a term of one-year imprisonment for any offense; current law provides a seven-year maximum for possession and life imprisonment for trafficking. In the United States, mandatory minimum sentences are imposed. Contemporary thinking also provides for a treatment alternative, an extension of a response that developed in the 1950s and 1960s to the opiate dependence problem (Peyrot 1984). Treatment programs solely for cocaine users and the incorporation of cocaine as a drug of abuse in general treatment facilities and psychiatric caseloads have been forthcoming. While the efficacy of treatment interventions for compulsive, self-destructive cocaine use remains to be established, the failure of criminal prohibition in preventing widespread access to cocaine seems incontestable (Wisotsky 1983; DiNardo 1993; Kennedy, Reuter & Riley 1993).

The Crack Era, 1985 and Beyond

In 1983, a Los Angeles basement chemist discovered how to use baking soda to make crack (Inciardi 1988). Originally called "cocaine-rock," it became popular in drug-using circles, especially among heavier cocaine users and marginal young people. When smoked, crack, which is easy to conceal and transport in small vials, is more rapidly absorbed than powder is when snorted. Also, small amounts can be bought as "rocks" for as little as $2 to $5. This means that younger users can buy cocaine for less than the cost of a movie ticket.

In the early 1980s, cocaine was used predominantly by sniffing the crystalline product. This so-called champagne of drugs, often available at parties and sophisticated gatherings, was not viewed uniformly by experts as a highly addictive drug. When crack appeared, however, it was portrayed as a drug that was immediately addictive, and its use was associated with disadvantaged and minority group members in the United States. Crack epidemics were soon reported in most large American cities.

Crack put drug abuse back on the public agenda in a forceful way. By the end of 1986, there had been more than 1,000 newspaper stories on it in the United States and hundreds of television reports, such as CBS's "48 Hours on Crack Street," one of the most highly rated documentaries ever (Inciardi 1988).

In Canada, crack first appeared in mid-1986, and some pockets of use emerged in the larger cities. Although it appeared to be used by only about 1 percent of adults and students in Canada and the rates were not increasing, crack was nevertheless portrayed as a great menace. This perceived crack epidemic contributed to the creation of Canada's Drug Strategy in 1987, renewed after five years with an eventual budget of about $500 million, far more than had ever been spent on drug abuse in Canada before, and led to greater provincial funding on drug abuse treatment, especially in Ontario and British Columbia (Fischer 1994).

Summary

This chapter has traced the introduction of cocaine to human societies from indigenous use by South American natives, through discovery by Europeans, to its popularity, decline, and contemporary reemergence in the New World.

The use of cocaine moved from acceptable to unacceptable and illegal behavior and eventually, with the help of vested interest groups, became the object of formal control. Four significant factors have been identified in the first cycle (1880–1911). First, an objective or undesirable condition appeared—reports about cocaine's adverse effects. Second, the interests of pharmacists and physicians helped legitimate the problem. Third, the realization that the use of cocaine was not confined to specific racial and occupational groups but was being used by various members of society fostered widespread concern. Finally, the moral climate of the era facilitated an outcome of reform that culminated in successful legislative control of cocaine use from 1911 to 1970.

In the second cycle, from 1970 to 1985, many similarities can be discerned. Initial praise for the drug from cultural heroes was followed by concern for its adverse effects. Medical legitimation of its problem status was accompanied by an awareness that cocaine use was increasing rapidly in a broad cross-section of the population. However, a number of differences in the new era can be noted that have prevented effective legal suppression of cocaine use. Some of the similarities and differences in the two cycles were noted.

In the third cycle, since 1985, cocaine use levels have been quite stable, but the introduction of crack heightened public concern. Crack users were portrayed as of lower status than cocaine users in the previous eras and received widespread media attention.

Public knowledge about and attitudes to cocaine are seldom derived from first-hand perusal of medical journals and legal statutes. The more usual channels are newspapers, books, magazines, radio, and television. The next chapter explores the diffusion via popular culture of both favorable and unfavorable images of cocaine into the public consciousness.

2

Cocaine in Popular Culture

Given the substantial attention devoted by the media to the use of cocaine and crack in recent years, the potential impact of this exposure merits consideration. Popular or mass culture consists of all widely accessible forms of transmission of the values, beliefs, and practices of a society. The forms have multiplied, from the simple fare produced by the early presses to the multimedia banquet provided by modern technology. Mass communication now performs a number of functions: surveillance or news, correlation of information (in the form of editorial activity), cultural transmission, and entertainment (Wright 1975). The study of the effects of mass communication is a difficult and complex enterprise (Weiss 1969). One important question is whether media content precedes or follows public concern, or if the two even influence each other.

On intuitive grounds, we would all agree that exposure to particular ideas or facts affects attitudes and behavior. Wright (1975) has posited that people consciously refer to the media as normative sources to guide their behavior.[1] It follows that "a mass medium can act as a vehicle for the dissemination of ideas about a particular kind of deviant behavior" (Winick 1978:7). Consequently mass media play an important, albeit covert, role in the definition of acceptable and deviant forms of behavior. The importance of popular culture in transmitting notions about cocaine is also indicated by the attention it has received from researchers (Ashley 1975; Grinspoon & Bakalar 1976; Phillips & Wynne 1980; Siegel 1984). In our first study of cocaine users in 1983, participants who were asked where they derived their expectations concerning cocaine cited media sources as second only to that of the influence of peers.

This chapter examines the portrayal of cocaine and crack in music, popular literature, newspapers, movies, and television. Our choice of material will be selective rather than comprehensive. We also report on newer, more systematic surveys of newspaper and magazine stories about cocaine and crack.

Music

Although illicit drug use has been a component of the musicians' milieu throughout this century (Winick 1959), it was not until the early 1960s that references to drug use in song lyrics became conspicuous. One of the few early exceptions was Cole Porter's "I Get a Kick Out of You," from the 1934 musical *Anything Goes*:

> I get no kick from cocaine
> I'm sure that if I took even one sniff
> It would bore me terrifically too,
> But I still get a kick out of you.

But with the emergence of the counterculture movement during the 1960s and 1970s, song lyrics depicting the use of drugs became prevalent and explicit. Cocaine was no exception. This era saw a number of songs with mentions of cocaine hitting the charts: "Buy and Sell" and "Poverty Train" (Laura Nyro, 1966 and 1967, respectively), "Casey Jones" (Grateful Dead, 1970), "Sweet Cocaine" (Fred Neil, 1971), and "Let It Bleed" and "Sister Morphine" (Rolling Stones, 1970 and 1971, respectively). Most song lyrics referred to cocaine use indirectly; an exception was "Cocaine":

> When your day is done and you want a run, Cocaine,
> When you got bad news you want to kick the blues, Cocaine,
> She's alright, she's alright, she's alright, Cocaine.
> If your thing is gone and you want to ride on, Cocaine
> Don't forget this fact you get it back, Cocaine
> She don't lie, she don't lie, she don't lie, Cocaine.*

---

*Writer J. J. Cale. Copyright 1975 by Audiogram Music. Reprinted with permision.

In the 1990s much rap music refers specifically to cocaine and crack, sometimes in a positive way, but more rap groups are now giving antidrug messages to young potential users with a "stay clean message."

Although few studies in the past examined the relationship between allusions to drug use in music and consequent use, the popular belief existed that drug references incited use among young people.[2] For this reason, in 1971, the U.S. Federal Communications Commission (FCC), acting on concerns expressed by the U.S. Army, attempted to regulate lyrics that tended to promote or glorify the use of drugs (Seiden 1974).

One early study (Schwartz, Feinglass & Drucker 1973) examined the issue of lyric content. Rather than focusing solely on the prevalence and frequency of drug lyrics, the researchers provided empirical data on the content and message of 129 drug-related songs. They found, contrary to popular belief, that popular music of the 1970s was not homogeneously in favor of drug use. For example, of the 26 songs that referred to cocaine specifically, 11 percent ($N = 3$) presented cocaine in a favorable light, but 50 percent ($N = 13$) presented it negatively. The balance of songs contained descriptive content judged to be neutral or lacking explicit lyrics. The types of music most likely to depict negative images of cocaine were rock, folk, and soul. The researchers also suggested that popular music was a reflection of contemporary society rather than a prod toward new practices. In particular, the frequency of lyrics mentioning drugs tended to follow peaks in use among the general population rather than the converse.

Literature

Another source of cocaine lore is popular literature. Perhaps one of the most illustrious cocaine users, next to Freud, is the fictional detective Sherlock Holmes. In the opening paragraph of *The Sign of Four* (1886), we find Holmes injecting himself with a 7-percent solution of cocaine while his colleague and companion, Dr. Watson, looks on:

> Sherlock Holmes took his bottle from the corner of the mantel-piece, and his hypodermic syringe from its neat morocco case. With his long, white, nervous fingers he adjusted the delicate needle, and rolled back

his left shirt cuff. For some little time his eyes rested thoughtfully upon the sinewy forearm and wrist, all dotted and scarred with innumerable puncture-marks. Finally, he thrust the sharp point home, pressed down the tiny piston, and sank back into the velvet-lined arm-chair with a long sigh of satisfaction. Three times a day for many months I had witnessed this performance, but custom had not reconciled my mind to it. On the contrary, from day to day I had become more irritable at the sight, and my conscience swelled nightly within me.[3]

Holmes' use of cocaine is portrayed as being intimately related to his need for mental stimulation:

"My mind," he [Holmes] said, "rebels at stagnation. Give me problems, give me work, give me the most abstruse cryptogram, or the most intricate analysis, and I am in my own proper atmosphere. I can dispense then with the artificial stimulants. But I abhor the dull routine of existence. I crave for mental exaltation."

Holmes was a recreational user, and any concerns about adverse consequences were voiced through the medium of Dr. Watson:

He [Holmes] smiled at my vehemence. "Perhaps you are right, Watson," he said. "I suppose that its [cocaine's] influence is physically a bad one. I find it, however, so transcendently stimulating and clarifying to the mind that its secondary action is a matter of a small moment."

"But consider!" I said, earnestly. "Count the cost! Your brain may, as you say, be roused and excited, but it is a pathological and morbid process, which involves increased tissue-change, and may at least leave a permanent weakness. You know, too, what a black reaction comes upon you."

Recently, other authors (Meyer 1974; Musto 1968) have speculated imaginatively about Holmes' cocaine use. In Meyers' *The Seven-Percent Solution*, Holmes seeks treatment for cocaine dependency from none other than Sigmund Freud. Indeed, Professor Moriarty, Holmes' archnemesis, is depicted as a figment of cocaine-induced psychosis:

"Have you heard of Professor Moriarty?" he [Holmes] asked, plunging headlong into the business after a sip or two of his drink. I had, in fact, heard the name, but did not say so. Moriarty was the appellation I had sometimes known him to mutter when he was deep in the throes of a cocaine injection. When the drug's effects had left him, he never alluded to the man, and, though I thought of asking him about the name and what significance it held for him, there was something in Holmes' manner that usually precluded such an enquiry. As it was, he knew how heartily I disapproved of his loathsome habit, and this was a difficulty I did not wish to exacerbate by referring to his behavior while under its influence. "Never." "Aye, there's the genius and the wonder of the thing." He spoke with energy though without shifting his position. "The man pervades London—the Western world, even!—and no one has ever heard of him."

Thus, the character of Holmes was transformed in the addiction-conscious 1970s from a man in control of his cocaine use to a man enslaved by it.

Modern novels and biography have also presented cocaine users. It is not uncommon to find examples of cocaine depicted as central to a glamorous world of status and intrigue. Robert Sabbag writes in *Snowblind*, subtitled, *A Brief Career in the Cocaine Trade*,

> Cocaine is the caviar of the drug market. On the street, where an equivalent amount of premium-import marijuana can be obtained for a mere $40 . . . cocaine commands a price in excess of $1,000 an ounce. And like high-quality caviar, it most frequently embellishes the diet of the avant-garde and the aristocratic, a leisure class—in New York, a Who's Who among actors, models, athletes, artists, musicians and modern businessmen, professionals, politicians and diplomats, as well as that sourceless supply of socialites and celebrities of no certifiable occupation. The common denominator is money. . . . Coke is status. (p. 68)

Another example is Robert Woodward's *Wired*, which chronicles actor John Belushi's life, especially the period prior to his "speedball" (mixture of heroin and cocaine) overdose death in 1982. Again cocaine use is portrayed as being omnipresent in the entertainment industry: "Later at the party, John played celebrity host to the crowd of stars, moving around rapidly, accepting and offering congratulations. Penny Marshall saw someone drop a vial of cocaine in John's pocket. Smokey saw it too and went over and had John lift his arms while he searched and got it. . . . No fewer than five people passed or dropped vials or packets in John's pocket—a standard Los Angeles way of sending best wishes" (p. 208).

The novel *Clockers*, by Richard Price, takes the reader into the life of Strike, a 19-year-old black inner-city drug dealer and his team of "clockers" (crack sellers). A nonuser himself, Strike says to his young apprentice, "I ever see you put this shit in your nose or in a pipe or in your arm? Shit, I'll come and kill you my *damn* self. . . . You probably asking yourself, how come I sell it, then? . . . Cause if I don't, somebody else will. Me not selling it ain't gonna stop nothing out there but my money flow" (p. 428). There is no sympathy in this milieu for the "pipeheads"—the users.

Newspapers and Magazines

Knowledge and perceptions of cocaine are also derived from the news media. One aspect is the presence, image, and representation of cocaine and its users. As Lazarsfeld and Merton (1948) have noted, the making of any issue into a news item confers status on it. Additionally, consistent exposure to negative portrayals of cocaine use serves to enforce the normative behavior of nonuse.

Sensationalized reporting has been widespread. Front-page headlines in a Toronto newspaper read as follows: "We're Cocaine City"; "Cocaine Epidemic in Metro."[4] Similar accounts can be found as cover material on popular magazines (Orcutt and Turner 1993). Rather than the photographic cover typical of *Sports Illustrated*, a dramatic account, depicting the cocaine use of football player Don Reese, was found on the cover of the June 14, 1982, issue.[5] Reese's exposé makes explicit the domination associated with cocaine use. Not only does cocaine appear to take control of peoples' lives, but it continues to be a dominating force: "it [cocaine] took control and almost killed me. It may yet." Reese maintains that cocaine use is widespread in the National Football League, and it "controls and corrupts the game." Such is a stereotypical example of cocaine use as portrayed in the popular press. Rarely have researchers attempted to demonstrate empirically the sensationalized nature of drug use reporting in the media. In an exceptional paper, Orcutt and Turner (1993) carefully analyze *Newsweek*'s numerical and graphical presentation of the Monitoring the Future Study's cocaine use estimates that result from annual national surveys of high school seniors for many years. They found "ample evidence of media workers snatching at shocking numbers for an ISR [the Institute for Social Research] press release, smothering reports of stable or decreasing use under more ominous headlines, and distorting the cocaine problem to epidemic proportions as high as 40 percent of high school seniors." (p. 203).

Negative images of cocaine also occur in the popular scientific press. *Discover* presented a cover story on cocaine, "Coke: The Random Killer," indicating that "the evidence is everywhere and people have to relearn it: cocaine isn't the champagne of drugs. Cocaine kills."

The examples illustrate the largely negative image of cocaine that pervades the news media. Frequent exposure to such portrayals is likely to have two effects. On the one hand, the public may derive misperceptions regarding cocaine use and its effects; on the other hand, it is likely that attitudes and beliefs unfavorable to its use will be strengthened.

A second issue of relevance is the extent to which the news media reflects or creates public opinion about cocaine use. Duster (1970) argues that, historically, sensationalized reporting of drug problems, which were often racially based, contributed to punitive legislative responses. This can occur regardless of the lack of correspondence between dramatic newspaper accounts and use of drugs in the population at large (Duster 1970), and also between the reporting of crime news and its associated crime rate (Dominick 1978). The news media, then, have the independent capacity to generate public outcry resulting in political action. Some empirical work (Behr & Iyengar 1985) suggests that the direction of the relationship is that television news influences public opinion, not vice versa.

Hill (1985) compared the political and social issues content of national news programs with personal agendas derived from a cross-sectional survey and found a weak relationship between the two. Of the 3,600 stories, "problems of drug abuse" was ranked seventeenth out of twenty political and social issues ($N = 42$; 1 percent of all stories). However, personal agendas, measured by the percentage of the sample that reported the highest level of interest, ranked problems of drug abuse fourth in importance. Thus, this study suggests that quantity of media exposure has little effect on the public's perceived importance of social issues.

Such findings, however, are mixed. Behr and Iyengar (1985) noted that real-world conditions partially determine levels of media coverage. Also, several studies indicate that the media agenda-setting effect is dependent on the issue (Behr & Iyengar 1985; MacKuen 1983). Thus, frequency of cocaine references in these media may in part be a response to the public agenda regarding use. Figure 2–1 compares the prevalence of cocaine use among American adults (Miller et al. 1982) and high school seniors (Johnston, O'Malley & Bachman 1984) with the number of cocaine-related magazine articles (derived from the *Readers' Guide to Periodical Literature*). Although causal processes cannot be inferred from these data, some interesting relationships can be noted. Between 1976 and 1982, the number of magazine articles tend to parallel the prevalence of use in the population (the exception is 1981). Indeed, the number of articles peaks in 1979 when cocaine use plateaus. After 1982, however, citations appear to escalate well beyond the level of cocaine use. This media escalation may be attributable to the responsive nature of the media, with an associated time lag—or it may be an example of the misalignment of media content with social reality.

FIGURE 2–1
Correspondence between Number of Cocaine-Related Magazine Articles and Percentage of Use in the Population in the United States.

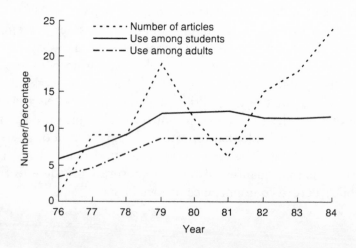

Contemporary Cocaine Stories

Since the early 1980s, there has been a large increase in the number of cocaine stories in Canadian media. The mainstay of news media incidence is the *Readers' Guide to Periodical Literature* and other periodical and newspaper indexes (e.g., Lidz & Walker 1980; Beninger 1984). Figure 2–2 shows three indicators of media coverage between 1980 and 1990: the number of newspaper stories involving "drug abuse," the number of news stories involving cocaine or crack (both derived from the Canadian News Index),[6] and the number of stories in Canadian periodicals as indicated by the Canadian Periodical Index.[7] These data are important in two respects. First, for both news stories and periodical coverage, they document increasing trends in media coverage in Canada. Changes in media coverage have shown little association with changes in cocaine use in the general population; however, increases in media coverage tend to lag closely behind increases in cocaine use in the United States.

In Figure 2–2, we display the percentage of cocaine news stories in comparison to all drug abuse stories. Here we get another reflec-

FIGURE 2–2

Number of Newspaper and Periodical Accounts of Drug Abuse and Cocaine Use in Canada, 1980–1990

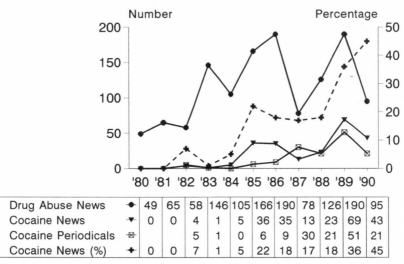

		'80	'81	'82	'83	'84	'85	'86	'87	'88	'89	'90
Drug Abuse News	●	49	65	58	146	105	166	190	78	126	190	95
Cocaine News	▼	0	0	4	1	5	36	35	13	23	69	43
Cocaine Periodicals	⊞			5	1	0	6	9	30	21	51	21
Cocaine News (%)	✛	0	0	7	1	5	22	18	17	18	36	45

Sources: Drug Abuse and Cocaine News, Canadian News Index, Vol. 4–14. Cocaine Periodicals, Canadian Periodical Index, Vols. 35–43.

tion of the influence of cocaine and crack relative to other drugs. Between 1980 and 1984, cocaine stories represented up to 7 percent of all drug stories. However, in 1985 this percentage had increased to 22 percent, remaining stable into 1988. In 1990, stories about cocaine represented 45 percent of all drug abuse news.

To examine whether the number of news stories about cocaine fluctuates disproportionately to the number of estimated cocaine users, we computed the number of cocaine stories per 100,000 cocaine users.[8] We found 2.8 cocaine stories per 100,000 users in 1984, 8.1 stories in 1988, and 33.4 stories in 1989. These data suggest a disproportionate increase in news stories about cocaine relative to the size of the cocaine-using population. Clearly, the concern and attention regarding cocaine use is driven by factors other than the size of the using population.

Media volume is one indicator of social concern; the shared collective image portrayed is another. Consider the following editorial:

> So some people claim the drug menace in Canada is being exaggerated. Perhaps. However it's impossible to exaggerate its devastation. Heroin, cocaine and crack are killers. [Former Prime Minister] Brian Mulroney has been criticized for appearing to jump on Ronald Reagan's anti-drug bandwagon. The critics say there's no drug problem here comparable to the one in the U.S. So Mulroney's just kowtowing again. They miss the point. Completely and tragically! They're ignoring the thousands whose lives have been stripped of all meaning and of all opportunities but three: Theft, prostitution and to try to escape in drugs. . . . To start with, we must do more to educate Canadians about the menace. And we must fight harder against those who profit from it. Major drug dealing is worse than murder because it destroys many people. It should be treated as mass murder. . . . Lawmen on the frontlines of the war against drugs have no hesitation backing Mulroney's tough anti-drug line. (*Toronto Sun* 1986)

A *Maclean's* cover story for April 3, 1989, read as follows: "A deadly plague of drugs: Inside the grim world of assassinations, gang wars—and addicts who will kill for a fix."

The public attention given to cocaine has been surpassed only by fears about cocaine in the form of crack, a problem of "the greatest threat to society, in general, of any single development over the past 15 years" (*Toronto Star* 1989a), and where "a very, very paranoid psychotic group" (*Globe & Mail* 1989) purchase a "one-way ticket to hell" (*Toronto Star* 1989b).

One likely explanation for Canadians' inflated perception of the drug problem is the influence of the American drug scene transmitted to Canada through the mass media.[9] Consider the following conclusion of an NBC television special, "Cocaine Country," that aired in October 1986, hosted by Tom Brokaw:

> As we have seen in this hour, now that we recognize just how destructive, even deadly, cocaine can be, how much it has corrupted our values, we still have no easy answers, no vaccine, no sure-fire political or legal solutions. Ultimately, this is a danger to us all, so it must be confronted by each of us, first individually, a decision to live drug-free, and then collectively, to make it possible for others to make that same decision and stick by it. Cocaine will always be there and people eager to supply it, but only if we lack the courage to fight it. Only if each of us surrenders.

Portrayal of Cocaine and Crack in Toronto Newspapers

Cocaine has been a major concern for newspapers and other media in Toronto, where much of the emergent cocaine and crack use in Canada was concentrated. In 1988–1989, a content analysis of the three major Toronto newspapers was conducted to examine and compare how two stimulant drugs, cocaine and tobacco, were portrayed (Erickson & Moreau 1990). About half of the articles mentioning cocaine were extracted during January and February 1989, just before the period of recruitment for the second study of cocaine users in this book, and the balance of articles during the remaining ten months. Thus, the portrayal reflects what our participants were exposed to in Toronto papers. This media study corresponded to a period when heightened concern and coverage of cocaine, and especially crack, had spilled over the border from the United States. "Devil Drug Has Metro in Its Grip" was not an atypical headline.

Over a twelve-month period, sixty-seven news stories about cocaine (including crack) were selected for analysis of themes and content. Half of the sources of information cited in the stories were the police or other criminal justice officials; scientific or health professionals were the sources only 6 percent of the time. Not surprisingly, two thirds of the articles emphasized crime, smuggling, and enforcement. Details of raids and seizures were regular fare. Health aspects of cocaine use, the focus of only one-sixth of all stories, included addiction more often than any other adverse physical or psychological effects. Thus, users might sense that the official reaction was concerned more with criminalizing them than with concern for their health.

Movies

Phillips and Wynne (1980) provide excellent coverage of cocaine in movies from the silent era to the 1960s. Indeed, the list of films referring to cocaine during this period is surprisingly lengthy, considering cocaine's legal status and the general conservatism of the time.[10] We will restrict our attention here, however, to contemporary movies and television.

References to cocaine are increasingly frequent in both movies and on television.[11] In restricting our attention solely to the frequency of references, however, we may lose sight of the portrayed image of cocaine and its users. As we have seen in other media, the contemporary image is largely negative; users are typically portrayed as addicted regardless of their level of use or social status. The public is left with the impression that all cocaine users are likely to be dependent on the drug.

In the 1983 movie *Scarface*, Al Pacino plays an upwardly mobile gangster who grew from the world of poverty to become a magnate of crime. Throughout this film, cocaine plays an important role, and near the climax Pacino buries his face in a mound of cocaine lying on his study desk. Dennis Weaver portrays a happily married and successful real estate agent who becomes addicted to cocaine in *Cocaine: One Man's Seduction*, a 1984 made-for-TV movie.

Several movies of the late 1980s and early 1990s have cocaine addiction as the central theme. In those movies, addicted cocaine users have to hit bottom in order to get treatment and eventually recover. For example, in *Bright Lights, Big City* (1988), Michael J. Fox plays a magazine editor who is addicted to cocaine. He loses his job and wife because of the drug. After many adverse reactions to cocaine, Fox realizes that he is addicted, and at the movie's end he starts a new life with new friends.

In the movie *Less Than Zero* (1987), several friends just out of college get involved in the cocaine party scene of Los Angeles. One becomes addicted to crack and is unable to quit, even with the help of family and professionals. Eventually, after a bad reaction to cocaine, Downey is able to quit with the help of his friends.

A large number of other movies include themes whereby users become addicted and suffer horribly before being rescued or seeing the light themselves. These themes occur in *Postcards from the Edge* (1990), *St. Elmo's Fire* (1985), and *My Own Private Idaho* (1992). The star of *My Own Private Idaho*, River Phoenix, recently died of a drug overdose involving cocaine and several other drugs.

Numerous other movies include references to cocaine or crack without being a main theme—*Colors* (1988), *City of Hope* (1990), and *Jungle Fever* (1991), among others. In general, recent movies are less likely to portray the recreational use of cocaine than its addictive side and the suffering that it causes.

Television

Some television portrayals of cocaine use leave the impression that use is often found among the privileged classes. Cocaine addiction in police officers was portrayed in both "Cagney and Lacey" and "T. J. Hooker" in the 1980s. Several episodes of the former series were devoted to the relationship between detective Chris Cagney and her lieutenant beau, who was attempting to deal with his dependence on cocaine. Indeed, it was largely his addiction that led to the dissolution of their relationship.

In the early 1980s, a number of talk shows had guests who extolled the virtues of cocaine and presented it as the champagne of drugs. However, after several entertainers publicly displayed problems with cocaine, this theme seemed to disappear. In the late 1980s and early 1990s, cocaine and crack themes again became staples in television programming. Talk show programs such as "Oprah Winfrey," "Geraldo," and "Shirley" often had programs about cocaine-addicted babies. Many news broadcasts focused on cocaine seizures, drug busts, and the shutting down of crack houses as television caught on to the drug epidemic. Several news journal programs have had hour-long programs about cocaine, "48 Hours," "Street Stories," and "The Fifth Estate," among them. In addition, police programs such as "Cops" show drug busts and dealer arrests as if they were one of the most common of all police activities. Tabloid journalism programs such as "Inside Edition," "American Journal," and "America's Most Wanted" often show cocaine drug busts, cocaine trafficking, and cocaine use among entertainers.

Many anticocaine commercials have appeared in the 1990s, including the "Stay Real" series by Canada's Health and Welfare and one on "cocaine frying your brain" by the National Citizens Coalition Against Drugs. Finally, several popular series "Blossom," "Beverly Hills 90210," and "Fresh Prince of Bel Air" contain characters who are former cocaine addicts. In general, television now presents cocaine use as usually leading to addiction but an addiction that can be overcome. Recreational use of cocaine is rarely seen on television, except in the occasional older movie.

Summary

There is little doubt that cocaine can become a powerfully addictive substance, and persons may become dependent in the extreme manner portrayed by some media exposure. Yet it is possible that too many such portrayals, with their emphasis on the addictive potential of cocaine, may lead to an exaggerated impression of the real problem in the community at large. This is particularly important from a Canadian perspective, with media exposure largely dominated by American sources. As we shall show in the next chapter, rates of cocaine use in Canada remain significantly lower than those found in the United States, yet Canadians are exposed to an American social reality that differs quantitatively and qualitatively from their own. Consequently, it is likely that Canadian perceptions with respect to cocaine and its problems are inflated.

References to cocaine in the media are frequent, but the image of cocaine is still a paradox. The mere presence of cocaine stories in the media confers importance to the topic and propels it into the public consciousness. With the same creative stroke, cocaine often embodies an aura of status and intrigue, while at the same time largely negative images of use and users abound. Since these negative images exceed the actual problem level, the community is left with a misperception of the nature of cocaine and its users.

3

Trends and Current Use of Cocaine and Crack

During the late 1960s, the use of cocaine rose in North America, South America, and some parts of Europe. Additionally, it began to appear at parties in polite society and was portrayed in movies and television programs. Until the mid-1980s, cocaine use was primarily restricted to the developed Western world and a few South American countries; now reports on cocaine use come as well from a variety of countries in North and South America and Europe.

Before describing the extent of cocaine use and related problems, it is instructive to review the nature and meaning of drug use indicators. The initiation, maintenance, and escalation of drug use is the result of a complex interplay of three factors: the *drug*, the user's *set* (intraindividual factors such as beliefs and personality), and the *setting* (interpersonal factors such as social relations and environmental factors). Consequently, in evaluating and measuring the scope of the cocaine problem we cannot rely solely on any single indicator of use or abuse.

Different drug use indicators tend to capture different components of the drug problem. It therefore follows that when we compare changes in one indicator with changes in another, we should not necessarily expect them to agree. But the absence of agreement does not suggest that either of the indicators is invalid. If consensus occurs, it suggests that the changes in drug use are robust since they are captured by different indicators. When survey indicators showed a downturn in cocaine use after 1985–1986, some questioned the results on the grounds that treatment admissions for cocaine were increasing (Clayton 1985). But because there is a lag time between onset of cocaine use and treatment admissions, we should not expect these two indicators to covary at the same time. As another example, some interpret increases in drug-related deaths as an indication of an increase in the size of the abusing population, but this need not be the case. Increases in deaths may also be caused by greater drug purity or different use patterns of a stable pool of drug users. The point is that we cannot ignore that different drug use indicators capture different components of the drug problem and different populations of users.

Cocaine Use in International Perspective

In the first edition of this book, we were able to identify only a few studies of cocaine use in general populations outside North America. That situation has changed. Several countries in Latin America and Europe, as well as Australia, were noted in studies in the period 1985–1993 (table 3–1). Clearly cocaine use has spread widely to countries where use was almost nonexistent before the early 1980s.

Latin America

Although coca chewing has been common among certain Andean groups for centuries, the use of cocaine and coca paste is a relatively new phenomenon. Most of the world's coca is grown and refined into cocaine in Bolivia, Colombia, and Peru. Thus, some people in these countries might be expected eventually to develop problems with cocaine and coca paste. Cocaine and coca paste problems affect chiefly young persons living in cities whereas coca chewing was and is a more rural phenomenon.

In Peru, both coca paste and cocaine use are relatively recent. Coca paste use was first noted in the early 1970s among a group of multiple-drug users and those being treated for drug abuse. Its use now has disseminated to high school and university students and to older professionals and middle-class people. A survey conducted in Lima in 1979 among residents 12 to 45 years of age showed that 6.5 percent of males and 4.4 percent of females chewed coca and

TABLE 3–1

Cocaine Use in General Populations Outside North America: Selected Recent Studies

Country	Year	Population	Percentage Using Cocaine
Europe			
Denmark[a]	1990	National sample: aged 16 plus	0.9 lifetime users, 0.07 last month
Sweden[a]	1989	National sample:	
		Aged 16–74	1.0 lifetime
		Aged 12–24	0.6 lifetime
Spain[b]	1989	National sample: Aged 18 plus	3.0
		Madrid sample:	
		Aged 14–64	6.1 lifetime
		Aged 14–64	0.5 last 30 days
Americas			
Bahamas[c]	1987	Students in junior and senior schools	1.7 lifetime
		Delinquents in a special school	11.0 lifetime
Bolivia[d]	1988	National samples of adults	4.4 lifetime
Colombia[d]	1987	National samples of adults	2.1 lifetime
Peru[d]	1987	National samples of adults	2.6 lifetime
Costa Rica[e]	1987	National study aged 14–60	1.0 or less lifetime
Ecuador[f]	1988	National study aged 10–65	1.0 used in lifetime
Mexico[h]	1991	National survey of high school students	1.0 lifetime, 0.4 last year
Peru[i]	1988	National study	
		Lima	13.4 coca leaves, 3.6 coca paste, 1.8 sniffed cocaine
		Highlands	30.5 coca leaves, 0.6 coca paste, 0.2 sniffed cocaine
Brazil[k]	1986	Saõ Paulo: Students 3rd–10th grades	0.9 lifetime users, 0.4 last month
Africa			
Nigeria[l]	1986	Students in one secondary school (Ogun State)	3.1 lifetime, 1.0 on retest
Oceania			
Australia[g]	1986	Sydney: Telephone survey of young adults aged 14–35 who used alcohol and tobacco weekly and had been offered or had tried at least one illicit drug.[g]	13.0 lifetime, 2.6 current users
	1986	Statewide study of secondary school students (New South Wales)[j]	1.1 lifetime

[a] Anta (1991).
[b] Pompidou Group (1990).
[c] Smart and Patterson (1990).
[d] Florenzano (1990).
[e] Murillo (1990).
[f] Aguilar (1990).

[g] Hall et al. (1991).
[h] Medina-Mora et al. (1990).
[i] Piazza (1993).
[j] Baker et al. (1987).
[k] Carlini-Cotrin (1988).
[l] Adelekan and Odejide (1989).

2.4 percent and 0.2 percent smoked coca paste, whereas only 1.4 percent and 0.4 percent, respectively, used cocaine. Between 1979 and 1984, police seizures of cocaine tripled and coca paste seizures nearly doubled. It has been estimated that about 30 percent of all private and state hospital psychiatric facilities in Peru are occupied by coca paste smokers (Jeri 1984).

A study by Piazza in 1988 showed that rates of coca and cocaine use had increased greatly in Peru since Jeri's 1984 study. Piazza showed that 13.4 percent in Lima chewed coca leaves, 3.6 percent used coca paste, and 1.8 percent sniffed cocaine. In contrast, in the highlands, 30.5 percent chewed leaves, and few used other forms of cocaine, which indicates that traditional use of coca is expanding. The newer routes of administration—smoking and sniffing— are more common in urban areas.

Colombia, a large producer of cocaine, experienced a large increase in both cocaine and coca paste usage in the early 1980s. A majority of inpatients being treated for drug dependency in Colombia now have primarily a coca paste, or *basuco*, problem. The proportion of clients reporting some *basuco* use increased from 1 percent in 1977 to 89.4 percent in 1984 (World Health Organization 1984). By 1987 about 2.1 percent of the adults in Colombia had used cocaine in some form. Climent and de Aragon (1984) found that 4.4 percent of psychiatric outpatients in Cali were dependent on coca paste. In Antioquia, hospital admissions due to coca paste use increased almost threefold, from 31.3 percent in 1981 to 86.3 percent in 1983 (De Pabon 1984).

National surveys of adults made in Bolivia, Colombia, Peru, Costa Rica, and Ecuador show that rates of cocaine or coca use are relatively low in general populations—much lower than in Canada or the United States (table 3–1). In Costa Rica and Ecuador, only about 1 percent have used coca or cocaine in their lifetimes; rates are higher in producer countries such as Bolivia (4.4 percent), Peru (2.6 percent), and Colombia (2.1 percent).

Surveys have also been made of student populations. In Mexico and Brazil, rates of cocaine use are low (1 percent) compared to similar groups in North America and have not increased in Mexico since 1982 (Sarinana, Maya & Aguitar 1982; Medina-Mora et al. 1990). Rates of use were higher among students in Medellín, Colombia; 5 percent had used *basuco* and 4.2 percent cocaine.

Usually use of coca paste was preceded by both alcohol and cannabis use. A preliminary survey of high school students in Calí, Colombia, also found that cannabis and *basuco* use levels were about equal, although the exact figures are not given (Climent & de Aragon 1984).

Coca paste smoking has become common despite the low level of coca and cocaine use in general populations among drug users in Bolivia, and a number of cases of dependency have been observed (Noya Tapia 1984). Coca users are also a very large proportion of the drug dependency cases being treated in most Latin American countries.

Europe

In 1968, there was only one small seizure of cocaine in Europe; however, by 1983 there were 728 seizures in fifteen countries involving 928 kilograms. The largest increase was from 1982 to 1983 (from 398 kilograms to 952 kilograms). In both Austria and Switzerland, the proportion of narcotics law infractions due to cocaine has increased greatly since 1976 (Uchtenhagen 1984). Also, treatment centers in Germany, Holland, Belgium, Italy, Portugal, England, and Switzerland have seen large increases in the proportion of drug abusers reporting cocaine use. A youth drop-in center in Zurich found that 4.1 percent used cocaine in 1981 compared with 11.4 percent in 1984 (Uchtenhagen 1984).

A variety of surveys done in European countries in the early 1980s, usually with youthful populations, have been summarized, although exact comparisons cannot be made because the survey methods differ. Rates of cocaine use vary from 0.3 percent among those 15 to 25 years of age in Zurich, to 4 percent in a national study in the Federal Republic of Germany (12 to 24 years of age) and 7 percent in a study in Bayern in southern Germany. It appears that, on average, about 3 to 4 percent of youth in Europe had some experience with cocaine. Only the study in Bayern has trend data—use increased from 3 percent in 1973 to 7 percent in 1980—but the population sample is not stated. (Uchtenhagen 1984).

More recent surveys of cocaine use in general populations in Europe found rates of use higher for young people and for males. Surveys in Denmark and Sweden showed that only about 1 percent of adults had used cocaine in their lifetime, whereas in Spain about 3 percent in a national sample and 6.1 percent in Madrid had used cocaine, although few had used it in the past thirty days. None of the European studies provides information on trends in cocaine use over time (Anta 1991; Pompidou Group 1990).

Africa, Asia, and Australia

Coca plants were grown in India and Java in earlier times. A legal cocaine industry supplying drugs to the pharmaceutical market existed between 1910 and 1930 (Tongue 1984), and large amounts of coca were grown in India between 1883 and 1925. Despite this, Africa and Asia are largely untouched by the current surge of interest in cocaine. There are few recent reports of use from African countries, although one survey of students in Nigeria showed that cocaine use involved 3.1 percent of students. In Asia, no known surveys have estimated the use of cocaine.

A limited amount of cocaine has been imported into Australia, and various sources suggest that use is increasing. For example, 556 grams were seized in 1977 and 8,700 grams in 1983. A few cocaine deaths have been reported, and some treatment facilities have found increased admissions for cocaine abuse. A survey of students in New South Wales in 1986 found that only 1.1 percent had used cocaine in their lifetime. More recently, a telephone survey of young adults aged 14 to 35 who used alcohol and tobacco weekly and had been offered or had tried at least one illicit drug found that 13 percent had used cocaine and 2.6 percent were current users (Hall et al. 1991). In that survey, rates of use were not related to gender, income, or education; however, cocaine users were more likely to be daily smokers and drinkers and to use other illicit drugs such as cannabis.

Treatment

Cocaine abusers have been seeking treatment in various countries (table 3–2). In Ireland, France, Spain, the United Kingdom, and Mexico, cocaine abuse rates are relatively low; 1 to 3 percent of those seeking drug abuse treatment are cocaine users. Rates are higher in Italy (10.6 percent). In Canada, the United States, and

TABLE 3–2

Cocaine Use in Admissions for Drug Dependency Treatment

Country	Year	Population	Percentage Using Cocaine
Spain[a]	1987–90	Outpatients in treatment	3.0 or less
Ireland[b]	1989	Outpatients in treatment	2.0 of all cases; 0.8 of new cases
France[b]	1989	Drug abusers in treatment	2.1
Italy[a]	1982–90	Drug abusers in treatment (Catanzaro)	10.6 all cases
	1986–90	Urine tests on drug abusers in treatment (Milan)	4.6 in 1986 and 3.2 in 1990 were positive for cocaine
United Kingdom[c]	1987–89	Drug abusers in treatment in London	1.0 had cocaine as main problem; 3.0 used cocaine in last month in 1987; 29.0 in 1989
Netherlands[e]	1985–89	Injection drug users in methadone program (Amsterdam)	10.0 freebasing in 1985; 48.0 freebasing in 1989
Mexico[d]	1986–88	Alcohol and drug abusers in treatment	1.6 lifetime in 1986; 4.0 lifetime in 1988

[a] Anta (1991).
[b] Pompidou Group (1990).
[c] Strang, Griffiths & Gossop (1990).
[d] Ortiz (1990).
[e] Hartgers et al. (1991).

the Netherlands, almost half of those seeking drug abuse treatment have cocaine abuse problems. In several countries with low rates of cocaine abuse (e.g., United Kingdom and Mexico), there are indications that cocaine abuse is becoming a larger problem than in the past.

Coca paste, an intermediate product in the extraction of cocaine from coca leaves, has become popular in Colombia, Peru, and Bolivia, and seizures of it have been made in Canada and the United States.

Several studies of coca paste smokers have come from Latin America, all involving patients in drug abuse treatment facilities.

One of the first to study coca paste was Jeri (1984), whose respondents were patients in Peruvian hospitals. Most of the smokers were male, and they had begun smoking between 11 and 20 years of age. Most had used other drugs such as cannabis before coca paste. Although some university students were included, most were dropouts from high school. Dependence on coca paste usually developed in three to six months, with users typically developing hallucinations and serious paranoidal thoughts. Jeri has described the "coca paste psychosis," common among heavy users in his study, involving hypervigilance, paranoid delusions, hallucinations, insomnia, and aggressiveness. Most of the users drank alcohol heavily at the same time as smoking, so as to control sweating, palpitations, and numbness brought on by coca paste.

A similar study in Colombia looked at 118 *basuco* (coca paste) smokers in treatment. About 84 percent were males, and the average age was about 26 years. Most were single. About three-quarters had not completed high school, and half of the group belonged to the lowest social class. Patients usually reported anxiety, compulsion to use coca paste, irritability, paranoia, hostility, hallucinations, and suicidal ideation. However, cases of coca paste psychosis are not referred to (Climent & de Aragon 1984).

Cocaine Use in North America

The General Cocaine-Using Population

In examining cocaine use among mainstream, general populations—civilian, noninstitutionalized individuals living in households—we pay particular attention to one American and three Canadian surveys.[1] One of the most comprehensive drug surveys conducted among a general population is the National Household Survey on Drug Abuse (NHSDA) sponsored by the National Institute on Drug Abuse (Substance Abuse & Mental Health Services Administration [SAMHSA] 1993). Initiated in 1971, this nationwide survey, employing a stratified multistage sample design, has maintained a sample of at least 5,000 Americans 12 years of age and older. The most recent survey, conducted in 1991, interviewed 32,594 respondents, with a participation rate of 84 percent. The three Canadian surveys also interviewed a probability sample of respondents residing in households. The most recent is the Health Promotion Survey (HPS), which interviewed 13,792 Canadians aged 15 years and older by telephone (Stephens & Fowler Graham 1993). Respondents were selected by random-digit-dialing (RDD) methods, and 78 percent of selected respondents participated in the survey. The second survey, the National Alcohol and Other Drug Use Survey (NADS), employed a similar method to the HPS. It interviewed 11,634 respondents in 1989, 79 percent of selected respondents (Eliany, Giesbrecht & Nelson 1990). The third Canadian household survey represents a series of cross-sectional surveys conducted by the Addiction Research Foundation (Adlaf, Smart & Canale 1991). This is the only household survey in Canada that has repeated cross-sectional measures of drug use in a Canadian population. The survey, first initiated in 1977 has surveyed approximately 1,000 Ontario adults aged 18 years and older six times (1977, 1982, 1984, 1987, 1989, and 1991).

Students are perhaps the most well-studied segment of the population regarding drug use, for several reasons. First, because of the developmental implications of early drug use, both the public and the government are more concerned with the consequences of drug use among youths than among adults. Second, student surveys are generally more cost-efficient and in many cases administratively easier to field than are adult surveys. The most comprehensive American survey, the Monitoring the Future Study, is conducted annually (Johnston, O'Malley & Bachman 1993a). Conducted on a nationwide basis since 1975, it interviews approximately 16,000 to 18,000 high school seniors drawn from a stratified multistage cluster design. Beginning in 1991, the survey was expanded to include eighth graders (approximately 18,000) and tenth graders (approximately 15,000) in addition to the twelfth graders.

In Canada, the provinces are responsible for a greater share of health matters, especially those involving treatment and education. Consequently, there has been no nationwide student survey of drug use in Canada; most student surveys have been completed under provincial mandates. The survey we draw on heavily is the Ontario Student Drug Use Survey, which since 1977 has been conducted every two years among 3,000 to 4,000 students enrolled in grades 7, 9, 11, and 13 (aged approximately 12, 14, 16, and 18 years) (Adlaf, Smart & Walsh 1993). The other surveys we rely on include one of 12,700 British Columbia students enrolled in grades 8 to 12 (British Columbia Ministry of Health 1991), a survey of 6,400 New Brunswick students enrolled in grades 7 through 12 (Alcoholism & Drug Dependency Commission of New Brunswick 1990), a survey of 3,400 Nova Scotia students enrolled in grades 7, 9, 11, and 13 (MacNeil et al. 1991), and a survey of 1,600 Prince Edward Island students enrolled in grades 7 through 12 (Killorn 1982).

CURRENT USE OF COCAINE

Rates of cocaine use in mainstream populations are higher by a factor of three to five times in the United States than in Canada (figure 3–1). The percentage of Americans aged 12 years and older who used cocaine in their lifetime was 11.5 percent in 1991, compared to 3 percent of Canadians aged 15 years and older in 1990. Differences in past-year use are of a similar magnitude, with 3 percent of Americans compared to 1 percent of Canadians reporting use during the past year. When we construct a more precise age and year comparison, we find that in 1991, 11.8 percent of Americans aged 26 and older used cocaine in their lifetime compared to 3.6 percent of similarly aged Ontarians. For use during the past

FIGURE 3–1

Percentage Reporting Cocaine Use, United States versus Canada

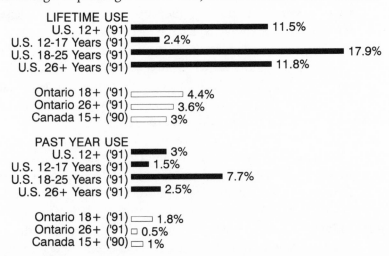

Sources: NHSDA (SAMHSA 1993); Ontario Adult Drug Use Survey (Adlaf, Smart & Canale 1991); HPS (Adlaf 1993)

TABLE 3-3
Percentage Reporting Cocaine Use from American Household Surveys, 1972–1991

	1972	1973	1974	1975	1976	1977	1978	1979	1980	1981	1982	1983	1984	1985	1986	1987	1988	1989	1990	1991
Lifetime use																				
12–17 years	1.5		3.6		3.4	4.0		5.4			6.5			4.9			3.4		2.6	2.4
18–25 years	9.1		12.7		13.4	19.1		27.5			28.3			25.2			19.7		19.4	17.9
26+ years	1.6		0.9		1.6	2.6		4.3			8.5			9.5			9.9		10.9	11.8
Past year use																				
12–17 years	1.5		2.7		2.3	2.6		4.2			4.1			4.0			2.9		2.2	1.5
18–25 years	—		8.1		7.0	10.2		19.6			18.8			16.3			12.1		7.5	7.7
26+ years	—		a		0.6	0.9		2.0			3.8			4.2			2.7		2.4	2.5

Source: SAMHSA 1993.
[a] Estimate less than 1 percent.

year, the respective comparison is 2.5 versus 0.5 percent. Although these differences are clearly sizable, we shall see that the variation in cocaine use between Canadians and Americans is partly dependent on the age of the population and the period under study.

TRENDS IN COCAINE USE

Cocaine trends in the United States divide into three periods: a preepidemic phase (1979 and earlier), an epidemic phase (1979–1989), and a postepidemic phase (1989 onward). During the preepidemic period, lifetime cocaine use in the United States increased from 1.5 to 5.4 percent among 12 to 17 year olds, from 9.1 to 27.5 percent among 18 to 25 year olds, and from 1.6 to 4.3 percent among those 26 and older (table 3–3). Cocaine use during the past year increased from 2.7 percent in 1974 to 4.2 percent in 1979 among 12 to 17 year olds, from 8.1 percent to 19.6 percent among 18 to 25 year olds, and from less than 1 percent to 2 percent among those 26 and older.

Canadian surveys estimating cocaine use are fewer in number and span a shorter time period than those in the United States. Only three nationwide surveys have estimated cocaine use, and these data do not indicate any significant change between 1985 and 1990 (table 3–4). In 1985, 0.9 percent of Canadians aged 15 and older reported using cocaine during the past 12 months, compared with 1.4 percent in 1989 and 1 percent in 1990. Data from the Ontario surveys, covering the period 1984 to 1991, similarly show stable cocaine use, with past-year use varying between 1.7 and 2.1 percent. Figure 3-2 displays trends in cocaine use during the past year among those aged 26 and older in the United States and in Ontario. What seems noteworthy is that differences between the United States and Ontario vary according to the epidemic phase. During the peak of the epidemic period (1982–1985) rates of cocaine use in the United States were significantly higher than were rates in Ontario (4 percent versus 1 percent, respectively). Differences in current rates of use between the United States and Ontario are clearly smaller (2.5 percent versus 0.5 percent).

SOCIAL DEMOGRAPHY OF USERS

The general population surveys in the United States and Canada showed that, like the use of other illicit drugs, *males* are approxi-

TABLE 3-4

Percentage Reporting Cocaine Use from Canadian Household Surveys, 1978–1991

	1978	1979	1980	1981	1982	1983	1984	1985	1986	1987	1988	1989	1990	1991
Durham region, Ontario: Lifetime use														
15–17 years	3.1													
18 + years	2.7													
Ontario Household Survey														
Lifetime use (18 + years)							3.3			6.1		5.6		4.4
Past-year use (18 + years)														
Total sample							1.7			1.8		2.1		1.8
18–29 years							4.1			4.7		6.1		5.5
30–39 years							2.5			1.8		1.1		a
40–49 years							a			a		1.1		a
50 + years							a			a		a		a
National Health Promotion Survey														
Lifetime use (15 + years)								—					3.0	
Past-year use (15 + years)								0.9					1.0	
National Alcohol and Other Drug Use Survey														
Past-year use (15 + years)												1.4		

Sources: Adlaf (1993); Adlaf, Smart & Canale (1991); Eliany, Giesbrecht & Nelson (1990); Gillies (1978); Larmarche & Rootman (1988).
a Estimate less than 1 percent

FIGURE 3–2

Percentage Reporting Cocaine Use During the Past Year, Ages 26 and Older, United States Versus Ontario, 1976–1991

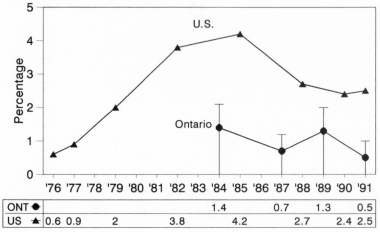

	'76	'77	'78	'79	'80	'81	'82	'83	'84	'85	'86	'87	'88	'89	'90	'91
ONT ●									1.4			0.7		1.3		0.5
US ▲	0.6	0.9			2			3.8			4.2			2.7		2.4 2.5

Note: Vertical bars represent 95 percent confidence intervals. Sources: NHSDA (SAMHSA 1993); Ontario Adult Drug Use Survey (Adlaf, Smart & Canale 1991).

mately twice as likely as females to report using cocaine (table 3–5). In the United States, 4.1 percent of males aged 12 years and older used cocaine during the past year, compared to 2 percent of females. Comparable figures for Ontario adults aged 18 years and older are 2.8 percent and less than 1 percent of females. Two national Canadian surveys have also demonstrated this consistent gender difference. The National Alcohol and Other Drugs Survey (Eliany, Giesbrecht & Nelson 1990) conducted in 1989 among Canadians aged 15 and older found that 2 percent of males and 0.8 percent of females reported using cocaine or crack during the past year, and the 1990 Canada Health Promotion Survey found that 4 percent of males aged 15 and older compared to 2 percent of females used cocaine or crack in their lifetime (Adlaf 1993).

Like gender, age is one more dominant demographic discriminator for cocaine use. The age group with the highest rate of cocaine use is those between 18 and 29 years of age (table 3–5). In the 1991 NIDA household survey, 7.7 percent of those aged 18 to 25 years reported using cocaine in the past year, compared to 1.5 percent of those aged 12 to 17 years, 5.1 percent of those aged 25 to 34 years,

TABLE 3-5

Characteristics of Cocaine Users, United States versus Ontario, 1991 (in percentages)

Characteristic	Ontario		United States	
Gender	Male	2.8	Male	4.1
	Female	a	Female	2.0
Age	18–29	5.5	12–17	1.5
	30–39	a	18–25	7.7
	40–49	a	26–34	5.1
	50–64	a	35 +	1.4
	65 +	a		
Region	Metropolitan Toronto	2.2	Northeast	2.9
	Toronto outskirts	a	North Central	2.7
	Eastern Ontario	2.3	South	2.3
	Western Ontario	a	West	4.6
	Northern Ontario	4.3		
			Large metropolitan area	3.4
			Small metropolitan area	3.0
			Nonmetropolitan area	2.3
Education	Elementary	1.5	Less than high school	3.8
	Secondary	1.7	High school	3.3
	Postsecondary	1.9	Some college	3.8
			College graduate	1.6
Race/ethnicity	Mother tongue			
	English	2.1	White	2.8
	Other	a	Black	3.9
			Hispanic	3.8
Frequency of cocaine use	Less than once a month	94.4	1–2 times	24.4
	Once a month or greater	5.6	3–10 times	30.0
			11–99 times	31.3
			100 + times	14.4

Sources: NHSDA (SAMHSA 1993): Adlaf, Smart & Canale (1991).

Note: Ontario population: adults 18 years and over; U.S. population: 12 years and older. All respondents were queried about their use of cocaine during the past year.

[a] Estimates less than 1 percent.

and 1.4 percent of those aged 35 and older. A similar relationship holds in Canada. In 1991, 5.5 percent of Ontario adults aged 18 to 29 years reported using cocaine during the past year compared to less than 1 percent for all other age groups (Adlaf, Smart & Canale 1991). Nationwide Canadian surveys also demonstrate higher cocaine use among young adults. The 1989 National Alcohol and Other Drug Use Survey found that 3.1 percent of those aged 20 to 24 years and 3.3 percent of those aged 25 to 34 reported using cocaine in the past year, compared to 1.9 percent of those aged 15 to 19 years and even lower estimates among all other age groups. The 1990 Canada Health Promotion Survey found the highest rate of cocaine use among those aged 25 to 34 years (7 percent), followed closely by those aged 20 to 24 years (5 percent), with lower rates among those aged 15 to 19 years (3 percent) and 35 to 44 years (3 percent).

Differences in cocaine use according to marital status are typically sizable. Among Ontario adults in 1991, 0.6 percent of married respondents reported using cocaine during the past year, compared to 4.9 percent of single respondents, 4.5 percent of respondents living as married, and 1.8 percent of respondents who were separated, divorced, or widowed (Adlaf, Smart & Canale 1991). The 1989 NADS survey also found similar differences: 1.8 percent of married respondents, compared to 7.4 percent of never-married respondents, 6.1 percent of divorced respondents, and 5.5 percent of separated respondents reported using cocaine during their lifetime. Much of the difference in cocaine use by marital status might be due to other demographic configurations. Adlaf, Smart, and Canale (1991) found that marital status was not significantly related to past-year cocaine use when factors such as gender, age, region, education, occupation, and native language were considered.

Geographical residence and population density are highly related to cocaine use in both Canada and the United States. The 1990 Canadian HPS found significant variation in rates of lifetime cocaine use according to provincial residence. From east to west, rates of use were as follows: Newfoundland (less than 1 percent), Prince Edward Island (2 percent), Nova Scotia (2 percent), New Brunswick (1 percent), Quebec (4 percent), Ontario (3 percent), Manitoba (2 percent), Saskatchewan (1 percent), Alberta (3 percent), and British Columbia (4 percent). A detailed study of provincial differences in cocaine use drawn from the 1989 Canadian NADS survey found that provincial differences in cocaine use were not significantly weakened when controlling for age, gender, religious affiliation, unemployment, occupation, income, education, and language spoken at home (Adlaf forthcoming). Respondents from Newfoundland and Prince Edward Island had rates of cocaine use significantly lower than the average, while respondents from Quebec and British Columbia had rates of use significantly higher than the average.

Regional differences are also sizable in the United States. The 1991 NIDA household survey found rates of past-year cocaine use highest among respondents from the West (4.6 percent) versus those from the Northeast (2.9 percent), the North Central (2.7 percent), or the South (2.3 percent).

Findings regarding socioeconomic factors—education, employment status, occupation, and income—are weaker and occasionally lack consistency compared to age and gender. Smart, Liban & Brown (1981), for example, found that cocaine use was unrelated to a respondent's employment status and income and negatively related to occupational status.

The relationship between educational level and cocaine use does not show strong or consistent results between Canada and the United States (table 3–5). Rates of past-year cocaine use did not differ by educational level among Ontario adults in 1991. Among those with elementary education 1.5 percent used cocaine versus 1.7 percent of those with secondary education and 1.9 percent of those with postsecondary education (Adlaf, Smart & Canale 1991). The 1990 Canada Health Promotion Survey found that those with elementary education were least likely to report cocaine use in their lifetime. Two percent of those with elementary education used cocaine compared to 4 percent of those with secondary education and 3 percent of those with university education (Adlaf 1993). The NIDA household survey, on the other hand, found that those with the highest education were the least likely to report using cocaine. In 1991, 1.6 percent of college graduates used cocaine during the past year, compared to 3.8 percent of those with less than a high school education, 3.3 percent of those with a high school education, and 3.8 percent of those with some college education.

The relationship between income and cocaine use appears to be stronger in the United States than it is in Canada. The 1991 NIDA household survey found that cocaine use declined with increasing income. Among those with total family income of less than $9,000, 4.8 percent reported cocaine use during the past twelve months, compared to 3.7 percent among those with incomes of $9,000–$19,900, 2.9 percent with incomes of $20,000–$39,900, 1.8 percent with incomes of $40,000–$74,900, and 1.9 percent of those with incomes of $75,000 and over. Among Ontario adults, rates of cocaine use are highest among those with family incomes between $15,000 and $19,900 (10.5 percent) versus 2 percent or under among all other income categories (Adlaf, Smart & Canale 1991). Nationwide, however, the relationship between income and cocaine use among Canadians is weak. The 1990 HPS found no strong relationship between a measure of income adequacy and cocaine use. Among those classified as very poor, 5 percent used cocaine, compared to 4 percent of those classified as poor, 3 percent classified as lower middle and upper middle, 4 percent classified as rich, and 5 percent classified as unknown (Adlaf 1993).

As with income, the relationship between occupation and cocaine use is weak. The highest rates of past-year use among Ontario adults were students (4.8 percent) followed by those in sales and clerical occupations (2.9 percent), professional and managerial occupations (1.8 percent), and labor occupations (1.6 percent); homemakers and the unemployed reported rates of less than 1 percent (Adlaf, Smart & Canale 1991). These differences, however, were not statistically significant. The 1990 HPS found that the highest rate of lifetime cocaine use was among those with no jobs (8 percent), followed by those in blue-collar occupations (5 percent), other white-collar occupations and students (4 percent), those in professional and managerial positions (3 percent), those keeping house (2 percent), and those who were retired (1 percent). The 1991 NIDA household survey also found that rates of cocaine use were highest among the unemployed than among those employed full time or part time (11.8 percent versus 3.2 percent and 3.2 percent, respectively) (SAMHSA 1993).

Survey findings paint a complex picture regarding the relationship between cocaine use and racial and ethnic factors. Native language showed nonsignificant variation in past-year cocaine use among Ontario adults in 1991: 2.1 percent of English-speaking respondents used cocaine compared to less than 1 percent among other respondents (Adlaf, Smart & Canale 1991). The 1991 NIDA household survey found that white respondents were significantly less likely to report past-year cocaine use than were black or Hispanic respondents (2.8 percent versus 3.9 percent and 3.8 percent, respectively). However, these differences were dependent on the age of respondent. Racial differences were nominal among those aged 18 to 25 years (8.2 percent among whites, 6 percent among blacks, and 7.1 percent among hispanics), whereas among 12 to 17 year olds, Hispanics reported higher rates of use than did blacks and whites (2.9 percent versus 1.5 percent and 1.3 percent, respectively), and among 26 to 34 year olds, blacks reported the highest rates compared to whites and Hispanics (7.5 percent versus 4.9 percent and 4.5 percent, respectively). The racial differences in cocaine use are prominent and have been consistently strong over time. However, these differences likely have more to do with environmental and socioeconomic factors than race. Indeed, analysis of the 1988 NHSDA found that after respondents were grouped into neighborhood clusters, racial differences in crack use among African Americans, Hispanic Americans, and white Americans did not differ (Lillie-Blanton, Anthony & Schuster 1993). Thus, it seems likely that social and environmental conditions underlie racial differences in cocaine use.

Regarding demographic characteristics of users derived from general population studies, two points are salient. First, studies are consistent in finding cocaine use significantly related to age, gender, employment status, region, and population density of survey respondents. Second, income, education, and occupational class do not reveal consistent patterns across different studies or populations. We must be cautious in attributing causal interpretations to the role of these factors. We have seen in the case of marital status and race that other factors are responsible for univariate differences in cocaine use.

PATTERN OF USE CHARACTERISTICS

General population surveys document that cocaine is infrequently used. The 1991 NIDA household survey found that about one-quarter of lifetime cocaine users (24 percent) used cocaine once or twice during the past twelve months (table 3–5). An additional one-third (30 percent) reported use three to ten times, 31 percent used eleven to ninety-nine times, and 14 percent used one hundred or more times. The same survey shows that cocaine is typically used less frequently than cannabis. Among lifetime cannabis users, 22 percent used once or twice, 25 percent used three to ten times, 25 percent used eleven to ninety-nine times and 28 percent used one hundred or more times during the past twelve months (SAMHSA 1993). The 1991 Ontario adult survey found that 94 percent of lifetime cocaine users used less than once a month, and 6 percent used once a month or more often (table 3–5).

Another consistent characteristic is that cocaine users are likely to have had experiences with other illicit drugs and are likely to be current users of drugs other than cocaine, in particular, cannabis. Among Ontario adults who reported lifetime use of cocaine, 90 percent reported also having used cannabis during the prior year (Smart & Adlaf 1984). We must note, however, that the reverse does not hold; among cannabis users, only 13 percent report using cocaine. Additionally, cocaine users are more likely to report using cannabis frequently in comparison to cannabis users who have not used cocaine.

USE OF CRACK COCAINE

Despite the ground that crack use has gained in inner cities, its use among mainstream populations has remained low and stable (table 3–6). The NIDA household survey, which first estimated crack use in 1990, found that 1.4 and 0.5 percent of Americans aged 12 years and older had used crack in their lifetime and in the past year, respectively. These rates of use remained largely unchanged in 1991 (1.9 and 0.5 percent). To date, no nationwide Canadian household survey has estimated the use of crack cocaine. The most readily available information comes from the Ontario household surveys. Lifetime crack use among Ontario adults remained under 1 percent between 1987 and 1991 (Adlaf, Smart & Canale 1991). The NIDA household survey shows a nominal change in the percentage of Americans aged 12 years and older reporting crack use between 1990 and 1991, with lifetime use increasing from 1.4 to 1.9 percent and past-year use remaining stable at 0.5 percent. However, the percentage of 18 to 25 year olds reporting lifetime crack use increased from 2.8 to 3.8 percent (SAMHSA 1993).

TABLE 3-6

Estimates of Crack Use Derived from Canadian and American Population Surveys, 1986–1993 (in percentages)

	1986	1987	1988	1989	1990	1991	1992	1993
Ontario adults 18 + Years								
Lifetime use		a		a		a		
Ontario students								
Past-year use								
Total sample		1.4		1.0		1.0		1.0
Males		2.1		1.0		1.1		1.5
Females		0.7		1.0		0.9		0.6
British Columbia students grades 8–12								
Past-year use		1.6			2.0			
Nova Scotia students, grades 7, 9, 10, 12								
Past-year use						1.8		
U.S. household 12 + years								
Lifetime use, total					1.4	1.9		
12–17 years					1.0	0.9		
18–25 years					2.8	3.8		
26–34 years					3.1	3.7		
35 + years					0.5	1.0		
Past-year use, total					0.5	0.5		
12–17 years					0.7	0.4		
18–25 years					1.4	1.0		
26–34 years					1.0	0.8		
35 + years					a	0.3		
U.S. high school seniors								
Lifetime use		5.4	4.8	4.7	3.5	3.1	2.6	
Past-year use		3.9	3.1	3.1	1.9	1.5	1.5	
Past 30-day use		1.3	1.6	1.4	0.7	0.7	0.6	
U.S. college students								
Lifetime use		3.3	3.4	2.4	1.4	1.5	1.7	
Past-year use	1.3	2.0	1.4	1.5	0.6	0.5	0.4	
U.S. 19–28 year olds								
Lifetime use		6.3	6.9	6.1	5.1	4.8	5.1	
Past-year use	3.2	3.1	3.1	2.5	1.6	1.2	1.4	
U.S. Grades 8, 10, 12								
Lifetime use								
Grade 8						1.3	1.6	
Grade 10						1.7	1.5	
Grade 12						3.1	2.6	
Past-year use								
Grade 8						0.7	0.9	
Grade 10						0.9	0.9	
Grade 12						1.5	1.5	

Sources: Adlaf, Smart & Canale (1991); Adlaf, Smart & Walsh (1993); British Columbia Ministry of Health (1992); Johnston, O'Malley & Bachman (1993a, 1993b); MacNeil et al. (1991); SAMHSA (1992).

a Estimates less than 1 percent.

Because the sample sizes of Canadian surveys are relatively small, there is no profile available of the population of adult crack users in Canada. The 1991 NIDA survey found that demographic characteristics of lifetime crack users are similar to those of cocaine users. Most notably, rates of lifetime crack use were highest among males (2.6 versus 1.3 percent of females), blacks (4.3 versus 2.1 percent of Hispanics and 1.5 percent of whites), residents of large metropolitan areas (2.3 versus 2 percent of residents of small metropolitan areas and 1.1 percent of residents of nonmetropolitan areas), the West (2.6 versus 2 percent of residents from the North Central, 1.8 percent of residents from the Northeast, and 1.5 percent of residents from the South), those with less than high school education (2.7 versus 2.1 percent of those with high school education, 1.7 percent of those with some college education, and 1.5 percent of those with a college degree), and unemployed respondents (7.2 versus 2.5 percent of those employed part time and 2.1 percent of those employed full time). We cannot interpret these differences in risk factors as causal forces.

For simplicity, we have described the profile of cocaine and crack users independently, but we do not wish to leave the impression that cocaine and crack users represent two independent groups. The 1991 NIDA household survey found that multiple routes of administration were reported by the same respondents. Among those who used cocaine at least once in the past year, 76 percent reported sniffing or snorting cocaine, 28 percent reported smoking (including freebase and crack), 11 percent reported oral ingestion, 11 percent reported injection, and 3 percent reported other methods of administration (SAMHSA 1993).

The Student Cocaine-Using Population

CURRENT COCAINE USE

The most comprehensive American survey conducted annually among high school seniors in the United States found that in 1992, 6.1 and 3.1 percent reported using cocaine during their lifetime and past year, respectively (Johnston, O'Malley & Bachman 1993a; *see* table 3–7). Cocaine use among American college students is similar in magnitude to high school seniors, with 7.9 and

TABLE 3-7

Estimates of Cocaine Use Derived from American Student and Adolescent Populations *(in percentages)*

	1975	1976	1977	1978	1979	1980	1981	1982	1983	1984	1985	1986	1987	1988	1989	1990	1991	1992
U.S. high school seniors																		
Lifetime use	9.0	9.7	10.8	12.9	15.4	15.7	16.5	16.0	16.2	16.1	17.3	16.9	15.2	12.1	10.3	9.4	7.8	6.1
Past-year use	5.6	6.0	7.2	9.0	12.0	12.3	12.4	11.5	11.4	11.6	13.1	12.7	10.3	7.9	6.5	5.3	3.5	3.1
Past 30-day use	1.9	2.0	2.9	3.9	5.7	5.2	5.8	5.0	4.9	5.8	6.7	6.2	4.3	3.4	2.8	1.9	1.4	1.3
U.S. college students																		
Lifetime use						22.0	21.5	22.4	23.1	21.7	22.9	23.3	20.6	15.8	14.6	11.4	9.4	7.9
Past-year use						16.8	16.0	17.2	17.3	16.3	17.3	17.1	13.7	10.0	8.2	5.6	3.6	3.0
19–28 year olds																		
Lifetime use												32.0	29.3	28.2	25.8	23.7	21.0	19.5
Past-year use												19.7	15.7	13.8	10.8	8.6	6.2	5.7
Grades 8, 10, and 12																		
Lifetime use																		
Grade 8																	2.3	2.9
Grade 10																	4.1	3.3
Grade 12																	7.8	6.1
Past-year use																		
Grade 8																	1.1	1.5
Grade 10																	2.2	1.9
Grade 12																	3.5	3.1

Sources: Johnston, O'Malley & Bachman (1993a, 1993b).

FIGURE 3–3

Cocaine Use by Grade of Student, United States (1992) versus Ontario (1993)

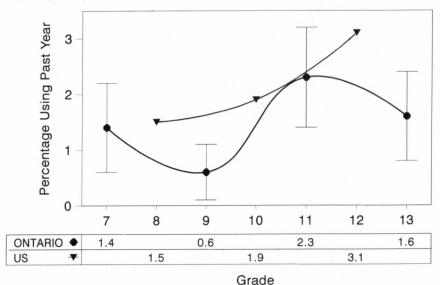

		Grade				
ONTARIO ●	1.4		0.6		2.3	1.6
US ▼		1.5		1.9		3.1

Note: Vertical bars represent 95 percent confidence intervals.

3 percent reporting lifetime and past-year use, respectively. Beginning in 1991, students from grades 8 and 10 have also been surveyed. In 1992, 2.9 and 1.5 percent of grade 8 students and 3.3 and 1.9 percent of grade 10 students reported cocaine use during their lifetime and the past twelve months, respectively. The national household survey (NIDA 1992) conducted in 1991 found that 2.5 and 1.5 percent of American youths from 12 to 17 years of age reported lifetime and annual cocaine use, respectively.

Within Canada, regional variation in cocaine use is evident (table 3–8). Annual cocaine use ranges from a high of 6.1 percent (in 1990) among students from British Columbia, followed by students from New Brunswick (3 percent in 1989) and students from Ontario (1.5 percent in 1993). One issue that reappears throughout this chapter is the nature of American-Canadian differences in cocaine use. In our first edition of this book, our review of the literature indicated that cross-national differences in cocaine use were substantial. Current rates of use, however, do not differ dramatically, as figure 3–3 shows.

TRENDS IN COCAINE USE

The three epidemic periods also characterize trends in student cocaine use (table 3–7). The first is a period of escalation in which the prevalence of annual use increased from 5.6 percent in 1975 to 12 percent in 1979. The second period, between 1979 and 1987, represented a period of stable but high rates of use, varying between 15.2 and 17.3 percent. This period of stability was followed by a period of steady declines in cocaine use. Between 1987 and 1992, annual cocaine use fell from 10.3 to 3.1 percent. The lifetime prevalence of cocaine use shows a similar pattern.

A similar growth curve occurs in survey data from NIDA's Household survey (table 3–3). Among 12 to 17 year olds, annual cocaine use increased from 1.5 percent in 1972 to 4.2 percent in 1979. Between 1979 and 1985, use remained stable at about 4 percent. During the postepidemic phase, use declined from 4 percent in 1985 to 1.5 percent in 1991.

Only three Canadian student surveys have trend data on cocaine use (table 3–8). Two of these surveys show no change in use; however, both cover short time spans. Cocaine use was 6.1 percent in both 1987 and 1990 among students from British Columbia and from 3.3 percent in 1986 to 3 percent in 1989 among students from New Brunswick. Both surveys, however, were conducted during the postepidemic period. The only survey that covers all three phases of the epidemic is the Ontario Student Drug Use Survey. The same secular change occurs among Ontario students as occurred among American students. Between 1977 and 1979 cocaine use increased from 3.8 to 5.1 percent. The epidemic period is roughly similar to the American trend: between 1979 and 1987 cocaine use remained stable varying between 5.1 and 3.8 percent. During the postepidemic period, cocaine use declined from 3.8 percent in 1987 to 1.5 percent in 1993.

Figure 3–4 compares trends in cocaine use among American grade 12 students and Ontario grade 11 and 13 students. Although we can see similar period changes for both groups, the difference between the two countries is largely a function of the epidemic

TABLE 3–8

Estimates of Cocaine Use Derived from Canadian Student Populations, 1976–1993 (in percentages)

	1976	1977	1978	1979	1980	1981	1982	1983	1984	1985	1986	1987	1988	1989	1990	1991	1992	1993
Vancouver: Grades 8–12																		
Lifetime use: Total sample			8.5				10.1											
< 14 years			3.9				6.7											
15–16 years			8.8				11.1											
17 + years			13.1				12.4											
British Columbia: Grades 8–12																		
Past-year use												6.1			6.1			
Ontario: Grades 7, 9, 11, 13																		
Lifetime use: Total sample								4.7		4.7		4.7		3.2		1.7		
Grade 7								2.9		2.7		2.5		1.1		0.8		
Grade 9								5.8		4.7		3.1		2.4		1.6		
Grade 11								5.1		5.2		5.2		5.0		2.8		
Grade 13								5.1		7.2		8.8		5.2		1.1		
Past-year use: Total sample		3.8		5.1		4.8		4.1		4.5		3.8		2.7		1.6		1.5
Grade 7		2.7		4.2		2.7		2.8		2.9		2.4		1.1		0.8		1.4
Grade 9		4.0		5.7		5.9		4.6		4.3		3.2		2.1		1.5		0.6
Grade 11		3.9		6.1		5.5		5.0		5.1		4.6		4.6		2.8		2.3
Grade 13		4.2		4.0		2.9		5.0		6.7		5.9		4.2		1.2		1.6
Montreal																		
Past six month use									3.8									

New Brunswick: Grades 7–12		
Past year use	3.3	3.0
Nova Scotia		
Past-year use		
Grade 7 males	3.1	2.1
Grade 7 females	—	1.3
Grade 9 males	—	1.2
Grade 9 females	1.2	3.5
Grade 10 males	5.8	3.5
Grade 10 females	3.0	3.4
Grade 12 males	8.3	3.8
Grade 12 females	5.1	2.2
Prince Edward Island: Grades 7–12		
Past six-month use	2.7	1.8

Sources: Alcoholism & Drug Dependency Commission of New Brunswick (1990); Adlaf, Smart & Walsh (1993); British Columbia Ministry of Health (1991); Desranleau (1984); Hollander & Davis (1983); Killorn (1982); MacNeil et al. (1991).

FIGURE 3–4

Cocaine Use, U.S. Grade 12 versus Ontario Grades 11 and 13, 1975–1993

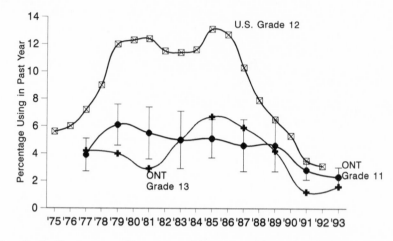

Note: Vertical bars represent 95 percent confidence interval for grade 11 students. See tables 3–7 and 3–8.

phase. Cocaine use differences are small during the preepidemic and postepidemic periods and large during the epidemic period. These epidemic-related differences also appear to occur among Vancouver students. During the preepidemic period, 13.1 percent of Vancouver students aged 17 years and older and 12.9 percent of American grade 12 students used cocaine in their lifetime. By 1982, this difference widened, with 12.4 percent of Vancouver and 16.5 percent of American students reporting use.

SOCIAL DEMOGRAPHY

Males are more likely to use cocaine than are females, although the relationship between gender and cocaine use is partly influenced by age. In the United States, 3.7 percent of male high school seniors reported use in the prior year in contrast to 2.4 percent of their female counterparts (Johnston, O'Malley & Bachman 1993a). However, gender differences are not sizable among younger students. Rates of use are similar among male and female grade 8 students (1.5 percent versus 1.5 percent) and grade 10 students (2 percent versus 1.7 percent). Among Ontario students, gender differences have been slowly weakening with time. In 1993, 1.5 percent of males and 1.4 percent of females used cocaine during the past year. In contrast, in 1979, 6.6 percent of males compared to 3.5 percent of females used cocaine (Adlaf, Smart & Walsh 1993).

Age is a critical factor in discriminating rates of cocaine use; however, age differences tend to weaken when the age range becomes restricted. Age differences in cocaine use are prominent among American students. Cocaine use during the past year increased from 1.5 percent among grade 8 students to 1.9 percent among grade 10 students to 3.1 percent among grade 12 students. This increase with age also held in 1991. Age differences among Ontario students have recently become less prominent. In 1993, none of the differences among the four grade cohorts differed significantly (1.4 percent, 0.6 percent, 2.3 percent, and 1.6 percent of grades 7, 9, 11, and 13, respectively, reported cocaine use during the past twelve months).[2] Age differences, however, have been influenced by period or time differences in cocaine use. Two grade trends have been particularly prominent. Cocaine use among grade 9 students showed a strong and steady decline from 5.9 percent in 1981 to 0.6 percent in 1993. The other trend occurs among grade 13 students, whose use increased from 2.9 percent in 1981 to 6.7 percent in 1985 and then declined to 1.2 percent in 1991.

As was the case for general populations, strong regional differences are also prominent among student populations. Johnston, O'Malley, and Bachman (1993a) found higher rates of past-year use among students from the western United States (4.3 percent), followed by the Northeast (2.8 percent), the South (3.2 percent), and finally the North Central (2.5 percent). This same pattern of regional differences held for both grade 8 and grade 10 students. Similar geographical differences in cocaine use also occur in Canada. Use of cocaine is significantly higher in Western Canada than it is in other parts of the country. In 1990, 6.1 percent of British Columbia students used cocaine during the past year, compared to 1.6 percent of Ontario students in 1991 and 3 percent of New Brunswick students in 1989.

PATTERN OF USE CHARACTERISTICS

Regarding patterns of cocaine use among students, many of the results found among the general population run parallel to student populations. Age of initiation, on average, is higher in comparison to other types of illicit drugs, and use is highly correlated with experience of other drugs. In both the United States and Ontario, the majority of cocaine users use infrequently. For example, 49 percent of Ontario students used cocaine fewer than six times during the past year.

CRACK COCAINE USE

Although crack use remains a serious problem among impoverished, inner-city adolescent populations (Smart et al. 1992; Williams 1989), its use among mainstream adolescents remained relatively low throughout the late 1980s and early 1990s. In 1987, the first year the Monitoring the Future Study surveyed students about crack use, 3.9 percent of American twelfth graders used crack in their lifetime (table 3–6). Crack use declined steadily into the 1990s. In 1992, only 1.5 percent of American high school seniors reported use during the twelve months before the survey. During this same period, lifetime crack use dropped from 5.4 percent in 1987 to 2.6 percent in 1992. Annual crack use declined similarly among American college students from 2 percent in 1987 to 0.4 percent in 1992. In Canada, crack use among student populations did not make inroads into the adolescent drug scene. To date, only two Canadian student surveys have documented crack use. Among British Columbia students, crack use remained stable between 1987 and 1990 (from 1.6 to 2 percent), and, among Ontario students, crack use fluctuated between 1 and 1.4 percent between 1987 and 1993.

In discussing American-Canadian differences in cocaine use, we noted with some interest that differences between the two countries seem to show a relationship to the epidemic phase of a drug. American-Ontario differences in cocaine use did not differ during the preepidemic or postepidemic periods but did differ during the epidemic period. Despite the shorter time period, the same pattern appears for crack use. During the epidemic period (1987–1989) differences in crack use were substantial, whereas differences are not large during the postepidemic period (1990 onward; see figure 3–5).

FIGURE 3-5

Percentage of Students Using Crack During the Past Year, Ontario versus United States, 1987–1993

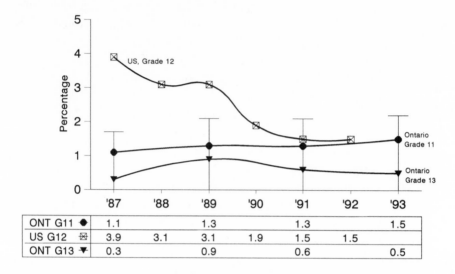

	'87	'88	'89	'90	'91	'92	'93
ONT G11 ●	1.1		1.3		1.3		1.5
US G12 ⊠	3.9	3.1	3.1	1.9	1.5	1.5	
ONT G13 ▼	0.3		0.9		0.6		0.5

Note: Vertical bars represent 95 percent confidence intervals for grade 11 students.

The Abusing Population

EPIDEMIOLOGICAL STUDIES

Whether a drug causes significant harm to society is partly a function of the interplay between the size of the using population and the size of the abusing population. Thus, the percentage of cocaine users who experience serious problems is an important epidemiological consideration. We noted earlier that general population survey methods are a useful means in estimating the size of the drug-using population. Increasingly, epidemiological survey methods are being used to estimate the size of the abusing population. For instance, in 1985, the NIDA household survey began asking drug users about problems experienced because of their cocaine use. Among respondents in the 1991 survey who used cocaine during the past year, the most commonly reported problems attributed to cocaine use were feeling nervous and anxious (14.3 percent) followed by becoming depressed (9.7 percent). All other problems are reported by fewer than 6 percent of users (SAMHSA 1993). Second, all of the ten problems surveyed increased between 1985 and 1991, with the most substantial increases occurring for feeling alone and isolated (from 1.6 to 5.7 percent), feeling suspicious and mistrustful of others (from 1.9 to 6.6 percent), and getting less work done at school or work (from 1.3 to 3.5 percent).

Despite the rhetoric holding that cocaine and crack are instantly addicting, there is little epidemiological evidence that users of cocaine or crack are significantly more likely to develop dependence than are users of other drugs. Table 3–9 shows findings from the 1991 NIDA household survey on self-reported indicators of dependence. It is important to note that criteria for a finding of dependence are not based on a single indicator but on various combinations of indicators. Here, however, we will restrict attention to the separate indicators. Among those who used cocaine at least once in the past year, 32 percent reported trying to cut down their use of cocaine, 10 percent needed larger amounts to get the same effect or for which they could no longer get high on the amount they used before, 8 percent used cocaine every day or almost every day for two or more weeks in a row, 8 percent felt dependent, and 7 percent experienced withdrawal symptoms (SAMHSA 1993). The percentages reporting these problems are higher among regular users; still, about half of cocaine users who used at least once a month did not report any of the five dependence indicators.

Perhaps the most striking point in table 3–9 is that the percentage of cocaine users who report indicators of dependence is not dramatically different from problems cited by marijuana users and substantially lower compared to cigarette smokers. These findings are similar to those from the Epidemiological Catchment Area surveys.[3] From a sample of 611 cocaine users drawn from a probability sample of 13,500 respondents over 1981–1984, recreational cocaine users, (those who used six or more times but never daily for two weeks) reports of dependence were low: 2.6 percent reported feeling dependent; 2.4 percent were unable to cut down the amount used; and 7.7% reported tolerance and 0.9% experienced withdrawal (Anthony & Petronis 1989). Moreover, dependence indicators were significantly lower than were those cited by 126

TABLE 3-9

*Percentage Reporting Dependence Indicators in the Past Year
Attributed to Cocaine, Marijuana, and Cigarettes:
U.S. 12 Years and Older, 1991*

	Cocaine Use	Marijuana Use	Cigarette Use
Among those who used cocaine in past year	(N = 1,279)	(N = 4,030)	(N = 9,765)
Tried to cut down	32	28	65
Need larger amounts	10	7	14
Used daily for two or more weeks	8	14	71
Felt dependent	8	8	63
Withdrawal symptoms	7	3	23
Among those who used once a month or more	(N = 482)	(N = 2,035)	(N = 3,172)
Tried to cut down	48	36	67
Need larger amounts	19	12	16
Used daily for two or more weeks	17	26	88
Felt dependent	17	14	81
Withdrawal symptoms	14	5	29

Source: SAMHSA (1993).

heroin users: 7.2 percent reported feeling dependent, 1.5 percent reported being unable to stop, 11.8 percent reported tolerance, and 10.1% experienced withdrawal. Differences in dependence were even more sizable when those who used daily for at least two weeks were compared.

Using the 1985 NIDA household survey, Adams and Gfroerer (1991) examined the predictors of cocaine abuse and dependence among 435 adults who used cocaine during the past year. They found that among males, four factors significantly increased the probability of dependence: being unmarried, having moved more than two times during the past five years, using cocaine twelve or more times in the past year, and having used cocaine fifty or more times in their lifetime. Among women, only two factors increased the likelihood of dependence: using cocaine intravenously and having used cocaine more than five years.

TREATMENT ADMISSIONS

One traditional indicator of the size of the abusing population is the number of users seeking treatment, but like any other measure, it has strengths and weaknesses. In addition to measuring the size of the abusing population, treatment admissions can be influenced by such factors as the available treatment slots and social norms, attitudes, and stigmatization about treatment. As well, few treatment agencies separate cocaine from crack in determining the major problem of abuse. Another complicating factor is that multiple drug problems are often the norm, so determining the client's primary problem may be far from straightforward.

Despite these problems, two observations regarding cocaine treatment seem apparent. First, cocaine and crack are currently the dominant drugs of abuse among treatment seekers. At the Addiction Research Foundation's Clinical Institute in Toronto, 18 percent of all clients seeking treatment (including alcohol) in 1991 cited cocaine as their major problem of abuse (Metro Toronto Research Group on Drug Use [MTRGDU] 1993). Figure 3–6 shows the percentage of nonalcohol treatment admissions in Toronto and nineteen U.S. centers (NIDA 1992). It indicates substantial variation in the percentage of clients seeking treatment primarily for cocaine, ranging from 20 percent in Los Angeles to 90 percent in Atlanta. Despite this variation, cocaine treatment activity is still prevalent; in fifteen of the twenty sites, cocaine is ranked as the primary drug of abuse (excluding alcohol).

The second observation is that cocaine has become a greater problem among the drug-using population than it was in earlier years. Indeed, cocaine users were not prominent in most treatment populations until the mid-1980s or after crack arrived. For example, data collected from 1977 to 1979 from a street-level drug and crisis center in Alberta indicated no cocaine users seeking assistance (Clark & McKiernan 1981). In Toronto, the percentage of clients seeking treatment for cocaine increased 200 percent, from 6 percent in 1984 to 18 percent in 1991 (MTRGDU 1993). In the Detroit area, the percentage of clients admitted for treatment who cited cocaine as their primary problem increased 140 percent, from 15 percent in 1986 to 36 percent in 1992 (NIDA 1993).

Although it is clear that treatment activity regarding cocaine and crack has increased, we cannot be sure what this increase means. It

FIGURE 3–6

Percentage of Nonalcohol Treatment Admissions for Primary Cocaine Abuse and Number of Emergency Room Mentions per 100,000

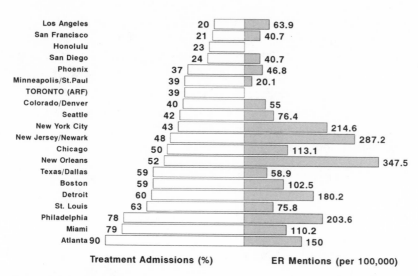

Treatment Admissions (%)   ER Mentions (per 100,000)

Source: NIDA Dec. 1993

may reflect an increase in the size of the cocaine-using population, an increase in the size of the cocaine-abusing population, or both, or it may mean that more users are deciding to seek treatment.

EMERGENCY ROOM INDICATORS

An indicator of acute drug abuse problems is the number of individuals attending hospital emergency rooms because of a drug-related problem. In Canada, no nationwide reporting network monitors such events. In the United States, these data are made available by the Drug Abuse Warning Network (DAWN). In 1990, the sample of hospitals was changed to a more scientifically rigorous probability sample, which includes over 500 hospitals nationwide. Although many of the weaknesses of DAWN's emergency room data were therefore improved, the disadvantage is that long-term changes in emergency room activity are no longer comparable to samples before 1990. In the right half of figure 3–6 we display the number of emergency room mentions per 100,000. As with treatment admissions, there is substantial variation in emergency room rates, ranging from 20.1 for Minneapolis–St. Paul to 347.5 for New Orleans (NIDA 1993). Again, cocaine is a dominant drug problem in emergency room mentions, ranking first in eleven of eighteen sites.

Cocaine, however, is not the most common drug cited in non-lethal emergency room episodes. In 1990, estimated total drug episodes were 371,208. The most common drug mentioned was alcohol, representing 31 percent of all drug episodes (DAWN 1991a). Alcohol was followed by cocaine (22 percent), narcotics (16 percent), analgesics (15 percent), and tranquilizers (14 percent). The remaining drugs were mentioned in less than 10 percent of emergency room episodes.

DRUG-RELATED DEATHS

Perhaps one of the more salient—and sensational—indicators of acute cocaine problems is drug-related deaths. This indicator, which can be difficult to interpret, can provide a rough indication of the relative contribution of cocaine to other drugs in drug-related deaths and under certain circumstances, can provide a rough estimate of changes in cocaine-related consequences. Trends are the more difficult to interpret. In addition to reflecting more drug users, increases in the number of deaths could be due to changes in such factors as purity, dosage, frequency of use, route of administration, and use of other drugs. Also complicating the picture is that more than one drug is typically involved in a drug-related death. Although the interpretation of changes in drug-related deaths is prone to ambiguity, the absolute number of deaths can still provide a rough indication of the size of the problem.

Estimates from the DAWN data show that narcotics are the most frequently mentioned in medical examiner reports of lethal episodes. In 1990, the DAWN data estimated 5,830 lethal drug episodes (DAWN 1991b). Of these, narcotics were mentioned in 60 percent of episodes, followed by cocaine (43 percent), alcohol (40 percent), antidepressants (23 percent), and tranquilizers (16 percent). Other drugs accounted for under 5 percent of lethal episodes.

As we saw with treatment admissions and emergency room episodes, rates of cocaine problems can vary dramatically among different cities. In 1991, the number of cocaine-related deaths—those in which cocaine was detected but was not necessarily the cause of death—was 1.1 deaths per 100,000 in Toronto, 1.3 in Phoenix, 1.6 in Minneapolis, 3.9 in San Francisco, and 10.4 in Miami (NIDA 1993). For drug-involved deaths—those in which cocaine was determined to be a significant factor—the figures were 0.5 deaths per 100,000 in Toronto, 1.5 in San Diego, 1.9 in Seattle, and 11.0 in New York. Clearly cocaine has not affected all urban centers with equal severity.

Purposive, Clinical, and Ethnographic User Studies

General population surveys are useful in establishing the size of the using population; however, their weakness is in capturing hard-to-reach populations and not collecting qualitative information about the character of drug use. Purposive, clinical, and ethnographic studies extend survey results in several ways. Most adult surveys, especially those in Canada, find relatively few cocaine users. Most survey-identified users are likely to be infrequent users with relatively few problems. Studies of heavy-using populations are necessary to establish the characteristics of heavy users, their rate of problems, and treatment requirements. They also help to establish the context of cocaine use, the way it is used, what other drugs are used at the same time, and a myriad of other details. Only with these studies can we gain sufficient depth of analysis with a wide variety of heavy cocaine users.

There should be no debate that general population surveys inevitably miss the populations that are at the greatest risk of using cocaine: individuals who are often without conventional and stable housing, such as the unemployed, street youth, and the homeless. For example, a 1992 survey of 217 Toronto street youth (those aged under 25 years who were homeless or using street-oriented social services) found that 53 percent used cocaine in their lifetime, 31 percent used it in the past year, and 3 percent used it daily (Smart et al. 1992). Regarding crack cocaine, 42 percent, 31 percent, and 5 percent used it in their lifetime, past year, and daily, respectively. When asked which drug caused the major problem for them, crack cocaine ranked first (by 44 percent of crack users) followed by inhalants (39 percents) and cocaine powder (30 percent).

This survey cannot be considered representative in the sense that the youth were not drawn by probability methods, but the sample was designed to produce a heterogeneous sample. Youth were derived from ten social-services agencies and from street contacts as well. The cocaine use of these street youth was compared to age- and gender-matched samples drawn from the Ontario Student Drug Use Survey. In total, three groups were compared: students who had not run away from home, students who had run away from home two or more times during the past year, and street youth. Among street youth, 31 percent reported using cocaine compared to 13 percent of runaways and 3 percent of nonrunaways; among street youth, 31 percent used crack cocaine during the past year compared to 5 percent of runaways and 1 percent of nonrunaways (Smart et al. 1992).

To understand the complexity and scope of cocaine problems, we cannot restrict our attention solely to general population surveys because many of those at highest risk for both use and abuse of cocaine are hard to reach. At the same time, we cannot necessarily conclude that because rates of cocaine use are dramatically higher in such hard-to-reach groups that general population estimates are necessarily downwardly biased. Whether population estimates are significantly affected by the hard to reach is a function not only of the difference in drug use between the two groups but also of the relative size of the two groups. For example, it is unlikely that including street youth in adolescent population surveys would significantly alter drug use estimates because the size of the population is extremely small. Analyses from the Epidemiological Catchment Areas program found that although the prevalence of cocaine use was significantly higher in the institutionalized population, their inclusion in the total sample had a small effect on the overall estimate of cocaine use (Trinkoff, Ritter & Anthony 1990).

Several early studies have provided extensive literature reviews interspersed with the experiences and feelings of users. Grinspoon and Bakalar (1976) conducted one of the earlier studies on cocaine. Using a snowball technique, they informally interviewed seventeen people who had used cocaine regularly at one time or were users at the time of the interview. The experience of these users varied from intermittent to heavy use for many years; most were primarily intranasal users. Although they experienced physical and psychological problems, such as insomnia, irritability, and anxiety, serious toxic or psychotic reactions were rare. Phillips and Wynne (1980) informally interviewed approximately one hundred self-reported cocaine users and dealers, again employing a snowball technique. As well, they solicited, via radio, letters written by users describing some of their personal experiences with cocaine. Both of these works provided excellent reviews of the literature in addition to the anecdotal information provided by users.

Spotts and Shontz (1980) have provided the best in-depth profile of intravenous cocaine users. Using a representative case method, they selected nine males whose preferred drug was cocaine, each depicting a variant life-style or "life adjustment pattern." The participants were selected from a pool of users suggested to the researchers by intermediaries from the criminal justice system and drug treatment programs. The researchers emphasized the selection of intravenous users; in this way they could obtain sufficient data to confirm or to refute the myths or realities surrounding the use of cocaine in its potentially most hazardous form. The following findings are of particular interest:

1. Most users felt a powerful attachment to cocaine but not to the extent of absolute necessity.
2. Cocaine unequivocally produced euphoric effects and a sense of well-being.
3. Low-dose users felt the drug enhanced social relationships; heavy users reported the converse.
4. All agreed that cocaine is not physically addicting; many reported temporary tolerance.
5. Users reported extreme differences in intensity between intranasal and intravenous administration.
6. Some users reported daily intravenous use of large doses for extended periods. For instance, one respondent reported daily intravenous use of 3 grams of pharmaceutical cocaine for two years.
7. Most intranasal users reported few serious adverse effects; nasal congestion and rhinorrhea were most common. Similarly, most intravenous users did not report severe medical complications associated with use. In fact, none had ever received emergency medical treatment for drug-related conditions.

Siegel (1985) conducted an early follow-up study of cocaine users. Initially he recruited 118 users for a study in 1976; 99 of them were social-recreational users using at least 1 gram per month for twelve months. Sixty-one users participated in all phases of the first four years, and fifty of these participated in a follow-up study in 1983. Although all users employed intranasal administration at the start of the study, by 1978 39 percent had smoked cocaine, or freebased (10 percent became primarily freebase smokers). All users reported episodes of cocaine abstinence, while twenty-five maintained their pattern of social-recreational use for nine years. However, four intensified their use, while five became compulsive users, most of them freebase smokers. Regarding prior drug experiences, all cocaine users had used marijuana and alcohol before the use of cocaine, and many had had experience with other illicit drugs.

Users in Siegel's study reported numerous adverse reactions, such as anxiety, paranoia, and irritability. Social-recreational users, however, tended not to report serious toxic or psychological crises, which were very common among compulsive users and intensive users. Few required treatment except for specific medical complaints, such as perforated nasal septa and skin disorders associated with intravenous use. However, users did report recognizing the need to "detoxify" or limit their use of cocaine. Most seemed to be able to develop strategies to do this adequately without professional guidance. This may, in part, explain why relatively few people are admitted to drug abuse treatment with cocaine as their primary problem. In general, Siegel's study suggests that most social-recreational users can maintain a low to moderate use pattern without escalating to dependency and that many users can essentially "treat themselves."

Several interesting findings have emerged from the 1-800-CO-CAINE help line, a telephone counseling service established in the United States (Gold 1984). Callers can dial a toll-free number to obtain advice about drug abuse, especially cocaine, although they are requested to complete a questionnaire over the telephone. A random selection of 500 callers found that 61 percent were using cocaine intranasally, 21 percent were freebasing, and 18 percent were injecting. Most had been using cocaine for about five years. The average caller was 30 years of age, and the majority calling were male (67 percent). The average number of years of education was 14.1 years; about 40 percent had incomes over $25,000. Regarding problems associated with use, most reported sleep disorders (82 percent), chronic fatigue (76 percent), headache (60 percent), depression (83 percent), irritability (82 percent), and memory problems (57 percent). Reports of losing jobs, spouses, or friends because of cocaine were not uncommon. Compared to the findings of several other studies, no relationship was found between adverse consequences and reported dose or frequency of cocaine use.

To examine the use of cocaine among high-income users, an additional analysis was made of fifty-seven males and thirteen females with annual incomes over $50,000 (Washton, Gold & Pottash 1984). Current use averaged 15 grams per week, and 70 percent said that they felt addicted. Despite their high incomes, 19 percent were dealing cocaine and 18 percent were stealing to support the habit. Some 13 percent had lost jobs because of cocaine.

Gold (1984) also reported findings regarding the use of cocaine by sixty adolescent callers (twenty-eight females and thirty-two males) with a mean age of 17 years. Most had been using cocaine for about fifteen months, and all started as intranasal users. The average caller reported twelve to twenty-two possible psychiatric effects, such as anxiety, depression, paranoia, and suspiciousness. A large proportion (42 percent) were dealing drugs, and 20 percent had been arrested for cocaine-related crime.

Cocaine users volunteering for experiments with the drug have been studied by Schuster and Fischman (1985). Employing a word-of-mouth referral system, they located 137 intravenous cocaine users who were from 21 to 35 years of age, male or nonpregnant females, and healthy. About 69 percent were male, and the average age was 27, as would be expected on the basis of surveys. A majority were high school graduates (59 percent) or college graduates (16 percent), and about 42 percent were employed. Of those accepted, almost all used alcohol, stimulants, and cannabis, and many had used opiates (46 percent) and hallucinogens (39 percent). Only 10 percent had used only cocaine, and most (72 percent) had used at least three other drugs. One of the most interesting aspects of this study is the large number of cocaine users rejected for heart problems, given the age of the sample. Some 25 percent were rejected for high blood pressure, 11 percent had heart disease, and 9 percent had an abnormal electrocardiogram. In addition, 7 percent had a major depression and 5 percent had other types of psychiatric illness.

By far, the most comprehensive ethnographic study of cocaine users was conducted by Dan Waldorf and his colleagues Craig Reinarman and Sheigla Murphy (1991). This work represents a study of three primary groups of cocaine users: (1) a main sample of 228 users (subdivided into 122 current users and 106 quitters), (2) a follow-up sample of 21 users who were first interviewed in 1974 and reinterviewed in 1986, and (3) a sample of 53 crack and freebase users. The most salient finding of this study was the wide variability found in the use-abuse continuum. For both cocaine and crack users, there was no uniform progression or pattern of use. Indeed, although many developed problems because of their cocaine use, about half of the participants maintained a controlled pattern of cocaine use, for some up to a decade.

More recently, Cohen and Sas (1993) reported on a six-year follow-up study of sixty four cocaine users reinterviewed in 1991, who were among 160 users first interviewed in 1987. They found that almost half of the 1991 participants had terminated their use of cocaine since 1987, while for the other half use had stabilized at a lower level. Only 6 percent of their follow-up sample sought assistance to help them control or quit using cocaine. Like Waldorf, Reinarman, and Murphy (1991), Cohen and Sas concluded that controlled use of cocaine was a common pattern exhibited among their 64 users.

Cocaine-Using Populations in Treatment

Studies of treatment populations give indications of the characteristics of cocaine-using groups whose use requires intervention. Such populations will contain higher proportions of heavy users and dependent persons than surveys or purposive samples. They also tend to contain more users experiencing social-psychological, legal, and coping problems. Nevertheless, studies of treated groups are necessary to provide a fuller picture for epidemiological information.

One of the early treatment studies, by Gawin and Kleber (1985), reported on thirty patients in a cocaine abuse outpatient treatment program at Yale University. The average educational level was 12.8 years, and about 70 percent were regularly employed. There were eleven intranasal users, thirteen intravenous users, and six smokers of cocaine. Intravenous users tended to use larger amounts of cocaine, to have longer drug-using careers, and to have had previous treatment experiences. About 30 percent of the total number of cocaine users were also alcohol abusers. This study suggests that intravenous users may be more likely to enter treatment, but they are more likely to report unsuccessful outcome.

Schnoll et al. (1985) studied 172 cocaine abusers in a combined inpatient and outpatient drug treatment program in Chicago. The percentage of clinic patients reporting cocaine dependency escalated from 6 percent in 1979 to 51.8 percent in 1983. About 69 percent were males and about 20 percent were unemployed. Almost all (84 percent) had completed high school. Some 44 percent were freebasers, 35 percent were sniffers, and 22 percent were intravenous users. About 56 percent were daily users of cocaine; in addition, 43 percent used cannabis nearly every day. Only 23 percent had been previously treated for alcohol or drug problems, but 30 percent had had outpatient care for psychiatric problems. A few had been arrested for dealing (5 percent) or possessing cocaine (10 percent). What is notable in this sample is the affluent nature of the population, probably due in part to the location of the clinic. It is also striking that so many respondents were freebasers. It is not clear whether freebasers are more likely to need treatment; perhaps affluent patient groups simply contain more freebasers.

Siegel's (1982b) study of thirty-two freebasers seeking treatment in California is one of the few works with this group of users. The majority were male (twenty-three males and nine females) and generally older (31.3 years of age) than most other survey- and treatment-identified groups. Ten were employed in entertainment, ten in business, and eight were cocaine dealers. All had initiated use intranasally before freebasing, and all were multidrug users. Most reported several physical and psychological symptoms typical of heavy cocaine users. Users engaged in cocaine smoking binges lasting up to fourteen days.

More recently Means and associates (1989) commented that many early studies of cocaine abusers in treatment used middle-class samples, often from private treatment centers. These clients tend to be well educated, employed, and well motivated for treatment. In contrast, Means and associates studied cocaine abusers seen in a public treatment agency near New York City. As expected, these clients were more often lower and lower middle class than those reported on by Gawin and Kleber (1985), Schnoll (1985), Siegel (1982), and others. For example, 66.6 percent were blue-collar workers; most had family incomes under $25,000, and 32 percent were unemployed.

Two studies have differentiated cocaine users in general from users in treatment. Chitwood and Morningstar (1985) compared ninety-five treatment clients and seventy-five nonclients selected through a snowball technique. No differences emerged with respect to demographic characteristics of marital status, sex, ethnicity, or occupation. As expected, users in treatment had a much higher level of cocaine use and also reported substantially more social problems. Those in treatment were more often unemployed, having been fired from jobs; they also were engaged in more illegal behavior and were more often arrested. Additionally, the treatment group was more socially isolated, reporting fewer friends than did users not in treatment. Clearly, cocaine users who sought treatment in this study differed substantially from users who do not.

Rose, Brown, and Haertzer (1989) compared cocaine-abusing volunteers in a research ward to those attending an outpatient treatment program. There were no differences in amount of cocaine used or the route of administration. Research clients, however, were older, more often black, and less often married, while treatment clients were more anxious and hostile on psychological tests but had less often been involved in crimes such as shoplifting and burglary.

Cocaine use by narcotic addicts has been noted in several studies. Hunt et al. (1984) examined cocaine use by 368 methadone clinic patients and 142 narcotic addicts who were not in treatment. Among the methadone clients, recruited from four treatment programs in three northeastern states, about 36 percent had used cocaine in the week prior to being interviewed. Even more striking, 7 percent used cocaine at least daily. Use was lowest among those who were doing well in treatment (19 percent) and highest among those who were in treatment but still using heroin (72 percent used cocaine in past week). Methadone clients used cocaine because it gave them an instant gratification, a "rush," that reminded many of the heroin rush; almost all injected their cocaine.

Kolar and associates (1990) examined 2,414 clients in eleven methadone programs in Baltimore. They reported that 47.9 percent of methadone clients in Maryland had problems with cocaine; however, only 15.1 percent of clients had a positive urinalysis during a one-month trial. The authors suggested that many of those with serious cocaine problems drop out early from methadone treatment and hence are not involved in many urinalyses.

Several studies have shown that crack abusers in treatment are more socially unstable than other cocaine abusers. For example, Wallace (1990b) found crack abusers at a special crack treatment center to be mostly high school dropouts (53 percent), black (90 percent), and unemployed (40 percent) because of crack. Most used crack only or crack and cannabis, usually daily. They came primarily from dysfunctional ghetto families with substantial social problems.

Several studies have shown that a large number of cocaine-dependent persons come from families with alcohol problems. For example, Miller and associates (1989) showed that 50 percent of cocaine addicts in treatment had first-degree relatives who were alcohol dependent, about the same rate as for alcoholics. Also, Wallace (1990a) found that 61 percent of crack addicts in treatment were children of alcoholics, and many had experienced violence in their families. Clearly, many cocaine addicts come from multiproblem families.

Summary

Since the first edition of *The Steel Drug* in 1987, the cocaine scene has changed dramatically. At that time, cocaine was at its apex of use; since then, use has declined. In Canada in 1987, crack cocaine was but a footnote in the drug scene; today crack has established itself as a dominant drug of abuse, especially in many inner-city communities in the United States. In summary, we note the following:

• Although cocaine, primarily powder, has spread to countries outside North America, the prevalence of use there remains low by North American standards. The exception is South American countries such as Peru, where the chewing of coca leaves is dominant. Despite a low prevalence of cocaine use in countries outside North America, there has been an increase in cocaine abuse among treatment populations in several countries.

- In the United States, the use of cocaine among the mainstream population showed a clear epidemic progression, characterized by an onset period about 1979, an epidemic period from 1979 to 1989, and a postepidemic period beginning in 1989. In contrast, there is no evidence that such an epidemic occurred in Canada. Moreover, an examination of the secular change in cocaine use between Canada and the United States leads us to wonder whether different drug epidemic potentials exist between the two nations.
- Crack's entry as a drug of abuse has been restricted to populations outside the mainstream, especially impoverished inner-city areas. Population surveys do not suggest a significant epidemic, and rates of crack use have remained low. The increasing harm caused by the use of crack has been restricted to indicators such as emergency room episodes, treatment admissions, drug arrests, and cocaine-related deaths. This does not imply that the size of the crack-using population has increased but rather than its harm has intensified among populations that are prone to problematic drug use.
- Although there is no doubt that crack has a high addictive liability, the evidence seems incontrovertible regarding controlled use of both cocaine and crack. Clearly, the notion that crack is an instantly addicting substance is without foundation.

Part II

Cocaine Users
in the Community

4

Study Design

B ecause social-recreational use of cocaine is a relatively new phenomenon, few studies have been done. We know from chapter 1 that cocaine was used in the early part of this century in a variety of over-the-counter medicines and tonics and was also available in pure form from drugstores without a medical prescription. The controls levied on cocaine in Canada in the 1908 Proprietary and Patent Medicine Act and the 1911 Opium and Drug Act effectively prohibited any but the most limited medical usage of the drug. There is little evidence of use of cocaine from these early years through to the end of the 1960s (LeCavalier 1983). Indeed, in 1969 when the LeDain Commission inaugurated Canada's first national survey of drug use, cocaine was not investigated specifically (LeDain 1973). In slightly more than a decade, however, cocaine convictions rose steadily. The Bureau of Dangerous Drugs reported 44 convictions in 1972, 592 in 1979, and 1,953 in 1984. Thefts of cocaine from doctors' offices, hospitals, and pharmacies also increased, from 17 in 1972 to 124 in 1983.

Although no national surveys had been conducted at the time we initiated our study in 1983, a later survey showed that 0.9 percent of Canadian adults had used cocaine in the past year (HWC 1985); moreover, a 1984 Ontario household survey indicated that 3.3 percent of adults had used cocaine at some time in their lives (Smart & Adlaf 1984). The conviction statistics, in conjunction with considerable anecdotal material presented in various media, suggested that cocaine use had become increasingly popular in Canada and thus warranted investigation. Representative surveys of the population tend to identify few cocaine users and very few heavy users, whereas studies of those in treatment include more heavy users and thus overestimate the extent of problems from cocaine use. Consequently, there is a need for studies of users in the community who are not currently in treatment or identified solely because of a cocaine problem.

This chapter presents the research design and selected findings of in-depth interviews with 111 users of cocaine. The research challenge was to locate a group of fairly typical cocaine users in the community rather than those who had presented themselves for treatment or had been in trouble with the law. The principal criteria for selection in the study, in addition to some experience with cocaine in the past three years, were that participants must be 21 years of age or older and must have been employed at least six of the past twelve months.

Method

Obtaining a Community-Based Sample of Drug Users

Locating subjects at large is always a difficult task, and one made more challenging when the activities of interest are illegal. There were four major hurdles to overcome in this study:

1. Locating cocaine users whose experience with the drug was appropriate for the purpose of the research.
2. Enlisting the cooperation of eligible users.
3. Establishing good rapport between subject and interviewer so that a full range and richness of personal material could be elicited.
4. Obtaining valid responses.

Successful removal of these obstacles is intimately connected with the protection of subjects' identities through the provision of meaningful guarantees of confidentiality.

A number of other studies in drug- or crime-related areas have also had to confront these issues. When Goode (1970) interviewed 200 marijuana smokers in 1967, the clandestine and relatively new activity of cannabis use offered a parallel to the secretive but emerging popularity of cocaine use in the 1980s (Murray 1984). In the 1970s, Plant's (1975) field study of different types of drug takers in an English town and Goldstein's (1979) interviews with female drug users and prostitutes in the United States placed similar demands on the researchers' ingenuity. In all of these studies, the primary task of locating willing subjects was undertaken by an expanding network of personal contacts—the snowball technique. The snowball technique was pioneered by Katz and Lazarsfeld (1955) and later applied by Coleman, Katz, and Menzel (1966) in sociological studies of communication flow. This method was seized upon by other sociologists as particularly useful for the study of illicit activities that are group oriented and widely undertaken (Biernacki & Waldorf 1981). As Becker (1963) had noted and Goode (1970) reiterated, the universe of drug users, which is large and unknown, does not readily become accessible for purpose of a random sample. To select as representative a cross-section of users as possible becomes the attainable objective. In so doing, we try to avoid the inherent bias of studying those who have already been the object of official attention by treatment or law enforcement agencies (unless, of course, this is the group of particular interest). A number of studies of cocaine users described earlier were built on personal contacts with potential subjects (Grinspoon & Bakalar 1976; Phillips & Wynne 1980; Waldorf et al. 1977).

Going to the community is the starting point. Goode (1970), Plant (1975), and Goldstein (1979) all broadcast widely their interest in obtaining subjects to friends, colleagues, and acquaintances. From initial sources, contacts were made, and then these interviewees were asked to supply names of others who might be willing to take part in the study. Sometimes the subject as intermediary negotiated the acceptance or refusal on behalf of the researcher; in other instances, the interviewer accompanied the subject to meetings with other potential interviewees. The importance of being perceived as both a serious researcher and an "okay guy" was essential to making this technique effective. While the nature of this technique precludes calculation of the usual refusal rate, noncompliance was rare once direct contact was made, and adequate samples were achieved.

Once contact was made and participation agreed, Goode, Plant, and Goldstein noted a number of features that helped establish rapport during the interview. Being attentive, nonjudgmental, knowledgeable about the subject matter (using slang terms, for instance), informal in dress, relaxed in manner, and able to inspire trust are all basic and essential interviewing skills. In addition, Goldstein commented that "the actual act of interviewing, however, has always seemed to be more a function of individual personality and creativity than of carefully planned tactics" (1979:19). In this kind of interviewing, what seems to be required, above and beyond the abilities necessary to good survey research, is an ability to be genuinely interested in and caring about the subjects.

Protection of subjects' identities was foremost in the minds of interviewer and interviewee alike in these studies, and a variety of strategies were employed to this end. No names or telephone numbers were recorded unless absolutely necessary, and then only on a separate scrap of paper that was destroyed as soon as the interview was complete. Interviews often took place on neutral territory (e.g., an office, a park, or a restaurant), with choice as to time and place largely in the control of subjects. Notes and responses were transcribed by Goode, Plant, and Goldstein, and Goode also used a tape recorder. These methods apparently posed no problem once trust was established. No researcher reported any breach of confidentiality or any effort by officials to investigate the records.

Finally, most of the techniques used to gain the subjects' cooperation and trust were also thought to contribute to the validity of the research. The investigators argued that the subjects had nothing to gain from the research, the interviewer had no power over their lives, and hence subjects had no motive to lie or distort answers. Of course, all self-report studies are open to question about the accuracy of recall, confusion, and the provision of socially acceptable replies, but there is nothing inherent in this method of recruiting subjects to raise doubts about validity. Quite the opposite may be true: if subjects feel particularly valuable and sought after, and participate primarily out of interest or at least curiosity, considerable confidence may be placed in the openness and honesty of their replies.

In sum, other studies have been conducted successfully in similar and equally sensitive areas as those contained in the current research. Obviously such studies are somewhat unpredictable and time-consuming, and they provide a relatively small sample; they are appropriate to generate rather than test hypotheses; and they place considerable demands on interviewers' resources and ingenuity. Yet experience shows such research can be done.

Advertising is a second strategy to consider when seeking a community-based sample of cocaine users. It does have drawbacks. Self-selected samples are highly unlikely to be representative; for instance, one would not expect the higher-status, older, and more affluent user of cocaine to volunteer for an interview about this illegal activity. With the exception of a treatment-seeking motivation (Gold 1984), there is little incentive for individuals to offer their services as research subjects to counterbalance a possible risk of detection. To provide payment for subjects introduces the possibility of attracting both those willing to fabricate a story and also a disproportionate number of unemployed and needy individuals. Nevertheless, studies of illicit drug users have been done successfully using this approach (Powell 1973; Blackwell 1983; Phillips & Wynne 1980). Advertising for subjects appears to have merit when the objective is to probe the variety and richness of experience of elusive subjects in a relatively uncharted area.

Sample Selection

The objective of this study was to examine the social-recreational use of cocaine among fairly typical adult users in the community. Students were deliberately excluded because as a group they are relatively detached from conventional adult roles and from community standards of drug use behavior. The criteria for sample inclusion were aimed at obtaining a wide variety of experience with cocaine. Specifically, use of cocaine at least once in the past three years was the minimum criterion, with no maximum limit. To meet the requirement of adult, each participant had to be at least 21 years of age. Respondents were screened as well, on the criterion of employment, which was operationally defined as spending at least six of the past twelve months in full-time employment. Housewives were considered employed.

A total of 111 participants were obtained from two separate sources: personal contacts and an advertising campaign. Potential participants were sought initially from friends and acquaintances of the researchers. These initial contacts led to additional interviews with the participants' friends, thus producing a snowball effect. When the personal contact network became exhausted after producing nearly fifty interviews, the advertising strategy was deployed, with advertisements placed in Toronto newspapers, announcements broadcast on radio and television programs, and posted advertisements in various Toronto business establishments. Although none of the advertisements offered payment to respondents, all participants obtained through this method were paid a stipend. The advertisement was worded as follows:

Experience With Cocaine

People experienced with cocaine are required for a social research project at the Addiction Research Foundation.

For some people, drugs have become a part of everyday life. We are interested in learning more about how this happens, and also what people like and do not like about various drugs.

Must be aged 21 or over and have used cocaine sometime in the past three years.

—One Private Anonymous Interview Required!

In total, forty-seven participants were obtained from the researchers' personal networks and sixty-four from the advertising campaign. A comparison of these two groups in terms of demographic characteristics and cocaine use showed no differences in gender, marital status, and cocaine use. However, compared to the personal network group, participants in the advertising group tended to be older and were more likely to report being unemployed or having a lower income.

The major safeguard adopted to ensure anonymity for participants was that a record of names, addresses, and telephone numbers was neither required nor maintained. The interviews were conducted in a face-to-face setting, either at the interviewer's office or at a place of the respondent's choosing, and usually lasted about one hour. At the completion of an interview, any questions raised by the participants were addressed. The interviewer provided material on the health effects and legal status of cocaine if the participant was interested. Also, if a participant asked how he or she could obtain treatment, the interviewer provided appropriate information.

Regarding the validity and accuracy of participants' responses, the interviewers assessed them to be truthfully given from cooperative respondents. Participation in the study was entirely voluntary. No advance remuneration was offered, and then only a stipend was provided upon completion of the interview. These factors, together with the safeguards concerning confidentiality and anonymity, strongly suggest that the responses are valid. Moreover, an examination of the consistency of the reported cocaine use increases confidence in the data. All participants were asked about their use of cocaine (lifetime, past year, past month) at two separate points during the interview: 85 percent of the participants reported *exactly* the same level of use at both times, with only minor variation in the balance of responses.

Comparative Survey Data

One limitation of the study is the purposive nature of the sample. Because it was derived from personal contacts and also by a process of self-selection, it may not be representative of the population of adult cocaine users. Comparisons, however, can be made with secondary sources of information regarding adult cocaine users. Included in table 4–1 are data based on a sample of cocaine users (N = 34) derived from a probability sample of Ontario adults 18 years of age and older (Smart & Adlaf 1984). Since this sample was derived from an essentially random process, it should be representative of adult cocaine users generally.

Overall, the characteristics of the community sample correspond with those identified in the provincial survey. Indeed, the male-female ratio between samples is remarkably similar: twice as many males as females are involved in each. Also, the age distribution in both samples is similar. Three exceptions, however, are worthy of mention. A prominent difference exists for education level. The participants in our study reported higher levels of education than those in the Ontario survey; 27 percent and 11 percent, respectively, obtained university degrees. Another difference is related to the overrepresentation of participants with a marital status of single.

TABLE 4-1
Demographic Characteristics of Two Samples of Cocaine Users

	Cocaine Users from Community (N=111)		Cocaine Users from Ontario Survey (N=34)[a]
	(%)	(N)	(%)
Gender			
Male	67.6	(75)	71
Female	32.4	(36)	29
Age			
21–25 years	27.9	(31)	24
26–30 years	34.2	(38)	44
31–35 years	22.5	(25)	24
36–40 years	7.2	(8)	6
41 + years	6.3	(7)	3
Not stated	1.8	(2)	—
Marital status			
Single	57.7	(64)	31
Common law	17.1	(19)	17
Married	9.0	(10)	37
Separated	5.4	(6)	—
Divorced	9.9	(11)	15
Not stated	0.9	(1)	—
Education			
Grade 9–11	15.3	(17)	20
Grade 12–13	27.0	(30)	23
Community college	18.0	(20)	40
Some university	12.6	(14)	6
University degree	19.8	(22)	—
Postgraduate degree	7.2	(8)	11
Gross family income			
$10,000 or less	18.9	(21)	12
$11–20,000	30.6	(34)	19
$21–30,000	26.1	(29)	16
$31–40,000	8.1	(9)	27
$41–50,000	9.0	(10)	—
$51–60,000	2.7	(3)	16
$61,000 and over	3.6	(4)	—
Not stated	0.9	(1)	9
Socioeconomic status of employed users (Blishen)			
I: Higher professions	11.0	(9)	—
II: Other professions	23.2	(19)	—
III: Managers/technicians	30.5	(25)	—
IV:White-collar clerical	20.7	(17)	—
V: Semiskilled/lower skilled	11.0	(9)	—
VI: Unskilled	3.7	(3)	—

[a] Based on a sample of cocaine users drawn from a Gallup probability sample of Ontario adults aged 18 and over. See Smart and Adlaf (1984).

More than half (58 percent) of the community sample were single, in contrast to 31 percent of cocaine users from the provincial survey. Differences in income between the two samples can partially be explained in relation to this finding. That is, since sample members who are single generally have lower incomes than those who are married or live in a common-law relationship, it is not surprising that the sample is overrepresented with individuals from lower income levels.

Sample Characteristics

Demographic Characteristics

Two-thirds (68 percent) of the 111 participants were male, with a mean age of 29.4 years. Most were single (58 percent), with the remainder being separated or divorced (15 percent), married (9 percent), or living in a common-law relationship (17 percent). About 40 percent had attended university, and of this group most had obtained an undergraduate or graduate degree. Half reported a gross income of $20,000 or less. Although all met the employment criterion by working full time for at least six of the previous twelve months, 26 percent were unemployed at the time of the interview.

In addition to education and income, a general measure of socioeconomic status was employed using Blishen (1967) scores derived from each respondent's occupation. This scale assigns a rank to each census occupational title in terms of education, income, and prestige. The Blishen scale can then be divided into six categories, from highest to lowest socioeconomic status. The range of occupational status of the participants varied as follows, with examples from each class:

Class I: lawyer, university professor.
Class II: financial analyst, radio broadcaster, nurse.
Class III: advertising salesman, commercial artist, musician.
Class IV: retail manager, actor.
Class V: sales clerk, auto mechanic, bartender.
Class VI: laborer, truck driver, courier.

Overall, one-third (32 percent) of the sample ranked in the top half of the scale, that is, in categories I, II, or III.

Cocaine Use Patterns Among the 111 Users

FREQUENCY AND QUANTITY

The participants were asked about use in lifetime, the past year, and the past month. They were also asked to estimate the size of dose of cocaine typically consumed, both in lines (or hits) and grams. [A line refers to the amount snorted per nostril; a hit is the amount injected.] The usual method of administration was snorting for 93 percent of those interviewed; the balance included those who injected (5 percent) and those who smoked it with cannabis or tobacco (2 percent). No regular freebase users were identified.

The data presented in table 4–2 suggest that experience with cocaine varied widely, with most using it relatively infrequently. Approximately 58 percent of the sample had used cocaine fewer than ten times during the past year; only 9 percent reported use on one hundred or more occasions. In the past month, over half of the sample (55 percent) reported no use, 25.2 percent had used it once or twice, and 13.5 percent had used it three to nine times. Thus, only a small minority of the sample (6.3 percent) were heavier, recent users of ten or more times in the past month.

Some users had difficulty estimating the quantity of cocaine they typically consumed per occasion. Among all users, 12 percent could not provide an estimate of the number of lines, or hits, taken, and 44 percent were not able to estimate the number of grams consumed. Of those who did estimate their typical consumption, the large majority reckoned it to be six lines or less and no more than half a gram. High-quantity consumption was relatively rare; none reported more than 3 grams on any given, protracted, occasion of use.

Based on the three frequency-of-use measures (lifetime, annual, and monthly), a cluster analytic technique was employed to establish an overall frequency-of-use variable.[1] This resulted in the formation of three clusters or groups of users, which we have labeled infrequent, intermediate, and frequent. On average, the frequent users ($N = 40$) reported use one hundred or more times during their lifetime, twenty to thirty-nine times during the prior year, and three to five times during the prior month. The intermediate group ($N = 48$), on average, reported use twenty to thirty-nine times during their lifetime, three to five times during the prior year, and almost none during the prior month. The infrequent users ($N = 23$), on average, reported using co-

TABLE 4–2
Use of Cocaine: Frequency and Quantity
(N = 111)

Frequency of Use	Use in Lifetime	Use in Past Year	Use in Past Month
Never	—	4.5 (5)	55.0 (61)
1–2 times	4.5 (5)	21.6 (24)	25.2 (28)
3–5 times	10.8 (12)	18.9 (21)	11.7 (13)
6–9 times	8.1 (9)	13.5 (15)	1.8 (2)
10–19 times	15.3 (17)	13.5 (15)	2.7 (3)
20–39 times	16.2 (18)	6.4 (7)	2.7 (3)
40–99 times	14.4 (16)	12.6 (14)	0.9 (1)
100 + times	30.6 (34)	9.0 (10)	0.0 (0)

Number of Lines/Hits Typically Taken per Occasion	Among All Users
1–2	19.8 (22)
2–4	19.8 (22)
4–6	27.9 (31)
6–10	9.0 (10)
10–20	9.0 (10)
20–30	2.7 (3)
Could not estimate	11.7 (13)

Estimated Grams Used per Occasion	Among All Users
Less than ¼ gram	19.8 (22)
¼–½ gram	21.6 (24)
½–1 gram	4.5 (5)
1–3 grams	9.9 (11)
Could not estimate	44.1 (49)

caine three to five times during their lifetime, once or twice during the past year, and not at all during the prior month.

LEVEL OF COCAINE USE AND DEMOGRAPHIC CHARACTERISTICS

The lack of association between most of the demographic characteristics and level of cocaine use is evident in table 4–3. Most studies on illicit drug use find that males typically use greater amounts and use more frequently than do females; this was not the case here. Among males, 25 percent, 37 percent, and 37 percent report infrequent, intermediate, and frequent levels of use, respectively, in

TABLE 4-3

Level of Cocaine Use by Demographic Characteristics

	Level of Cocaine Use			
	Infrequent (%)	Intermediate (%)	Frequent (%)	(N)
Total sample	20.7	43.2	36.0	(111)
Gender				
Male	25.3	37.3	37.3	(75)
Female	11.1	55.6	33.3	(36)
$X^2 = 4.350$ n.s.				
Age				
21–25 years	19.6	35.5	45.2	(31)
26–30 years	23.7	50.0	26.3	(38)
31 + years	37.5	42.5	20.0	(40)
$X^2 = 2.775$ n.s.				
Marital status				
Single	21.9	43.8	34.4	(64)
Married/common law	24.1	44.8	31.1	(29)
Separated/divorced	11.7	41.2	47.1	(17)
$X^2 = 1.713$ n.s.				
Education				
Grade 9–11	29.4	35.3	35.3	(17)
Grade 12–13	10.0	40.0	50.0	(30)
Community college/some university	11.8	52.9	35.3	(34)
University degree	36.7	40.0	23.3	(30)
$X^2 = 11.390$ n.s.				
Family income				
Less than $10,000	28.6	38.1	33.3	(21)
$11–$20,000	20.6	41.2	38.2	(34)
$21–$30,000	17.2	41.4	41.4	(29)
$31,000 and over	19.2	53.8	26.9	(26)
$X^2 = 2,584$ n.s.				
Socioeconomic class				
I: Higher professions	38.5	38.5	23.1	(13)
II: Other professions	16.7	40.0	43.3	(30)
III: Managers/technicians	12.9	45.2	41.9	(31)
IV: White collar/clerical	20.0	45.0	35.0	(20)
V and VI: Semiskilled/lower skilled/unskilled	33.3	46.7	20.0	(15)
$X^2 = 6.862$ n.s.				

n.s. = not significant

comparison to 11 percent, 56 percent and 33 percent among female users. The other demographic characteristics, except for education, show this lack of association with level of use.

When age of first use was examined by level of use, no significant differences were found. The mean age of first use was 23.6 years among infrequent users, 21.8 among intermediate users, and 21.9 among frequent users. At least in this sample, age of first use was not positively associated with level of use. Similarly, exposure of use, the difference between age of first use and current age, did not differentiate frequent from intermediate-level users, although infrequent users showed the shortest period of exposure (5.6 years for infrequent users, 7.5 years for intermediate users, and 7.5 years for frequent users).

PATTERN OF USE

The mean age of initiation to cocaine was 22.2 years (table 4–4). The largest number ($N = 50$) reported first using cocaine between 16 and 20 years of age; however, most of this group were aged 18, 19, or 20 at the time of first use. Generally, it is uncommon to find the initiation of a given drug occurring beyond the age of 30. Thus, the number ($N = 8$) who reported first use at a relatively older age (31–40 years of age) is noteworthy.

Related to age of first use is the users' exposure (the difference between age of first use and current age) to cocaine. On average, users' exposure was about seven years and was distributed as follows: less than three years (25 percent), four to six years (28 percent), seven to nine years (17 percent), and ten to seventeen years, (30 percent).

When asked about the time involved in occasions of cocaine use, the majority reported not extending their use beyond one day. Most remembered duration of use as three to six hours ($N = 22$) or seven to twelve hours ($N = 23$). A relatively large group of users ($N = 32$), however, reported having used cocaine continuously for two or more days. Users were also asked the number of times they had done runs, that is, continuous duration of use: 30 percent reported never having done runs, 23 percent reported doing runs one to two times, 21 percent reported them two to four times, 9 percent reported them five to ten times, and 17 percent reported doing them eleven or more times.

TABLE 4-4
Pattern of Cocaine Use
(N = 111)

Characteristic	Percentage	(N)
Age at first use		
13–15 years	3.6	(4)
16–20 years	45.0	(50)
21–25 years	30.6	(34)
26–30 years	13.5	(15)
31–35 years	2.7	(3)
36–40 years	4.5	(5)
Mean age 22.2 years		
Longest interval of use		
Less than 1 hour	5.4	(6)
1–2 hours	11.7	(13)
3–6 hours	19.8	(22)
7–12 hours	20.7	(23)
12 hours–1 day	9.0	(10)
2–3 days	18.9	(21)
4 + days	9.9	(11)
Could not say	4.5	(5)
Where typically used		
Own home	32.4	(36)
Friends	36.0	(40)
Work	6.3	(7)
Home/friends/work	11.7	(13)
Nightclub	1.8	(2)
Anyplace	11.7	(13)
Time of day		
Morning	1.8	(2)
Afternoon	3.6	(4)
Night	76.6	(85)
Whenever/varies	17.1	(19)
All day	0.9	(1)

Cocaine was typically used at a friend's home (36 percent) or at the respondent's own home (32 percent). Although the majority restricted its use to private settings, 12 percent reported using cocaine at the workplace. Eighty-five users (77 percent) typically used cocaine in the leisure hours of the evening, although a substantial number (N = 19) reported using cocaine whenever they could obtain it. Almost half (48 percent) cited sociability (especially at parties) as the main basis for use during these periods; other reasons cited were leisure or relaxation (23 percent), availability (9 percent), fatigue reduction (6 percent), and aiding work (4 percent).

Other Drug Use

A substantial percentage reported experience with drugs other than cocaine at least once during their lifetime. All had used cannabis, 95 percent had used hallucinogens other than LSD or PCP, 86 percent had used LSD, 61 percent had used narcotics other than heroin, and 29 percent had used heroin (table 4–5). Other than alcohol and cannabis, many reported current use (during the past year or past month) of four substances in particular: stimulants, hallucinogens other than LSD or PCP, tranquilizers, and LSD. About a third were near daily users of both alcohol and cannabis (at least twenty to thirty-nine times during the past month). Alcohol, cannabis, and cocaine, respectively, were the three drugs most frequently used by participants. A large number reported concurrent use of these substances, that is, use within a couple of hours of each other; 52 percent said that within a couple of hours of using cocaine, they usually consumed alcohol, and 39 percent usually used cannabis within the same period.

The respondents in this study had experience with an array of drugs, and most were recent users of alcohol and cannabis. They were also asked to describe the order in which they had first used psychoactive substances in their lives. Almost all (90 percent) had used alcohol and tobacco first or second, followed by cannabis (64 percent). Hallucinogens such as LSD tended to be used next, and the prescription drugs (stimulants, tranquilizers, and barbiturates) if used were likely to follow in the fifth or sixth positions. Interestingly, the position of cocaine was nearly always last, regardless of the number of other drugs ever used. That is, if someone had used only tobacco, alcohol, and cannabis, cocaine would be number four; if people had used all or most of the drugs on the list provided, cocaine would be ninth or tenth. It was never the first or second drug used. This chronology was due in part, no doubt, to cocaine's relatively recent arrival on the drug scene. Experimentation with other drugs, especially for the older (25 years and up) sample mem-

TABLE 4-5

Percentage of Cocaine Users Reporting Use of Other Drugs
(N = 111)

Drug	Ever in Lifetime (%)	Ever in Past Year (%)	Ever in Past Month (%)	Estimated Daily[a] (%)
Alcohol	100.0	98.2	92.8	32.4
Cannabis	100.0	95.5	85.6	30.6
Stimulants/amphetamines	84.7	62.8	27.0	0.0
Barbiturates	52.3	19.8	3.6	0.0
Tranquilizers	58.6	28.8	10.8	0.9
Heroin	28.8	8.1	1.8	0.0
Narcotics other than heroin	61.3	18.9	3.6	0.0
PCP	45.0	5.4	0.0	0.0
LSD	85.6	27.0	5.4	0.0
Hallucinogens other than LSD or PCP	94.6	49.5	13.5	0.0

[a]Daily use estimated as at least 20–39 times during the prior month.

bers, was likely to have occurred in the distant past. Cocaine's later place on the list is likely also a reflection of the ease with which cocaine can be introduced into cannabis-using social networks. Most of those interviewed were also regular cannabis users who operated in the same social milieu for both drugs.

Summary

This chapter has described the rationale for the study and the methodology employed in obtaining a community-based sample of cocaine users. The 111 participants were recruited from personal contacts and an advertising campaign. The sample's demographic characteristics were a fairly close approximation of cocaine users identified through random selection in a provincial survey. As cocaine users, the community sample members fell into a predominantly social-recreational mode, snorting the drug less than once a month, on average, in the past year. Only a very small proportion of the sample could be classified as current heavy users. Most cocaine users were also regular users of cannabis and alcohol and had experience with a variety of other drugs.

5

The Appeal of Cocaine

All psychoactive drugs have appeal, and cocaine is no exception. In fact, its appeal is probably greater than that of any other illicit drug, including cannabis. There are more users of cannabis, but cocaine users regard this drug as superior in a variety of ways.

The reported popularity of cocaine among various celebrities has glamorized its use. In some circles, cocaine has become the "great differentiator" (Stone et al. 1984:15) between who is "in" and who is not. For some, coke is high status.

Some of the responses from the participants in our study indicate that the popular status of cocaine is one of its appealing features. For instance, what someone liked most about his first experience was that he could now "brag about having done it." Someone else remembered that it meant that he was "now in the group." Another referred to the "thrill of just knowing I was doing coke." And someone made this analogy: "It's a special drug, like caviar." Still others said they tried it because it was "in vogue" and "the chic thing to do."

That the use of cocaine has increased since the early 1970s indicates that it has a special appeal now. Recall that Freud had recommended the medicinal use of cocaine as a cure for depression, fatigue, and many other ailments. He reported that under the effects of cocaine, "one feels more vigorous and more capable of work" (Freud 1884:60). And one hundred years later, similar beneficial effects of the drug have been reported by the participants in our study. When asked what they liked most about cocaine, some typical comments were:

> "I like the energizing feeling."
> "Your mind is alive, everything is intensified, everything is wonderful."
> "You feel invincible—anything is possible, you can do it all."
> "You're on top of the world."

Although cocaine has stimulating properties, some users' subjective impressions are of a calming effect. One of the participants remarked, "It calms you down, even though it sends you up." Freud (1884:60) reported that under the influence of cocaine, "one senses an increase of self-control. . . . One is simply normal, and soon finds it difficult to believe that one is under the influence of any drug at all." One of our participants who used it exclusively, in large, daily doses, observed that cocaine is "not an insulting drug." Some participants questioned whether the use of the term *high* was appropriate as far as the euphoria associated with cocaine is concerned, and they expressed sentiments similar to Freud's:

> "It's a controlled high."
> "The effects are very subtle—people may not realize they are high."
> "It makes me feel more like myself."

Although pleasurable effects are associated with the use of other psychoactive drugs, those effects may be counterproductive when the environment is not conducive to recreation, for example, when conversing with a "straight" person or trying to perform work tasks. However, under the influence of cocaine, users indicated not only that they could conceal that they had taken cocaine but also that they actually found it facilitated interaction. We have already noted that people feel that they can accomplish more under the influence of cocaine because of the lift and energy it provides. Additionally, we were told of such beneficial effects as these:

> "You can function."
> "It sharpens perceptions."
> "It gives you confidence."
> "It makes you feel more comfortable with others."

"It facilitates communication with others."
"You have the ability to conceal it and feel good—you could do business at the bank for a loan."

Many users particularly appreciated that they could benefit from the various appealing effects of cocaine without a feeling of loss of control.

First Experiences

We posed several questions to elicit information about the participants' initial experience with cocaine. From their responses, it is clear that little coaxing had been required for that first snort. Virtually all were with friends when cocaine was first offered, and most accepted the initial invitation. All of them had other prior drug-taking experiences and were curious to see what all the fuss was about. They were encouraged by the good reviews their friends had given cocaine. Consider, for example, the following explanations for accepting the initial invitation to use cocaine:

"People I know and trust said it was just amazing and wonderful."
"I was tempted from what I'd heard—you could go out and conquer the world."
"I wanted to see what the 'hype' surrounding coke was about."

It seems that it was not so much if they were going to try it but when the opportunity would present itself. This readiness was characterized with the remark that society has produced "a generation to whom testing a new drug is as routine as sampling a new season's Beaujolais" (*The Journal* 1985:1).

Although some of the respondents did not make special efforts to obtain cocaine, their readiness to use it when it was offered is illustrated by the following accounts of why they accepted the invitation:

"I had always wanted to try it but the cost deterred me until this time when it was offered."
"It was free."
"It was there, and I was offered it."
"I had used most other 'street' drugs."

"Why not? I'm always searching for a high and it was a new drug that had good reviews."

When probed for details about what they specifically liked and disliked about their first experience, most identified something appealing, and half could not think of anything objectionable. Even among those who identified something they disliked, some expressed this more as a qualification, with responses such as, "It was over so quickly" and "liking it too much." The positive responses regarding initial exposure to cocaine varied from a "sense of well-being" to "loved everything." One respondent remembered thinking, "This is the drug of the future."

The Cannabis-Cocaine Nexus

All participants had used alcohol, and many had tried other drugs prior to their initial experience with cocaine. All had used cannabis, and most continued to use it at least as often as cocaine. As well, the two drugs were often used concurrently during the same social event.

It has been suggested that the use of cocaine may be

> best understood with reference to use of other drugs, particularly the gateway drug marijuana. . . . An overwhelming majority of those who have used cocaine have previously used marijuana. . . . [Moreover,] extent of use of marijuana is strongly related to the probability that one will use cocaine. . . . [Consequently,] the best way to insure that people will never use cocaine is to prevent them from becoming heavily involved with marijuana. (Clayton, 1985:21–24)

Clearly, the relationship between cannabis and cocaine can be considered as a possible source for understanding the appeal of cocaine. The social circumstances under which these drugs are taken are quite similar: "Underlying both of these substances . . . are similar social bases of use. Both . . . are social-recreational drugs; typically, use of [cannabis and cocaine] involves sharing the drug with others" (Murray 1984:666). Thus, the use of one of these substances in such a setting is conducive to the use of the other.

The interest and status that cocaine enjoys in a cannabis-using network is illustrated by excerpts from *High in America: The True Story behind NORML* and the Politics of Marijuana:

> The year was 1977. The occasion was the big party which climaxed NORML's annual conference. . . . It was destined to be Washington's party of the year . . . the moment when "the drug culture met the establishment—everybody came out of the closet." . . . [The guests included] drug-using crazies, eminent scientists, and influential politicians. . . . [There were marijuana millionaires, celebrities, people from the news media, and more.] To have the President's drug adviser present added a final touch of legitimacy to the party. . . . [The President's adviser arrived at the party and a close friend of his approached the party's host.] He's on his way up here, and he wants to do some coke. . . . [The host, the head of NORML, took command of the situation and quickly obtained some good cocaine. He suggested that a few of his guests join him upstairs in a private room.] It took a few minutes to get everyone upstairs . . . some people were invited and others were not. . . . Most NORML parties had a room like that, where the elite could partake of their favorite drugs in private. (Anderson 1981:10, 19–20)

The Social Context of Use

The account of cocaine use among cannabis users in a party situation is instructive. The status of cocaine as a favorite drug is indicated, as is its presence and availability in this social setting. Also, the social nature of this drug-taking behavior is evident: people were invited to share in this activity. Within that setting, the idea of purchasing cocaine is not an issue. For some, it is not different from offering a person a drink; however, it is a more expensive gesture and tinged with the excitement of the forbidden.

The use of cocaine was a social event for the participants in our study. It seems to have been both available and offered in social gatherings that they attended. In fact, more than a quarter of the users in our sample had never purchased cocaine themselves, yet

---

*National Organization for the Reform of the Marijuana Laws

some were able to use it as often as weekly. On the other hand, nearly half of our participants had returned the favor at some point; 45 percent had given cocaine to friends or acquaintances.

We asked a number of questions regarding the circumstances in which cocaine was used. No one typically used it alone, and only two said they rarely used it in the company of others. The majority indicated that they knew a few other people who used cocaine, usually ten or more individuals.

We have mentioned that the effects of cocaine may facilitate social interaction. The participants reported that they felt more comfortable with others and more talkative. Even socializing with nonusers was not problematic and was not always a constraint on use. Users felt they were able to conceal the fact that they had taken cocaine. About two-thirds said they would use cocaine in the company of nonusers, mainly because the effects of cocaine would not be obvious to others; the effects can be controlled, and the drug is odorless. The third of respondents who said they avoided using cocaine when they were in the company of nonusers provided a variety of reasons for this decision, including less enjoyment, social discomfort, and the taboo nature of the drug in some circles. About half the participants said they did care whether others knew they used cocaine, but most qualified this reticence with respect to particular individuals, such as parents, other family members, and employers.

Ready initiation to use and the many social settings in which cocaine is taken highlight the social-recreational nature of its use. Controlled use during leisure hours—evenings, weekends, and special occasions—was possible for many users. In conjunction with the basically favorable view of cocaine's effects, endorsed by most respondents, it is not difficult to account for cocaine's popularity.

The Attraction for Women

A relatively high proportion of the sample (about a third) were female. This finding should not be too surprising in view of other available information. For instance, surveys indicate that a large proportion of cannabis users, though not a majority, are female. Second, there is a link between cannabis and cocaine use. Third, there is no obvious reason to expect that cannabis-using females

TABLE 5-1
Most Appealing Aspects of Cocaine Use, by Gender

Most Appealing Aspect	Male (N = 74) (%)	Female (N = 35) (%)
Euphoria	12.2	11.4
Controlled high	16.2	8.6
Cognitive energy	9.5	8.6
Confidence	5.4	11.4
Physical energy	25.6	17.1
Sociability[a]	8.1	25.7
Liked nothing	10.8	5.7
Physical sensation	5.4	11.4
Other[a]	6.9	0.0
Total	100.1	99.9

[a]$p < .05$.

have less interest in using cocaine than do their male counterparts.

The physical characteristics of powder cocaine are also well disposed to female access. A container holding a gram of cocaine, for example, would be unnoticed in a purse that held cosmetics. As well, cocaine is odorless and looks like any one of a number of inert white substances, such as saccharin. The paraphernalia associated with snorting cocaine could also go unnoticed in a purse. Certainly a compact mirror for powdering the nose would not be suspect. Cocaine use among women lends new meaning to the terminology describing this age-old practice. As one male respondent said when describing his wife and other female friends, "They're not much interested in cannabis or other drugs, but they really dive into that powder [cocaine]."

We did ask both men and women what they liked most about cocaine. There were some contrasts in the responses of these two groups, and these are apparent in table 5-1. Women were most likely to report that cocaine made them more comfortable and sociable in social situations. They were three times as likely to report this as males, and this was the only statistically significant difference. A related response was that females were twice as likely as males to identify the confidence cocaine elicited in them as what they liked most. On the other hand, they were only half as likely as males to report the "controlled high" as the most appealing aspect of cocaine use. There were other differences as well: females were less likely to like nothing about cocaine, less likely to enjoy the physical energy associated with use, yet more likely to find physical sensations appealing. We can gain further insight into what females find appealing about cocaine by examining what they do not like and noticing what they do not mention as unappealing aspects. In the next section we will return to this issue.

Unappealing Aspects of Cocaine

There were several aspects about cocaine that some participants considered unappealing. An examination of these dislikes provides an instructive contrast from which to judge the importance of cocaine's appealing factors. The most common response from men to the question regarding what they liked least about cocaine was its high financial cost. Since cocaine cost about $100 to $150 per gram at the time of our study, this response is not surprising and is compatible with our earlier finding that the participants would use cocaine more often if it was less expensive. A number of people were also concerned about effects related to the technique of snorting, particularly "dripping in the back of the throat" and "burning in the nose." As well, many disliked the transition period of coming down from the high.

Although females were most likely to find appealing the increased sociability and confidence during social interactions as a result of cocaine, no female participants reported concern about negative social consequences (table 5–2). However, women were significantly more likely to say that cocaine produced undesirable psychological or physical effects, such as insomnia, depression, nausea, and paranoia. Another interesting finding was that they were not very likely to report concern over effects related to the technique of snorting.

Certain unappealing aspects of cocaine play a role in the intention to continue or cease using the drug (table 5–3). Although the high financial cost was the most commonly reported response, the intended quitters were half as likely as the continuers to indicate that this was the least-liked factor. Those who planned to continue using cocaine were prepared to incur the financial burden. They

TABLE 5-2

Least Appealing Aspects of Cocaine Use, by Gender

Least Appealing Aspect	Male (N = 74) (%)	Female (N = 36) (%)
Coming down	14.9	11.1
Cost	25.6	19.4
Technique	20.3	8.3
Addiction/risk of addiction	12.2	13.9
Negative social consequences[a]	10.8	0.0
Psychological/physical effects[a]	12.2	36.1
Other	4.1	11.2
Total	100.1	100.0

[a] $p < .05$

were not pleased with the high price, but it did not seem to present a barrier to use, although it may have placed constraints on the frequency and quantity of their purchases and their use. In the same way, those who intended to continue using were more likely to report unfavorable psychological or physical effects of cocaine. Nevertheless, they were prepared to live with the unappealing aspects of cocaine, which were outweighed by its appealing factors. On the other hand, those who planned to quit were much more likely to cite addiction (or the potential for addiction) and negative social effects, such as being labeled a user and becoming "self-centered and insensitive to others" as reasons for quitting. They were also more likely to express concern about "coming down" and about effects associated with the technique of using. None of these differences was statistically significant.

We also examined reported dislikes in relation to frequency of use (table 5–4). Although the high cost of cocaine was mentioned by a similar proportion of participants in each category of use, there were discernible differences in other factors. For instance, none of the least frequent users stated "coming down" as something they specifically disliked, yet it was one of the major complaints of the intermediate users. The most striking finding was that nearly half of the infrequent users cited concern over effects related to the technique of use. They were several times more likely than frequent and intermediate users to identify this factor as the quality

TABLE 5–3

Least Appealing Aspects of Use
by Intention to Use or Cease Using Cocaine

	Intention to Use in the Next 12 Months	
Least Appealing Aspect	Unlikely (N = 23) (%)	Likely (N = 86) (%)
Coming down	17.4	11.6
Cost	13.0	26.7
Technique	21.7	15.1
Addiction/risk of addiction	17.4	11.6
Negative social consequences	17.4	4.7
Psychological/physical effects	13.0	22.1
Other	0.0	8.1
Total	99.9	99.9

they liked least about cocaine. It would seem that awareness of addiction and addiction potential, as well as experiencing undesirable psychological or physical effects, increases with level of use. For these more frequent users, the myth that cocaine is a safe, harmless drug has been dispelled.

Summary

This chapter has defined and illustrated the appeal of cocaine from the subjective vantage point of the user. Attractive features include its status, invigorating effects, retention of self-control under its influence, and facilitation of social interaction. First experiences generally elicited favorable responses. Further use continued primarily in a social-recreational way with a circle of friends who also used it. Few dramatic differences were found between men and women in their assessment of cocaine's appeal. Female users were more likely to highly rate its effect on sociability, and they found the undesirable physical or psychological side effects more unpleasant than male users did. Men were more likely to consider the high financial cost of cocaine its least appealing feature.

Intention to continue using was not related to cost, nor were any

TABLE 5–4

Least Appealing Aspects of Use by Frequency of Cocaine Use

Least Appealing Aspect	Frequent Use (N = 40) (%)	Intermediate Use (N = 48) (%)	Infrequent Use (N = 22) (%)
Coming down	10.0	22.9	0.0
Cost	22.5	25.0	22.7
Technique	10.0	8.3	45.5
Addiction/risk of addiction	22.5	6.3	9.1
Negative social consequences	7.5	6.3	9.1
Psychological/physical effects	25.0	22.9	4.5
Other	2.5	8.4	9.1
Total	100.0	100.1	100.0

of the other unappealing aspects significantly related to likelihood of continued use. More frequent users of cocaine expressed a higher perceived risk of addiction than did less frequent users. Users expressed clear likes, dislikes, and concerns about cocaine, but for most the pluses outweighed the minuses.

6

Problems with Cocaine

One of the major goals of the study was to examine cocaine-related reactions among varying levels of social-recreational use. For convenience and consistency, we shall refer to the entire domain of effects, problems, and adverse reactions as *reactions*. In this context, reactions are categorized into two groups: primary reactions—those subjectively pleasurable effects for which the drug is intended—and the array of side effects that includes both acute reactions (those occurring shortly after administration) and chronic reactions (those occurring upon repeated exposure), positive or negative.

Although several investigations have provided excellent reviews of the literature coupled with anecdotal information (Grinspoon & Bakalar 1976; Phillips & Wynne 1980; Waldorf et al. 1977), few have provided empirical data concerning cocaine reactions. Exceptions include a study (Washton, Gold & Pottash 1984) conducted among seventy upper-income users (incomes over $50,000 annually) contacting the 1-800-COCAINE telephone service, which found that 84 percent reported chronic fatigue, 91 percent insomnia, 83 percent depression, 87 percent irritability, and 65 percent paranoid feelings. The relatively high level of adverse reactions, however, is likely attributable to the nature of the sample—that is, users concerned enough to seek informal or formal guidance with respect to their use of cocaine.

Two other studies (Spotts & Shontz 1980; Siegel 1980) have also

115

examined reactions among different populations. Employing a representative case approach, the former study extensively profiled cocaine use among nine males, each representing a unique life-style. Spotts and Shontz noted five distinct patterns of reaction among their participants:

1. Reactions common at all usage levels, such as loss of fatigue, increased mental activity, dry mouth, increased heart rate, sweating, loss of appetite, increased pulse rate, increased activity and restlessness, increased talkativeness, and insomnia.
2. Reactions common among heavy and intermediate users, including buzzing in ears (tinnitus), diarrhea, weight loss, tightness in chest, increased feelings of self-control, depression, and anxiety.
3. Reactions common among heavy users only, including the feeling that everything was perfect, and distortions of reality, such as auditory hallucinations and paranoid ideation.
4. Reactions unrelated to level of use, such as excessive pupil dilation, headaches, prolonged sexual performance, increased physical strength, and olfactory hallucinations.
5. Reactions generally uncommon at all levels: visual hallucinations, physical orgasm with rush, and tactile hallucinations.

Spotts and Shontz's results, however, are generalizable only to a limited group of participants who were exclusively male and primarily intravenous users. The sample was largely derived from individuals who had come into contact with the criminal justice system or treatment agencies. Clearly, this group of cocaine users is not representative of cocaine users generally. Indeed, surveys of general populations indicate that the majority of self-reported users use infrequently (Miller et al. 1982). Moreover, those seeking treatment differ with respect to level of use, consequences of use, and criminal behavior (Chitwood & Morningstar 1985).

Siegel's (1980) longitudinal study, on the other hand, examined cocaine reactions among ninety-nine (eighty-five males and fourteen females) social-recreational users at six-month intervals over a four-year period (1975–1978). On average, participants used 1–4 grams per month intranasally through the duration of the study. The findings most relevant to our study involve the reporting of acute positive and negative effects. With respect to the former, all of Siegel's participants reported euphoria and stimulation; 83 percent reported reduced fatigue, 67 percent diminished appetite, 62 percent garrulousness, 23 percent sexual stimulation, and 15 percent increased mental ability and increased sociability. Among the negative effects, 70 percent reported restlessness, followed by 34 percent reporting anxiety, 28 percent hyperexcitability, and 16 percent irritability. The most commonly reported positive long-term effects were increased energy (65 percent), increased sensitivity to cocaine (60 percent), general mood elevation (50 percent), and weight loss (21 percent). Negative long-term effects were restlessness and irritability (44 percent), attentional or perceptual changes (44 percent), nasal problems (28 percent), and fatigue (26 percent).

One of the more striking findings of Siegel's study was the decline in many long-term positive and negative effects over the four-year period. All effects declined dramatically between 1975 and 1978: increased energy dropped from 65 percent in 1975 to 32 percent in 1978, sensitivity to cocaine from 60 percent to 8 percent, general mood elevation from 50 percent to 16 percent, and weight loss from 21 percent to 4 percent. Only two of the four negative long-term effects declined with time; attentional and perceptual changes, from 44 percent in 1975 to 11 percent in 1978, and nasal problems, from 28 percent to 12 percent. Restlessness and fatigue remained largely the same across years.

This chapter will be a departure from the rest of the book in some ways. Much of the following analysis on cocaine reactions is technical. Cocaine reactions and their consequences are the result of the combination of pharmacological, individual, and social-environmental factors and, thus, by their nature are complex. The numerical measures employed to assess reactions enabled this analysis. Methodological details are kept to a minimum, with accompanying notes provided for those interested. Before the quantitative analysis, we examine three cases, intended to impart a subjective sense of how reactions to cocaine may be manifested by a single individual.

Case 1 describes a participant who used cocaine moderately frequently, experienced frequent acute and chronic reactions, and sought medical attention due to use of cocaine. This participant, a male in his mid-30s, was married and had obtained a postgraduate degree. He had a broad range of lifetime drug use experience, having used nine other drugs, including heroin, on a largely experimental basis. His method of cocaine use was intranasal, and although his lifetime experience was substantial (one hundred or more times during his life), current use was moderately infrequent (once or twice during the prior year and none within the prior month). He first used cocaine at age 26 and typically consumed about half a gram per occasion. Alcohol was used with cocaine most times. The most frequent acute reactions were increased heart rate and restlessness. Although rarely experienced, sensory distortions such as ringing or buzzing in ears and fuzzy vision did occur. The most frequent chronic reactions were congested nose and the inability to relax. The overall negative effect on his life eventually led to his seeking medical attention, which took the form of psychiatric counseling. No other medical attention for other drugs was ever sought. He expressed concern over the feeling of helplessness brought about by his use of cocaine: "You know it's not good for you but you can't get out."

Case 2 profiles a participant who used cocaine frequently and experienced frequent reactions but did not seek any form of medical attention. This participant was a male in his early 30s, employed as a skilled technician, who lived in a common-law relationship. He had a lifetime experience with eight other drugs (including heroin), although use was largely experimental. His lifetime experience with cocaine was substantial, having used it one hundred or more times. Current use was frequent: forty to ninety-nine times during the prior year but only once or twice during the prior month. He typically injected about 1 gram per occasion. Both alcohol and cannabis were used concurrently with cocaine. First use of cocaine occurred at age 23. The most frequent acute reactions were increased heart rate, restlessness, nervousness, buzzing in ears, and fuzzy vision. Chronic reactions were numerous. The most frequent, which he experienced most times or always after using, were insomnia, physical and mental exhaustion, inability to relax, weight loss, and uncontrollable desire or craving to use. He had never sought medical attention for his use of cocaine or any other substance.

Case 3 describes a participant who used cocaine frequently but did not experience substantial acute or chronic reactions. This participant, a divorced mother in her early 40s, had come recently to the cocaine scene. Her first use occurred at age 40. Moreover, she did not have wide experience with other drugs; only three others (alcohol, cannabis, and hallucinogens) were ever used. Her use was intranasal, on average consuming a quarter gram per occasion. She had used cocaine one hundred or more times during her lifetime, forty to ninety-nine times during the prior year, and only once or twice during the prior month. Both alcohol and cannabis were typically used concurrently with cocaine. Despite this rather frequent level of use, she reported few reactions. The most frequent acute ones were largely primary effects: increased self-confidence, talkativeness, energy, and sexual arousal. Chronic reactions were generally infrequent; the most common (occurring sometimes after use) were congested nose, insomnia, and the inability to relax.

Thus, reactions to cocaine vary among individuals. For instance, although the participant in case 1 used less frequently and consumed less than did case 2, he felt the need to seek psychiatric counseling. Similarly the participant in case 3 was generally a frequent user but experienced few negative consequences.

Descriptive Results

In order to quantify experiences with respect to cocaine reactions, participants responded to a list of questions indicating the frequency with which they had experienced any of the twenty-four reactions.[1] These items were categorized into two broad groupings: seventeen indicating reactions experienced during occasions of cocaine use and seven experienced subsequent to use. Responses were based on a five-point scale: 1—never, 2—rarely, 3—sometimes, 4—most times, 5—always. Table 6–1 presents the percentages, means, and standard deviations of these data; for simplicity, the responses of "rarely" and "sometimes" and of "most times" and "always" were combined.

The most commonly reported reactions are those attributable to the stimulative properties of cocaine. The most frequently cited reactions—those experienced most times or always—are feeling energetic (77 percent), feeling talkative (75 percent), feeling self-confident (67 percent), experiencing increases in heart rate (66 percent),

TABLE 6-1
Frequency of Cocaine Reactions (in percentages)

Variable	Never	Rarely/ Sometimes	Most Times/ Always	Mean[a]	SD
Experienced while using					
Energy	5.4	16.2	77.4	3.98	1.02
Talkativeness	1.8	23.4	74.7	3.91	0.92
Increased heart rate	8.1	22.5	65.7	3.86	1.20
Self-confidence	7.2	26.1	66.6	3.68	1.16
Restlessness	7.2	42.3	50.4	3.51	1.19
Sexual arousal	10.8	44.1	44.1	3.27	1.21
Dry mouth or throat	9.0	52.2	37.8	3.22	1.08
Acute insomnia	18.0	42.3	38.7	3.05	1.31
Nervousness	14.4	57.6	27.9	2.82	1.51
Self-consciousness	37.8	54.9	6.3	1.93	0.91
Buzzing in ears	55.9	36.9	6.3	1.75	1.03
Nausea	53.2	43.2	3.6	1.67	0.83
Lights in vision	63.1	33.3	3.6	1.59	0.88
Fuzzy vision	64.9	30.6	4.5	1.51	0.84
Paranoia	76.6	23.4	0.0	1.31	0.60
Aggression or violence	82.9	17.1	0.0	1.20	0.46
Hallucinations	84.5	14.5	0.9	1.21	0.58
Experienced reactions					
Congested nose	9.0	58.5	32.4	3.09	1.03
Unable to relax	27.0	57.6	15.3	2.42	1.13
Uncontrollable desire or craving to use	48.6	31.5	19.8	2.16	1.36
Chronic insomnia	28.8	54.9	16.2	2.35	1.15
Physical/mental exhaustion	30.6	54.9	14.4	2.29	1.07
Sore or bleeding nose	47.7	45.9	6.3	1.95	1.05
Weight loss	56.8	31.5	11.7	1.89	1.20

[a] Response Scale: 1 — never; 2 — rarely; 3 — sometimes; 4 — most times; 5 — always.

and experiencing restlessness (50 percent). Following this group, the next most frequently reported are acute insomnia (39 percent), dry mouth or throat (38 percent), and congested nose (32 percent).

Psychological disturbances and medical complications were not uncommon: 23 percent reported ever experiencing paranoia, 17 percent aggressive or violent behavior, and 15 percent hallucinations. The least frequently reported reactions were nasal sores or bleeding nose (6 percent), buzzing or ringing in ears (6 percent), fuzzy vision (4 percent), and nausea (4 percent). Although about half the users ever experienced nasal problems (42 percent), only a small minority (6 percent) report this occurring most times or always after using. The absence of substantial nasal problems is likely a reflection of the low frequency and quantity of use among the majority of the intranasal users. Nonetheless, serious nasal problems among occasional users may develop with time and would not be identified in a cross-sectional study such as ours.

Although the most commonly reported reactions appear to be minor, many users reported adverse reactions. In particular, about half of the users (51 percent) reported having experienced an uncontrollable urge or craving to use cocaine; moreover, about 20 percent reported experiencing this urge most times after using. In fact, during our interviews with users, many commented that they were aware of the addictive potential of cocaine.

Reactions by Gender, Age, and Frequency of Use

Few reactions varied significantly by participants' gender or age. Of the total set of reactions, one-way analysis of variance indicated that only self-confidence varied significantly by age of participant ($F[4,10] = 2.61$; $p = .040$). The oldest users, aged 41 years and over, reported the highest mean score (4.86 ± .38 SD) in comparison to younger age groups (means ranging in values from 3.39 to 3.81). Because this effect is marginal and the only significant finding among over twenty reactions, we must be cautious in interpreting the effect too literally. Yet for whatever reasons, use among these older users may be more intimately connected to positive self-image in comparison with younger users. Indeed, motivation for using cocaine may differ qualitatively between these groups.

With respect to gender differences, five reactions varied significantly. In contrast to males, females reported higher mean reactions for talkativeness, dry mouth or throat, and weight loss. Males, on the other hand, reported higher aggression and heart rate than did females.[2] As we will indicate later, however, these gender differences largely disappear when several other factors are considered simultaneously in the analysis.

Figures 6–1 through 6–3 present the percentage of participants reporting each reaction "most times" or "always" when using co-

FIGURE 6–1

Reactions Showing No Linear Relationship to Use: Percentage Reporting Reaction Most Times or Always

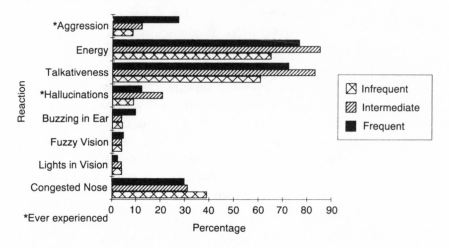

FIGURE 6–2

Reactions Showing Moderate Relationship to Use: Percentage Reporting Reaction Most Times or Always

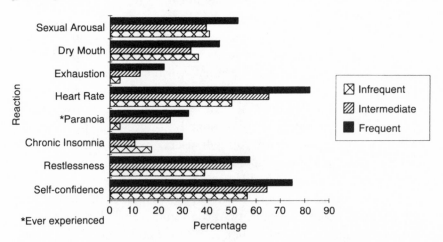

caine, by frequency of cocaine use. The three categories of use are infrequent, intermediate, and frequent, as based on the three-group cluster solution. In addition to the actual percentages portrayed in the graph, group means and related one-way analyses of variance are presented in table B–1 in the Appendix.

FIGURE 6–3

Reactions Showing Strong Relationship to Use: Percentage Reporting Reaction Most Times or Always

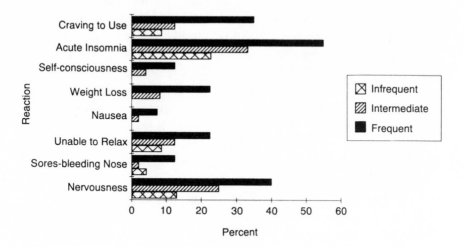

Three major patterns emerge from these data: a set of reactions that shows little association to frequency of use, a set that shows a nonlinear relationship to use, and a set that shows a positive linear relationship. With respect to the first set (figure 6–1), five reactions (congested nose, lights in vision, fuzzy vision, buzzing in ears, and hallucinations) are clearly unrelated to frequency of participants' use of cocaine. For example, among infrequent users, 39 percent reported experiencing congested nose most times after using, in comparison to 31 percent of intermediate users and 30 percent of frequent users. Analysis of variance conducted on these reactions indicated no significant differences among user groups.

The second pattern consists of a nonlinear relationship between frequency of use and reported reactions. Figure 6–1 shows that intermediate users were more likely than frequent and infrequent users to report talkativeness and increased energy. Most times or always when using cocaine, 83 percent of intermediate users, in contrast to 61 percent of infrequent users and 73 percent of frequent users, reported increased talkativeness. Although analysis of variance indicated no significant differences across groups, a test for nonlinearity (the sum of squares due to a nonlinear component) approached significance.[3] Increased energy, on the other hand, showed a significant nonlinear relationship to frequency of use, which was highest among intermediate users (85 percent reported increased energy most times or always) in comparison to 77 percent of frequent users and 65 percent of infrequent users. Mean reported energy was as follows: 3.43 among infrequent users, 4.17 among intermediate users, and 4.07 among frequent users. Analysis of variance on mean energy indicated a significant group effect ($F = 4.52$; $p = .013$); moreover, the test for linearity, indicating departures from linearity, was significant ($F = 4.51$; $p = .036$). Although aggressiveness also exhibited a nonlinear relationship, distinguishing frequent from intermediate and infrequent users, this difference was not statistically significant. Thus, of all the reactions examined, only talkativeness, energy, and aggression appear to be related to frequency of use in a nonlinear manner and only increased energy displays this relationship significantly.

The remaining sixteen reactions, as seen in figures 6–2 and 6–3, tend to exhibit a linear relationship to frequency of cocaine use, that is, on average, increases in cocaine reactions occur as frequency of use increases. The sixteen are:

elevated self-confidence	increased self-consciousness
nervousness	paranoia
nasal sores/bleeding nose	acute insomnia
inability to relax	uncontrollable desire to use
restlessness	increased heart rate
nausea	physical and mental exhaustion
chronic insomnia	dry mouth and throat
weight loss	heightened sexual arousal

With the exception of sexual arousal and dry mouth or throat, all remaining reactions were statistically significant beyond the .05 level. The four reactions that show the strongest relationship to frequency of use were adverse ones. First, nasal sores or bleeding nose was reported as occurring most times or always subsequent to use by 4 percent of infrequent users, 2 percent of intermediate users, and 13 percent of frequent users. Analysis of variance on this mean reaction indicated significant group differences (means of 1.26, 1.79, and 2.52 among infrequent, intermediate, and frequent users, respectively ($F = 14.21$; $p < .001$). Similarly, uncontrollable desire or craving to use cocaine was reported by 9 percent, 13 percent, and 35 percent of the infrequent, intermediate, and frequent users, respectively. These differences were highly significant (respective means for infrequent, intermediate, and frequent users were 1.39, 1.89, and 2.93; $F = 13.39$; $p < .001$). The third most strongly related reaction to frequency of cocaine use was weight loss, reported by less than 1 percent of infrequent users, 8 percent of intermediate users, and 23 percent of frequent users (means of 1.04, 1.83, and 2.45, respectively; $F = 12.16$; $p < .001$). Acute insomnia also showed a strong linear relationship to frequency of use, reported most times or always by 23 percent of infrequent users, 33 percent of intermediate users, and 55 percent of frequent users (respective means of 2.09, 3.02, and 3.62; $F = 11.62$; $p < .000$).

Interrelationships and Patterns of Reported Effects

We expected that cocaine reactions would be multidimensional in character. For this reason we began by examining Pearson product-moment correlations among the twenty-four reactions. A brief visual inspection of this zero-order correlation matrix shown in table 6–2 suggests at least five groups of reactions that are highly intercorrelated: self-confidence, talkativeness, and energy; increased heart rate, restlessness, and nervousness; fuzziness in vision, lights in vision, and hallucinations; aggressiveness and paranoia; and physical and mental exhaustion, unable to relax, weight loss, and uncontrollable desire or craving to use.

Since the correlation matrix suggested that cocaine reactions among participants appeared to be multidimensional in nature, that is, measuring more than a single construct, these data were factor analyzed.[4] Several advantages accrue from the application of factor analysis. First, this technique offers data reduction and consequently greater parsimony in analysis. Second, the structure of the data with respect to their multidimensionality can be examined, and the new variable will have greater reliability than any single variable. On the other hand, since information is combined to form fewer variables, some information is lost; however, overall, the advantages, such as increased reliability, far exceed the cost of loss of information.

A total of seven factors or dimensions were extracted (table 6–3). The factor loadings indicate the weight that the given factor

TABLE 6-2
Bivariate Correlation Matrix of Reaction Items

Reaction	1	2	3	4	5	6	7	8	9	10	11	12	13	14	15	16	17	18	19	20	21	22	23
1. Self-confidence	*																						
2. Talkativeness	.58	*																					
3. Energy	.42	.45	*																				
4. Increased heart rate	.24	.28	.19	*																			
5. Restlessness	.17	.20	.46	.44	*																		
6. Nervousness	.04	.14	.19	.39	.49	*																	
7. Buzzing in ear	.09	.04	.07	.24	.17	.37	*																
8. Fuzzy vision	-.03	-.05	.07	.14	.10	.28	.64	*															
9. Lights in vision	.08	.10	.12	.14	.09	.23	.53	.70	*														
10. Nausea	.02	.03	.00	.19	.13	.29	.22	.27	.19	*													
11. Dry mouth or throat	.09	.19	.26	.32	.34	.38	.29	.22	.14	.15.	*												
12. Paranoia	.01	.04	.04	.15	.14	.33	.37	.24	.18	.20	.19	*											
13. Aggression or violence	.14	.12	.14	.17	.17	.24	.31	.11	.15	.13	.16	.54	*										
14. Acute insomnia	.08	.10	.22	.20	.37	.53	.16	.28	.19	.34	.29	.19	.13	*									
15. Self-consciousness	-.04	-.05	.15	.25	.31	.50	.33	.38	.24	.36	.08	.36	.31	.53.	*								
16. Sexual arousal	.30	.21	.22	.22	.13	.00	.12	.21	.37	.07	.09	.00	.08	.18	.13	*							
17. Sore or bleeding nose	.19	.13	.14	.22	.20	.41	.11	.19	.20	.20	.03	.34	.15	.43	.38	.23	*						
18. Congested nose	.12	.09	.21	.04	-.04	.08	.09	.16	.14	-.06	.03	.08	.11	.22	.16	.11	.23	*					
19. Chronic insomnia	.19	.10	.09	.08	.18	.35	.21	.19	.15	.30	.22	.06	.09	.65	.31	.17	.18	.08	*				
20. Physical/mental exhaustion	.31	.18	.24	.28	.28	.35	.32	.30	.24	.26	.24	.21	.19	.36	.44	.26	.40	.24	.36	*			
21. Unable to relax	.24	.12	.21	.25	.34	.49	.31	.23	.18	.35	.23	.30	.26	.47	.46	.17	.17	.00	.71	.42	*		
22. Weight loss	.17	.19	.29	.30	.27	.28	.22	.24	.25	.23	.23	.08	.05	.36	.44	.24	.32	.17	.35	.51	.46	*	
23. Craving to use	.18	.20	.17	.32	.19	.33	.28	.21	.25	.34	.20	.30	.20	.47	.49	.25	.48	.24	.39	.38	.46	.50	*
24. Hallucinations	-.07	.10	.09	.13	.17	.27	.29	.45	.40	.12	.06	.31	.25	.26	.31	.16	.20	.10	.15	.27	.21	.14	.15

Note: Correlations greater than or equal to .16 are significant beyond .05.

TABLE 6–3

Cocaine Reactions: Factor Loadings

Reaction	Factor						
	1	2	3	4	5	6	7
Acute Insomnia and Nasal Disorders							
Acute insomnia	.69		.50				
Sore or bleeding nose	.48						
Sensory and Perceptual Distortions							
Buzzing in ear		.65					
Fuzzy vision		.97					
Lights in vision		.77					
Hallucinations		.46					
Stimulating Effects Dimension							
Chronic insomnia			.90				
Unable to relax			.74				
Aggressive and Paranoic Reactions							
Paranoia				.83			
Aggression or violence				.65			
Positive Social Effects							
Self-confidence					.78		
Talkativeness					.69		
Energy					.41	.39	
Acute Physiological Reactions							
Increased heart rate						.45	
Restlessness						.79	
Nervousness						.51	
Dry mouth or throat						.45	
Chronic-Problematic Reactions							
Physical/mental exhaustion							.43
Weight loss							.62
Uncontrollable desire or craving to use							.41
Nausea[a]							
Self-consciousness[a]							
Sexual arousal[a]							

[a] Factor loadings < .35.

or dimension has in generating the observed score; thus, they can also be interpreted as regression beta weights, or correlation coefficients. Acute insomnia and nasal sores or bleeding nose loaded

FIGURE 6–4

Profile of Cocaine Reaction Factors by Frequency of Use

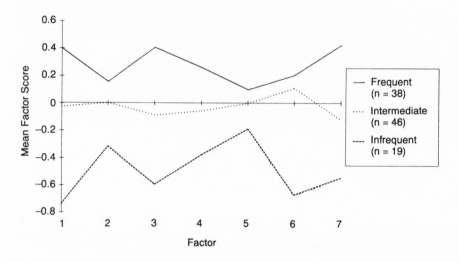

heavily on the first factor. This dimension is indicative of mild effects experienced by intranasal users. The second factor measures a dimension of sensory and perceptual distortions. Here four items loaded heavily: buzzing in ears (tinnitus), fuzzy vision, lights in vision, and hallucinations. Factor 3 is a composite of three items indicating the sleep- or relaxation-disturbing effects of cocaine: acute and chronic insomnia and being unable to relax. A fourth dimension consists of only two items, paranoia and aggression. Factor 5 is indicative of a dimension of social-stimulatory effects; reported self-confidence, talkativeness, and energy loaded highly. Physical-stimulatory effects are prominent in factor 6. Five items loaded highly on this dimension: energy, increased heart rate, restlessness, nervousness, and dry mouth or throat. The seventh and final factor extracted is related to three items and seems to be indicative of physical and psychological problems: weight loss, physical and mental exhaustion, and uncontrollable desire or craving to use. Finally, four items (nausea, self-consciousness, increased sexual arousal, and congested nose) did not load highly (beyond .35) on any of the above dimensions of cocaine reactions.

Level of Use and Dimensions of Reported Effects

The frequency of cocaine use should engender differences in the extent and nature of reported reactions. The mean factor scores are profiled in figure 6–4. Clearly, frequency of cocaine use shows a strong relationship to frequency of reported reactions.

Frequent users (that is, those who reported use on average over ninety-nine times during their lifetime, twenty to thirty-nine times during the prior year, and three to five times during the prior month) obtained the highest factor scores on all dimensions. Intermediate users (who on average reported using cocaine about twenty to thirty-nine times during their lifetime, more than three to five times during the prior year, and no use during the prior month) showed scores along the mean zero line. Infrequent users (on average using three to five times during their lifetime, once or twice during the past year, and not at all during the prior month) consistently obtained the lowest mean factor scores in comparison to the two groups.[6]

Multivariate Relationships

Although frequency of use is an important factor in determining the nature and extent of experienced reactions, it is likely neither the sole nor the most important determinant in comparison to other factors, such as social and psychological characteristics. Bearing in mind this multivariate framework, that is, the simultaneous consideration of several independent variables on a single dependent variable (in our case, cocaine reactions), we regressed each of the seven reaction factors on several independent variables or regressors.[7] Multiple regression allows us to examine the net effect of a given independent variable (or regressor) on a dependent variable, in our case, reaction scores, by holding constant the effect of other independent variables included in the model. Moreover, we are able to include both quantitative (e.g., age, years of use) and qualitative (e.g., gender, marital status) independent variables into the model or equation.[8]

Independent variable regressors were grouped into four major blocks. The first consisted of four demographic variables: a dummy variable indicating participant's gender (coded 0 = female, 1 = male), age of participant, socioeconomic status score (Blishen 1967), and a set of two dummy variables representing the three categories of marital status (married or common-law relationship, separated or divorced, and single as the reference category).

The second block of variables contained five use-related items. The first was a set of two dummy variables indicating the frequency of use (infrequent users providing the reference category). The second variable, exposure to use, indicated the length of time, measured in years, that the participant was exposed to cocaine (specifically, exposure = age - age of first use). The remaining three dummy variables indicate multiple drug use in combination with cocaine. Participants who reported using alcohol, tobacco, or cannabis most times when using cocaine were assigned a value of 1 and others a value of 0, resulting in the three variables—cocaine with alcohol (alcopoly), cocaine with cannabis (canpoly), and cocaine with both alcohol and cannabis (poly2).

The third block of variables represented three social factors that may differentially affect cocaine reactions. The first, others present, indicates how frequently others were present when cocaine was used. This variable was measured on a five-point scale ranging from never to always. The second variable, proportion of users in group, asked participants, "Of the people you usually socialize with, would you say that none, only a few, about half, or almost all use cocaine sometimes?" This variable suggests the degree of social approval among the participant's social network. A third, and related, variable indicated the actual number of individuals known to the participant who sometimes use cocaine.

The final block of variables represented a psychological domain, indicated by two items, perceived risk and perceived high. The former is a composite variable consisting of nine items indicating the degree of perceived harm associated with the use of drugs. Participants indicated perceived level of risk (no risk, slight risk, moderate risk, and great risk) for three substances (cannabis, cocaine, and heroin) by three levels of use (once or twice, occasionally, and regularly), resulting in a four-by-nine matrix. The reliability coefficient of this nine-item summated score was .82. The second psychological variable, perceived high, was a single item indicating how high participants usually got after consuming cocaine. This variable was measured on a four-point scale ranging from "not at all high" to "very high."

Table 6–4 presents the proportion of variance accounted for by each of the independent variables for each of the seven reaction-factors (see tables B–2 to B–8 in appendix B for regression coefficients). The first column (z) indicates the zero-order variance (the proportion of variance in the dependent variable linearly accounted for by the independent variable singly) and the second (U) the proportion of unique variance accounted for by the variable. The unique variance indicates the increase in the total proportion of explained variance (R^2) when the variable is added to all other independent variables included in the model. Also presented in table 6–4 is the block R^2 associated with each of the four independent variable domains.

Beginning with Factor 1 (Acute Insomnia and Nasal Disorders) we see that the inclusion of all regressors accounts for 34 percent of the variation in acute insomnia–nasal disorder scores (omnibus $F = 2.42$;[9] $p = .005$). As a group, demographic characteristics do not significantly account for the variation of this factor; indeed, the four variables account for only 3 percent of the zero-order variance. In contrast, use and social and psychological variables account for a significant proportion of zero-order variance; in each case, however, the unique contribution is nonsignificant. Two variables, frequency of use and number of friends who also use cocaine, are significantly related to this factor.

The more important of the two was frequency of use, which uniquely accounted for 7 percent of the variance. The second variable, number who also usually use cocaine, accounted for 4 percent of the variance and shows a negative relationship to Factor 1: holding constant other variables in the model, with each additional friend who also uses cocaine, on average, participants' Acute Insomnia and Nasal Disorders scores decline by .011 units (standardized coefficient = -.26). Psychological variables account for 10 percent of the zero-order contribution but only 3 percent of the unique variance. None of these variables contributes uniquely to Acute Insomnia and Nasal Disorders (Factor 1) scores.

Overall, the sixteen regressors capture 34 percent of the variation in Sensory and Perceptual Distortions (factor 2) scores (omnibus $F = 2.43$; $p = .005$). This factor shows significant zero-order

TABLE 6-4

Cocaine Reactions: Zero-Order and Unique Contribution
of Selected Independent Variables by Factor Type

Variables	1 z	1 U	2 z	2 U	3 z	3 U	4 z	4 U	5 z	5 U	6 z	6 U	7 z	7 U
Demographic characteristics														
Gender		.02		.01		.01	.02	.01	.02	.02			.03	.01
Age		.01							.02				.05*	.02
Marital status						.03						.01	.02	
Blishen score			.04*	.03	.03	.02		.03*	.05	.04	.04*	.04*	.04	
Block R^2	.03	.02	.07	.05	.05	.05	.05	.04	.05	.04	.08	.06	.08	.08*
Use variables														
Frequency of use	.21*	.07*	.02		.14*	.08*	.09*	.02	.03	.01	.12*	.08*	.21*	.08*
Years of use	.15*		.15*	.07*	.04		.06*		.05*		.07*		.04*	.02*
Cocaine + alcpoly							.04*	.03*	.01	.01				
Cocaine + canpoly	.01		.01			.01		.02	.02		.01			.01
Poly²							.04*		.04*					
Block R^2	.22*	.08	.17*	.09	.15*	.12*	.19*	.10	.12	.06	.17*	.09	.26*	.12*
Social Variables														
Others present	.12	.02	.06*	.02	.06*	.03	.16*	.06*	.01		.02		.10*	.01
Proportion of users in group	.03		.01	.04*				.03						.01
Number who use		.04*			.05*	.02	.05*	.02			.02			
Block R^2	.17*	.06	.09*	.07	.08	.05	.20*	.10*	.01	.01	.03	.01	.12*	.05
Psychological variables														
Perceived Risk					.06*	.06*	.03	.01			.03	.02	.02	.02
Perceived High	.10*	.03	.10*	.04*	.04		.09*	.02	.11*	.07*	.12*	.03	.23*	.08*
Block R^2	.10*	.03	.10*	.04*	.10*	.07*	.11*	.03	.12*	.07*	.15*	.05	.24*	.11*
Total R^2	.338		.338		.330		.397		.234		.312		.519	

* $p < .05$.
Note: Empty cells = value less than .01.

relationships with socioeconomic status (Blishen score), exposure to use, presence of others when using, and perceived high. The unique contribution is maintained, however, only for exposure to use and perceived high, accounting for 7 percent and 4 percent of the unique variance, respectively. The partial regression coefficients indicate a significant positive relationship between Sensory and Perceptual Distortions and exposure, which is expected to have a net increase of .081 units for every additional year participants are exposed to use and also for perceived high, where with every unit increase in perceived high, Sensory and Perceptual Distortions (Factor 2) are expected also to increase by .320 units. Also worthy of mention is the suppression effect,[10] seen for proportion of the participants' social network who also use. Here the zero-order contribution is both weak and nonsignificant, 1 percent, but after holding constant the effects of other variables, the unique contribution becomes significant, although not strong, accounting for 4 percent of the variance. The net effect here is inversely related; Sensory and Perceptual Distortions (factor 2) scores decrease by .270 units as the proportion of cocaine users in the participant's social network increases. Thus, as was the case for Acute Insomnia and Nasal Disorders (Factor 1), here we also find that the effect of social environmental factors tends to ameliorate the impact of experienced reactions.

As noted in the univariate analysis, sensory-perceptual distortions did not differ significantly according to frequency of use, and table 6–4 shows that this lack of relationship was maintained for the multivariate case.

Turning now to the Stimulating Effects Dimension of cocaine reactions (Factor 3), table 6–4 shows that the regression model accounted for 33 percent of the variance in Factor 3 scores (omnibus $F = 2.34$; $p = .007$). Here the variables frequency of use, others present when using, and perceived risk accounted for a significant zero-order contribution (14 percent, 6 percent, and 6 percent, respectively). Only frequency of use and perceived risk maintained a significant contribution after the inclusion of all other variables (8 percent and 6 percent of the unique contribution, respectively). Perceived risk exhibited a significant positive association with sleepless reactions (Factor 3), indicating that with every unit increase in perceived risk, Factor 3 will, on average, increase by .064

units. In this instance controlling for other variables changed the magnitude of cluster means, but the relationship to use remained similar to the univariate case; that is, Factor 3 scores increased significantly with cluster subtypes (frequency of use).

With respect to Aggressive and Paranoiac Reactions (Factor 4), the regression model accounted for approximately 40 percent of the total variation (omnibus $F = 3.13$; $p < .001$). Six variables (frequency of use, exposure, combination use with alcohol, presence of others, number of friends who also use, and perceived high) had significant zero-order contributions for the model, two of which contributed uniquely (alcohol combination use, 3 percent; presence of others while using, 6 percent). Additionally, socioeconomic status indicated significant unique contribution (3 percent), although the zero-order effect was suppressed. Unlike the univariate case, when the other variables in the model were held constant, the effect of frequency of use diminished.

Socioeconomic status was inversely related to Aggressive and Paranoiac Reactions; with every unit increase in participants' status, reaction scores declined by .015 (standardized coefficient = -0.21). This effect, however, was marginal ($p = .049$). Although frequency of use was unrelated to this dimension of cocaine reactions, participants who reported usually combining alcohol with cocaine use were, on average, more likely to obtain higher factor scores ($b = .452$; standardized coefficient = 0.21; $p = .049$). Finally, the frequency with which participants used cocaine in the presence of others was negatively related to Aggressive and Paranoiac Reactions. On average, the net effect of each additional unit in frequency of the presence of others was expected to result in a decline of .383 in Aggressive and Paranoiac Reactions (Factor 4). Thus, the more frequently participants used cocaine in the presence of others, the less likely they were to experience this type of reaction.

Factor 5, Positive Social Effects, indicative of generally positive if not primary effects, especially sociability, was generally not well explained by the variables in the model in comparison to the other factor reactions. Here only 23 percent of the variation was accounted for (omnibus $F = 1.45$; $p = .142$). Moreover, only three variables (years of experience, combination drug use, and perceived high) contributed a significant zero-order variance. Of these, only perceived high showed a unique contribution (7 percent), indicating a significant positive effect ($b = .389$; standardized coefficient $= 0.30$).

For Acute Physiological Reactions (Factor 6), the regression model accounted for 31 percent of the total variation (omnibus $F = 2.15$; $p = .014$). Four variables (socioeconomic status, frequency of use, years of use, and perceived high) contributed a significant proportion to the zero-order variance. Only two (frequency of use and socioeconomic status) of these, however, contributed uniquely (8 percent and 4 percent, respectively). Thus, frequency of use maintained a significant relationship as in the univariate case. Socioeconomic status was positively and significantly related to Factor 6 reaction scores: on average, with every unit increase of status, reaction scores increased by .016, net of the other independent variables (standardized coefficient $= 0.23$). More generally, those with higher socioeconomic status were most likely to experience Acute Physiological Reactions.

Factor 7, Chronic-Problematic Reactions, is of particular interest. Recall that three items—physical and mental exhaustion, weight loss, and uncontrollable desire or craving to use cocaine—loaded highly. As seen in table 6–4, the regression model did exceedingly well in explaining this dimension, accounting for 52 percent of the variation (omnibus $F = 5.14$; $p < .001$). Here five variables—age, frequency of use, years of use, frequency of presence of others, and perceived high—contributed a significant proportion of the zero-order variance. Of these, three retained their unique importance: frequency of use, accounting for 8 percent of the unique variance; years of exposure, for 2 percent; and perceived high, for 8 percent. As we saw earlier in the univariate case, frequency of use retained its significant effect net of the other independent variables. Years of exposure showed a marginal positive net effect indicating that with each additional year of exposure, Chronic=Problematic Reaction scores, on average, increased by .044 points (standardized coefficient $= .218$; $p = .050$). Perceived high similarly showed a positive effect but much stronger: for every unit increase in perceived high, Chronic-Problematic Reactions (Factor 7) increased by .429 points (standardized coefficient $= .33$; $p = .004$).

Summary

For the majority of participants, few reactions brought about dele-
terious consequences. The most commonly reported reactions—increased energy, talkativeness, and self-confidence—were largely
primary or desired effects. Considering that most were intranasal
users, few serious nasal conditions were indicated. Also, psychological reactions such as paranoia and hallucinations were reported infrequently. A minority, however, did appear to exhibit patterns of
use and associated consequences that could develop into a more
hazardous state. In particular, 20 percent reported an uncontrollable urge or craving to use cocaine after ingestion on most occasions.

Few reactions varied significantly by age or gender of participant. Level of use, on the other hand, proved to be an important
factor associated with reactions. Of the twenty-four reactions examined, sixteen showed a significant positive relationship (see figures 6–2 and 6–3). The analysis of the relationship between use and
reactions is hampered by the cross-sectional nature of our data. Implicitly we make the assumption that use is causally prior to experienced reactions. Although this specification must be the case initially, the subsequent direction of influence, or the possibility of
mutual dependence, cannot be unraveled by these data. For example, pleasurable experiences may serve to increase or maintain subsequent use; thus, reactions may also directly affect use.

In summary, Acute, Insomnia and Nasal Disorders (Factor 1)
were positively related to frequency of cocaine use and negatively
with the number of participant's associates who also use cocaine.
Sensory and Perceptual Distortions (Factor 2) were unrelated to
level of use in the multivariate analysis; they were, however, related
positively with exposure to use and perceived high and inversely
with the proportion of cocaine users in the participant's social network. The Stimulating Effects Dimension (Factor 3)—acute and
chronic insomnia and inability to relax—was positively related to
frequency of use and perceived risk of drug use. Aggressive and
Paranoiac Reactions (Factor 4), although unrelated to frequency of
use, were positively related to the combined use of alcohol with the
ingestion of cocaine and inversely related to socioeconomic status
and the frequency with which others were present when cocaine

was used. The Positive Social Effects (Factor 5)—self-confidence, talkativeness, and energy—were generally weakly related to the variables in the model; the only exception was a positive relationship to experiencing highs from use. Acute Physiological Reactions (Factor 6) were positively related to frequency of cocaine use and socioeconomic status. Finally, Chronic-Problematic Reactions (Factor 7)—physical and mental exhaustion, weight loss, and uncontrollable desire or craving to use cocaine—were positively related to frequency of cocaine use, exposure to use, and perceived high.

These seven dimensions are not engraved in stone. Although they adequately represented the data, they were derived from an exploratory mode of analysis. Not only is replication required to establish stronger confidence, but also confirmatory stage of analysis is required. It is also possible that these seven dimensions are a reflection of a single second-order common factor or dimension.[11]

Use variables, most notably frequency of use, were by far the most prominently associated with cocaine reactions. Indeed, this group of variables was strongly related in six of the seven reaction dimensions. Demographic factors, including gender, were generally weakly related. Following use variables, psychological variables were related in four of the seven dimensions; the most notable was perceived high. The frequency of cocaine reactions was not independent of the users' social environment and network. Social variables were strongly related in three dimensions. Moreover, these variables tended to lessen the likelihood of frequent negative reactions and thus cushion users to some extent.

Many of our findings are consistent with other research; others are not. For instance, Spotts and Shontz (1980) found that auditory hallucinations, such as buzzing in the ears, were common among heavy and intermediate users; our data did not uncover a strong relationship between frequency of use and reported sensory distortions. In contrast to our sample of 111 intranasal users, Spotts and Shontz's sample consisted of only 9 intravenous users. Siegel (1978), examining hallucinations among a sample of recreational users, found that 43 percent of the 85 users reported some form of sensory distortion. Participants in our study reported similar experiences; 44 percent experienced ringing in the ears (tinnitus), 35 percent buzzing in the ears, and 37 percent noted lights in vision.

In the light of the generally infrequent use among our participants, it is interesting that 23 percent reported feelings of paranoia, while 17 percent became violent or aggressive. As Spotts and Shontz also noted, reporting of these behaviors was significantly related to frequency or level of cocaine use. Other studies have noted a higher prevalence of paranoia. Washton, Gold, and Pottash (1984) indicated that 65 percent of upper-income users reported such feelings.

Spotts and Shontz found that such effects as increased talkativeness and dryness in the mouth and throat were invariant to level of use; our results replicate this finding. In contrast, however, they observed that increased heart rate, restlessness, and insomnia were also invariant to level of use. These reactions among our participants were significantly related to frequency of use.

The interpretation of many of these cocaine reactions is not independent of phenomenological constraints. Users actively weigh the rewards and negative consequences in a subjective perspective. Indeed, a traumatic experience for one may be another's pleasure. For instance, weight loss, reported by 43 percent in our study, appeared to reflect a negative dimension of cocaine reactions (loading highly with physical and mental exhaustion and uncontrollable craving or urge to use cocaine). Participants in Siegel's (1980) study, however, reported weight loss as a long-term positive effect.

In all, few participants experienced serious chronic reactions. On the other hand, even among a sample of social-recreational users, adverse reactions, including hallucinations, paranoia, aggressiveness, and psychological craving, did occur, albeit infrequently. Physical reactions, such as nasal congestion and cardiovascular changes, were by far the norm. Yet negative reactions among users appeared to be outweighed or ignored in the light of the appeal of cocaine. The next chapter deals with a different problem area for users: the risks inherent in obtaining and using this illegal drug.

7

The Legal Barrier

The first federal controls in Canada over drugs, including co-caine, came about in 1908 with enactment of the Opium Act and the Proprietary and Patent Medicine Act.[1] Today there remain two major federal statutes to control illicit drugs, the Narcotic Control Act [NCA] and the Food and Drugs Act [FDA]. Cocaine is covered under the NCA, along with cannabis, heroin, opium, phencycladine [PCP], and more than one hundred other drugs. Under the NCA, cocaine has been legally defined as a narcotic but is pharmacologically classified as a stimulant. Other stimulants (e.g., amphetamines, or "speed") are covered under part III of the FDA. In 1993, a new omnibus bill (C-85), The Psychoactive Substances Control Act, was considered. It made no changes specific to cocaine but did create a new offense, offering drugs for sale. The proposed law was much criticized (Usprich & Solomon 1993). The bill did not become law when Parliament was dissolved for an election. In early 1994, the new government introduced an almost identical bill (C-7) The Controlled Drugs and Substances Act, whose fate will be determined sometime in 1994.

All current federal offenses may be divided into one of three categories: summary, indictable, and dual procedure (or hybrid) offenses. Under the NCA, possession of a narcotic (or simple possession) is a hybrid offense, and thus the prosecution can proceed either summarily or by way of indictment. Table 7–1 describes the offense categories and penalties provided under the NCA. It por-

TABLE 7-1

The Narcotic Control Act, Canada:
Offenses, Definitions, and Maximum Penalties

Offense	Definition	Maximum Penalty
Possession	To knowingly have a narcotic on your person; To knowingly control a narcotic in another place or within another person's possession; Knowledge, consent and some control over a narcotic in the possession of a fellow group member.	Summary conviction: First offense, 6 months and $1,000 fine; subsequent offense, 1 year and $2,000 fine Indictment: 7 years
Trafficking	To manufacture, sell, give, administer, transport, send, deliver, or distribute any narcotic or substance held out to be a narcotic; To offer to do any of these things	Indictment: Life
Possession for the purpose of trafficking	To possess any narcotic for the above-mentioned purposes.	Indictment: Life
Cultivation	To knowingly grow or assist the growth of opium or cannabis.	Indictment: 7 years
Importing or exporting	To knowingly transport or arrange for the transport of any narcotic across the Canadian border.	Indictment: life (7 years mandatory minimum)
Prescription shopping	To obtain or attempt to obtain a narcotic from one doctor, without disclosing a prescription for a narcotic obtained from another doctor within the previous 30 days	Summary Convictions: 6 months and $1,000 fine for first offense; one year and $2,000 fine or both for subsequent offenses

Source: Based on material from Solomon et al. (1985).

trays a rather grim picture of the possible fate of Canadian drug offenders; someone who is caught smoking "pot" or "sniffing coke," for example, could be subjected to seven years' imprisonment if convicted under indictment. However, maximum penalties are rarely imposed. Probation, fines, and absolute or conditional discharges are other sentencing options.

The sentencing practices for possession of cocaine may be compared to those for other drugs.[2] Although the NCA does not distinguish among cocaine, cannabis, and heroin, the discretion exercised by the judiciary indicates that community standards associated with various drug problems are not the same.[3] Data up to 1985 show that people who are found guilty of possession of a narcotic are treated more leniently if the substance is cannabis than if it is cocaine, and heroin possessors receive the most severe dispositions. The current data (table 7–2) show that those possessing heroin are more likely to be jailed than those possessing cocaine or LSD. The possible sentences for possession of LSD, under part IV of the FDA, are similar to those for cocaine, but in fact a much lower proportion of those convicted for possession of LSD receive jail terms.[4]

Table 7–2 also shows that although possession of a narcotic such as cocaine may incur a maximum penalty of seven years (if treated as an indictable offense), 56.9 percent of those convicted for possession of cocaine in 1991 were given a fine. However, 32.3 percent received a jail term; for most the length of incarceration was less than one month.

Table 7–3 also shows that Canadian courts have been changing their view of the seriousness of cocaine. Penalties were much more severe in 1991 than in the early 1980s. In the early 1980s, about 70 to 75 percent of those convicted of cocaine possession were fined;

TABLE 7–2

Sentences Awarded for Possession of Cocaine, Heroin and LSD in Canada, 1991

Sentence	Cocaine	Heroin	LSD
Fine	56.9%	36.0%	61.4%
Suspended/probation	8.1	22.7	16.6
Absolute discharge	0.3	-	1.2
Conditional discharge	2.4	0.6	1.7
Jail			
Less than 1 month	18.2	25.0	10.4
1 month to less than 6 months	11.6	12.8	5.4
6 months to less than 1 year	1.7	1.7	5.4
1 year +	0.8	1.2	0.8
Other	0.1	-	-
Total	100.0	100.0	100.0

Source: Information Services Division, Bureau of Dangerous Drugs, Ottawa, Canada.

TABLE 7-3

Percentage Contribution of the Various Sentences to Total Sentences Awarded for Simple Possession of Cocaine, Canada, 1977–1991

		Nonimprisonment			
Year	Fine	Suspended Sentence/ Probation	Absolute/ Conditional Discharge	Total	Total Imprisonment
1977	61.2	7.2	4.8	73.2	26.8
1978	68.9	5.7	6.1	80.7	19.3
1979	67.0	3.1	8.0	78.1	21.9
1980	66.9	4.3	9.6	80.8	18.6
1981	68.4	3.6	9.2	81.2	18.4
1982	71.2	4.0	6.7	81.9	17.4
1983	74.2	3.1	7.2	84.4	15.3
1984	74.2	3.0	8.0	85.3	14.7
1985	72.7	3.3	7.5	83.5	16.5
1986	72.5	4.4	5.3	82.2	17.7
1987	68.1	5.1	5.8	79.0	20.8
1988	67.5	4.7	5.1	77.3	22.5
1989	60.7	5.6	3.5	69.8	30.0
1990	56.8	6.8	3.3	66.8	33.0
1991	56.9	8.1	2.7	67.6	32.3

Source: Bureau of Dangerous Drugs (annual reports).

only about 17 percent received a jail term. However, by 1991, barely half were fined, and almost a third went to jail, and there were far fewer discharges. It may be that the appearance of crack cocaine in the mid-1980s and the hysteria around it influenced judges to be stricter on cocaine possessors. However, systematic data are not available to show whether those possessing crack as opposed to other types of cocaine were treated differently in court. A pilot study in Toronto, however, suggests that this is indeed the case (Erickson & Cohen 1994).

An overview of drug enforcement statistics should monitor trends in convictions over a substantial period of time. Table 7–4 provides an assessment of changes between 1965 and 1991. Enforcement against cocaine is relatively new. Cocaine use was virtually absent from the criminal justice system in the 1960s, a time

TABLE 7-4

Convictions for Cocaine, Cannabis, Heroin and LSD in Canada, 1965–1991

Year	Cocaine	Cannabis	Heroin	LSD
1965	3	60	266	n/a
1966	1	144	221	n/a
1967	0	586	348	n/a
1968	2	1,429	279	n/a
1969	1	2,964	310	n/a
1970	12	6,270	383	1,558
1971	19	7,498	502	1,644
1972	44	11,713	923	1,161
1973	123	19,929	1,290	970
1974	237	29,067	798	1,482
1975	289	27,367	511	1,570
1976	363	39,259	708	989
1977	420	41,982	636	710
1978	507	36,079	580	712
1979	592	36,103	509	1,272
1980	850	40,781	309	2,076
1981	1,255	43,880	261	2,232
1982	1,353	34,886	289	1,806
1983	1,630	28,955	303	1,460
1984	2,365	26,193	324	1,188
1985	2,793	22,510	344	920
1986	3,355	n/a	326	936
1987	4,268	n/a	274	926
1988	6,090	n/a	338	804
1989	8,167	n/a	356	673
1990	8,282	n/a	422	697
1991	6,902	n/a	412	487

Source: 1965–1985: Bureau of Dangerous Drugs (compiled from published annual reports). 1986–1991: unpublished data supplied through the courtesy of the Information Services Division of the Bureau of Dangerous Drugs. It should be noted that, commencing in 1980, the BDD started compiling their data covering a five-year period in which the first of the five years is a final figure and the last four years are estimates. Thus, in 1991, 1987 is a final figure, and the years 1988 through 1991 will be altered in succeeding reports. Further, LSD was not prohibited until 1970, under part IV of the Food and Drugs Act, and, in 1985, the Bureau stopped publishing data on cannabis.

when a generation of young people were smoking marijuana. Since 1970, however, the number of cocaine convictions has risen steadily and at a far faster rate than for any other drug since cannabis peaked in 1979. The peak for cocaine convictions was 1990, with a slight decline in 1991. Cocaine convictions have outnumbered convictions for heroin and LSD for several years. Cocaine convictions first exceeded heroin in 1979 and have continued to do so. Not until 1983 did convictions for cocaine offenses reach a higher level than LSD offenses. Cannabis convictions continue to be the most numerous, as cannabis dominates the offense statistics; however, convictions have not been reported since 1985 (Erickson 1992). Convictions for heroin and LSD have fluctuated over the past decade and have recently begun to decline. Although there have been fewer total convictions for cocaine than for cannabis, the direction of the pattern over time is similar: cocaine convictions have reached successively higher levels since a single conviction was recorded in 1969.

Convictions for cocaine in each province (table 7–5) do not display identical recent trends. In Ontario, Quebec, British Columbia, and Alberta, the largest provinces, we do find the same consistent pattern of successively higher levels of convictions over time. However, Ontario and Quebec together account for about three-quarters of the total convictions in Canada. What is especially interesting is that almost half of Canada's cocaine convictions were handed down in Quebec over the past five years or so. Ontario is larger in population than Quebec, yet Quebec usually had more convictions over the past decade. The number of convictions for cannabis, on the other hand, has been far higher in Ontario than in Quebec, with some recent levels being as much as three times higher. Cocaine has scarcely appeared in some provinces according to the conviction statistics; there were fewer than twenty a year in Newfoundland, Prince Edward Island, Yukon, and Northwest Territories in the past five years.

Availability of Cocaine

Prohibition is meant to decrease drug availability by suppressing any legitimate access and keeping black market prices high and the commodity scarce. In a U. S. study, "increases in the presence and

TABLE 7-5
Convictions by Province for Cocaine, Heroin and LSD
in Canada, 1987–1991

Province	Year	Cocaine	Heroin	LSD
Newfoundland	1987	9	0	29
	1988	11	0	27
	1989	14	0	16
	1990	17	0	15
	1991	11	1	20
Prince Edward Island	1987	3	0	7
	1988	2	0	4
	1989	7	0	6
	1990	7	0	6
	1991	2	0	8
Nova Scotia	1987	71	0	71
	1988	63	0	49
	1989	105	3	46
	1990	88	0	56
	1991	116	0	25
New Brunswick	1987	26	0	41
	1988	55	0	31
	1989	65	0	19
	1990	39	0	47
	1991	63	2	31
Quebec	1987	2,047	82	269
	1988	2,993	93	264
	1989	3,391	108	213
	1990	3,013	119	196
	1991	2,814	111	131
Ontario	1987	1,212	62	538
	1988	1,904	107	445
	1989	2,834	131	377
	1990	3,207	159	389
	1991	2,606	164	290
Manitoba	1987	65	0	86
	1988	68	1	97
	1989	92	1	85
	1990	97	1	77
	1991	85	0	61
Saskatchewan	1987	41	0	88
	1988	48	0	77
	1989	57	0	51
	1990	72	4	45
	1991	21	5	22

TABLE 7–5 *(continued)*

Province	Year	Cocaine	Heroin	LSD
Alberta	1987	299	12	286
	1988	261	4	240
	1989	361	3	216
	1990	464	2	209
	1991	408	6	138
British Columbia	1987	490	118	308
	1988	672	130	314
	1989	1,223	111	204
	1990	1,264	136	162
	1991	762	123	124
Yukon	1987	4	0	9
	1988	6	0	7
	1989	10	0	3
	1990	9	0	3
	1991	11	0	8
Northwest Territories	1987	1	0	2
	1988	7	0	1
	1989	8	0	2
	1990	5	0	1
	1991	3	0	3
Canada	1987	4,268	274	1,734
	1988	6,090	338	1,556
	1989	8,167	356	1,238
	1990	8,282	422	1,206
	1991	6,902	412	861

Source: Unpublished data supplied through the courtesy of the Information Services Division, Bureau of Dangerous Drugs.

accessibility of cocaine were cited by 53 percent of respondents as the primary reason for escalation during their period of heaviest use. Thirty-two percent said they increased use because cocaine was more available, 15 percent because they had more money and 6 percent because people gave them more cocaine" (Chitwood 1985). Intelligence data prepared by the Royal Canadian Mounted Police (RCMP) indicate that the availability of cocaine has been increasing in recent years. Stamler, Falman, and Keele (1984:45) attribute this increase to "a vast overproduction of the raw materials needed to produce cocaine in coca-growing areas of South America and the activities of sophisticated trafficking organizations with large operations and profits." These distribution networks are based largely in Colombia, the main supplier of cocaine to Canada and the United States (Drug Enforcement Administration [DEA] 1985). The major producers of raw materials needed for cocaine are Bolivia and Peru.

Montreal, Toronto, and Vancouver are the main transit centers for cocaine coming into Canada. They are the major market and serve as regional distribution points for other parts of the country. Each of these cities has an international airport, and air transportation has been the primary mode for smuggling cocaine into Canada until recently. "In 1983, air transportation was used for an estimated 44 percent of the cocaine destined for Canada, a decline from 75 percent in 1982. The use of sea transportation remained unchanged at one percent, but land transportation increased from 24 percent in 1982 to 55 percent in 1983. The RCMP attributes this change to the increased use of North American cities as transit points between South America and Canada. This trend continued in 1984 with Miami, San Francisco, Los Angeles, New York, Mexico, and more recently the Bahamas and Jamaica, as the primary transit points for cocaine en route to Canada" (DEA 1985:16). This diffusion and expansion of illicit traffic suggests that the availability of cocaine in Canada would increase in the coming years, and, it did so. It would appear from the intelligence data that cocaine has been widely available in Canada.

A similar picture of accessibility emerges when we examine the reports of our cocaine-using sample in the first study.[5] The majority of participants reported that it was easy or very easy to obtain cocaine and that the average cost per gram was between $100 and $150 (in 1983–1984). We asked participants how they typically acquired cocaine. Most reported friends as a primary source, and thus the transaction typically occurred in a private residence. Other sources were siblings, spouse, boyfriend, cousin, neighbor, or work associate.

As well, a significant number of people were given cocaine. In fact, a quarter of the sample had never purchased cocaine, yet some had used it often in the past twelve months. Female participants were overrepresented in the group of nonbuying users.

Some of those who did purchase cocaine had, on occasion, given it as a gift to friends or relatives. One person purchased a gram for a friend's wedding present, and another bought it as a birthday gift. Still others provided cocaine for friends on less significant occasions. One beneficiary who was introduced to cocaine for the first time by a birthday present was not a drug user at the time and would not have considered buying cocaine himself. Yet the day after this first experience, he purchased $1,000 worth of cocaine and became a heavy daily user (in excess of a gram per day) for a few years until he was arrested for trafficking. While he was awaiting trial, he was abstinent, a proclaimed quitter. He was "relieved that it was over" but also indicated that cocaine was still there if he desired it. He said, "It's all around me, at work, my lawyer, girlfriend."

Many cocaine users do not make a special effort to obtain the drug. Cocaine is often offered in a social setting, much as alcohol is. Sometimes those in attendance may have no knowledge that cocaine might be offered to them and may have had no intention to use. In other situations certain individuals might expect, and even hope, that it would be offered to them during the course of their visit.

In addition to purchasing cocaine and getting it free, some users reported that they bartered for it. A fashion designer said that she often gave her dealer outfits she had made for the coke she needed. A restaurant owner said that half the time he acquired cocaine in exchange for meals served to certain customers. There were also a few participants who attended parties in which someone would supply cocaine while others would take care of the food and beverages.

Noncash exchanges help defray the high financial cost of cocaine, "the major constraint on cocaine" use consistently given by users calling the 1-800-COCAINE help line in the United States (Gold 1984:28). Although high price was one of the barriers to use reported by our participants, it was not quite as important as Gold indicated for his sample. Again, our sample was derived from the community. The majority of respondents had used cocaine fewer than ten times in the past year, and thus the financial costs incurred were not excessive. If they purchased cocaine for all those occasions, the cost would have been a maximum of $750 for that year. (This figure was reached by multiplying the average cost of $150 per gram by the typical quantity consumed on any given occasion, about half a gram, according to our findings). About half reported spending $50 or less a month on cocaine; only one-quarter spent more than $100 a month, and almost all of these spent less than $300 over that length of time. We had little indication that our participants resorted to criminal activities to obtain money for cocaine, as a U.S. study reported:

> When cocaine is readily available and accessible, the high cost of the drug frequently creates financial problems for users whose use exceeds their budgetary limits. High level users are more likely than low level users to report both money problems and a history of socially unacceptable, sometimes criminal activities designed to obtain (funds to purchase) cocaine. (Chitwood 1985)

Most users bought cocaine fewer than five times in the past year, and the typical quantity of cocaine purchased was 1 to 3 grams. Consequently, most respondents did not usually have cocaine on hand. In fact, half said the quantity they purchased was depleted on a single occasion, involving less than one day, a matter of hours, minutes, or as one user said, "a couple of seconds." The time spent in cocaine use for many users may be relatively insignificant compared to the time they devote to other recreational activities, and so it is not surprising that many cocaine users have a take-it-or-leave-it attitude about the drug.

Users' Knowledge, Attitudes, and Experience with the Legal System

Participants were questioned about their knowledge of the law relating to cocaine, their attitudes regarding the law, and their experience with the legal system. Most of them were ignorant of the relevant legislation. Only a third correctly identified the Narcotic Control Act as the legislation prohibiting cocaine use. Moreover, less than a quarter knew that the maximum sentence for possession is a seven-year term of imprisonment. Their knowledge of the actual sentences handed out in court, however, was fairly accurate. When asked what the most likely sentence would be if they were charged and found guilty for possession, only 14 percent believed they would receive a jail term. This perception compares favorably with the national statistics published by the Bureau of Dangerous

Drugs (1984) showing that 14 percent of such offenders actually received jail terms. Nearly half (41 percent) thought they would get a fine, fewer than the Bureau's figure of 75 percent. A discharge option was thought to be about as likely an outcome as a fine, but the actual figure of 8 percent is substantially lower.

Despite the unfamiliarity of most participants with the details of the law prohibiting the use of cocaine, two-thirds were of the opinion that it should be changed, and in the direction of leniency. Nevertheless, a substantial proportion of the sample (26 percent) supported the existing legislation.

As far as their personal involvement with the legal system is concerned, we find what appears to be, at first glance, a paradox. Although almost half of the participants had friends who had been arrested for possession of cocaine and a few had been caught themselves, only two thought that there was any likelihood of their being caught by the police if they continued use during the next year. In the light of their knowledge of friends who had been arrested, why did they deny the likelihood of being caught themselves? It may be that a sense of security, or even invincibility, arises when one continues to break the law and legal repercussions do not follow. After all, more than three-quarters of the participants had engaged in this illegal behavior at least ten times, and nearly half of those had done so one hundred or more times. Perhaps also the accounts of detection provided by their unlucky friends generated strategies for avoiding the same fate.

We asked them why the prospect of arrest was so unlikely. Their responses exude confidence:

"I have a lot of years experience of getting away with it."
"There is no reason for the police to suspect me."
"As soon as I get it, it's gone."
"I never carry more than I can eat."

Typically, their confidence was related to the precautions they took. They said, for example, that they were "discreet," "very careful," or used "only in a private residence."

An interest in deterring, preventing, or controlling cocaine use directs us to consider why some people stop using it. A preventive orientation is facilitated by an understanding of the factors related to cessation of use. Virtually all those who have used cocaine have previous experience with cannabis. There may be specific and identifiable reasons why they have disengaged from such a life-style.

Of the few studies that have examined cessation of cannabis use, the findings have been inconsistent, although it is clear that quitting marijuana cannot be attributed primarily to fear of legal consequences (Goodstadt, Sheppard & Char 1984; Meier & Johnson 1977; Singh 1978). Certainly extralegal influences have been shown to be more important (Bishop 1984; Meier & Johnson 1977). The same finding has been reported for cessation of alcohol and other drugs. Lanza-Kaduce and associates (1984:89) found that "peer associations [was] the most important variable." In any event, it appears that no earlier study has considered cessation of cocaine use in particular (Erickson & Murray 1989).

We asked participants to tell us how likely they were to use cocaine in the next year.[6] Twenty-four said it would be "very unlikely" or "unlikely"; these "quitters" were coded as 0. Eighty-six said it was "likely" or "very likely"; these "continuers" were coded as 1. One person said he did not know. Ten factors that may have influenced the decision regarding future use are presented in a correlation matrix (table 7–5). The data show that only half of these variables are linearly and significantly related to cessation of cocaine. Support of the existing law (Support Law), friends' use of cocaine (Peer Use), whether they had ever purchased cocaine themselves (Purchase), perceived risk of harm to oneself if one uses cocaine regularly (Perceived Risk), and frequency of cocaine use in their lifetime (Cokelife). Compared to those who will continue to use cocaine, quitters are more likely to support the law, less likely to have many friends who use cocaine, less likely to have purchased cocaine, more likely to associate serious risks with regular use of cocaine, and less likely to have used cocaine frequently.

The finding that neither perceived certainty nor perceived severity of legal sanctions is related to cessation of use may be surprising. The recent literature, however, has shown that the effects of fear of legal consequences are either negligible (Minor & Harry 1982; Saltzman et al. 1982), or much less important than extralegal factors (Bishop 1984; Meier & Johnson 1977). Additionally, there is virtually no variability in the measure of perceived certainty.

Only 2 percent of participants admitted any likelihood of detection. Thus, we could not have expected this item to be statistically useful as a predictor of other behavior.

In order to assess the relative and cumulative importance of the ten predictor variables, an ordinary regression analysis (OLS) was conducted. Since the relationship between perceived risk and cessation may be dependent on frequency of use, an interaction term was included to test for this possibility. One of the assumptions of OLS regression is linearity, and initial residual plots indicated some departure in these data. Thus, a logistic regression was chosen as the most appropriate technique to deal with these data.[7] However, the findings from the logistic regression are essentially the same as those obtained from the least-squares one, and since the least-squares approach is more widely known, we report the results of that procedure.

Table 7–6 presents the results of the regression analysis. The interaction effect of the frequency of use and perceived risk was not statistically significant and was therefore excluded. Only three of the predictor variables were found to be significant in explaining cessation of use: Purchase, Uncontrollable Urge, and Perceived Risk. "Quitters" are most likely to be users who have not purchased cocaine, those who feel an uncontrollable urge to use it, and those who feel that regular use constitutes a serious risk. By way of

TABLE 7–6

Regression Analysis (OLS) Predicting Cessation of Use

Independent Variables[a]	Beta	Significance
Purchase	.372	.001
Perceived Risk	−.257	.011
Uncontrollable Urge	−.221	.032
Cokelife	.150	.264
Medical Attention	−.100	.293
Perceived Certainty	−.057	.545
Support Law	−.056	.576
Availability	.045	.631
Peer Use	.043	.665
Perceived Severity	.013	.888
R^2 = .304		

[a] See page 151 for description of variables.

comparison, those who said they would no longer use cocaine were three times as likely to have never purchased it as those who planned to continue using the drug. Those who planned to discontinue using were also three times as likely as confirmed users always to report an uncontrollable urge to use cocaine and twice as likely to associate a great risk with regular use.

What is it about buying the drug that makes the difference? Does the purchasing behavior signify some kind of commitment to the drug-taking activity? Is it the next step removed from a take-it-or-leave-it attitude? Or is it simply that the use of cocaine is prohibitive for many people because of its high cost? Those who do not plan to purchase it are unlikely to use it unless they intend to frequent an environment where it will be offered.

We did not pose a specific question to determine if financial cost was a barrier to use; however, when asked if consumption would change if the law were made more lenient, about a third raised the issue of financial cost in responding. They indicated that their consumption would increase if cocaine became less expensive. Some thought that if the law were made more lenient, the price would go down; nevertheless, it seems that for many users the high cost of the drug, more than the threat of the law, acts as a barrier to use.

Summary

This chapter has provided an overview of national enforcement and sentencing trends for cocaine. Convictions for cocaine under the Narcotic Control Act have risen steadily since 1970, although convictions declined between 1990 and 1991. Of the more than 8,000 recorded in 1990, about half were for simple possession and the balance for trafficking and importing offenses. Cocaine possession has been treated more leniently by the courts than heroin possession and more severely than cannabis possession. RCMP drug intelligence indicated that cocaine is readily available in Canada, has become more so in recent years, and forecasts no decline in the near future.

This chapter also reported on the experience of the 111 cocaine users in obtaining cocaine and the extent to which the law functioned as a barrier to use. Respondents usually acquired cocaine from people they knew, not faceless dealers. The financial outlay was relatively low (averaging less than $100 per month for three-quarters of the sample) partly because of their fairly infrequent use and partly because of the amounts obtained gratis or by bartering. Their knowledge of the law and penalties regarding cocaine was generally inaccurate, and the threat of legal repercussions to them personally was viewed as negligible. Respondents felt insulated and safe in their use of cocaine among friends and regarded the law as irrelevant except in the sense of maintaining the high price of the drug. Their disregard of the law notwithstanding, nearly a quarter expressed little interest in continuing to use cocaine in the next year. In regression analysis, these likely "quitters" were found to be those who had never purchased cocaine, those who reported an uncontrollable urge to use it, and those who felt regular use presented a serious risk. Thus, the legal barrier was a minor obstruction to these users, but once hurdled, other considerations could still lead to discontinuing use.

8

Case Histories

Much of the material presented in previous chapters has been in the nature of a statistical overview, a format necessary in order to arrive at some general conclusions about cocaine use. Inevitably, the identity and experience of each participant in the study becomes submerged in a greater whole. We now counter this somewhat by presenting detailed case histories that remind us of the unique character of each participant. Minor alterations have been made to protect the identities of respondents. No case is typical in a sample of 111 individuals, although some experiences with cocaine may be shared. We have selected cases that fall along a continuum of involvement with cocaine. In a broadly based community sample such as ours, these portrayals serve as a reminder of the variety of interactions that may occur among individual, drug, and society.

Dave Dabbler

Dave was a self-employed businessman in his mid-30s. Although he had not completed high school, he earned close to $30,000 a year and lived alone in a comfortable downtown apartment. Divorced and with a teenage daughter, he described his life as "regular" and himself as "health conscious."

He was first offered cocaine at a friend's party and tried it out of curiosity. He had been told, "you could go out and conquer the

155

world," but he was disappointed with the effects. "I got very speedy; if that's it, it's not for me. I went off to ride my bicycle to get rid of the energy." Dave said he might try cocaine again if it was offered but would not make any effort to obtain it.

He used cannabis occasionally on the weekends, at parties with close friends. Other than infrequent use of alcohol and one experience with psychedelic mushrooms, he had not used other drugs. Dave gave the impression of a successful person with a well-ordered life, one in which drugs played a minor role.

Pam Party Goer

This single woman in her mid-20s worked as a makeup artist. Despite an annual income of less than $10,000, she was able to use cocaine often because it was "readily available at parties." She had bought the drug only once. She reported snorting cocaine about once or twice a month over the past year. For Pam, the attraction was in the stimulation and alertness she felt from the drug. She anticipated continuing use of cocaine at her current level. Her attitude was one of take it or leave it—but if it was around, she would rather take it.

Peter Party Goer

This divorced man in his early thirties had a university degree and worked as a self-employed producer in the entertainment industry. His income was in the mid-$20,000 range. Since his introduction to cocaine several years ago, he had adopted a routine of buying a gram twice a year, for "special occasions." He emphasized that cocaine was "always combined with doing other things" over the course of an evening. There were many situations in which he would avoid it, and he cited examples of business meetings and sports. Suitable occasions for use might be a birthday or "with cognac on Christmas Eve."

Peter described the effects as "very subtle . . . it opens up a more direct or intimate communication." About two years ago, someone had sent him 2 grams, and he used this daily for a week. He had no desire to repeat this experience. Cocaine, to him, was one way to spend extra disposable income, but for the price, "it wasn't worth it." He intended to continue using cocaine occasionally, but the drug did not have a high priority in his life.

Paul Party Giver

This high-income (over $50,000) manager in his 30s was married with children. Fairly new to cocaine, he bought a gram about every other month to share with his wife and sometimes a few close friends. What he liked most about cocaine was the "thrill" and feeling of being "in control." In his perception, the drug had changed his life for the better because it provided "another recreational outlet that I enjoy." Paul emphasized that cocaine was "a special drug—like caviar," and that he used it at times and places that did not "interfere with other obligations." He considered that he was not under the scrutiny of police because he was not a dealer and he had a middle-class life-style and associates. He had experimented with most other drugs in the past but was not currently using any of them. Alcohol and cocaine were his drugs of choice. He intended to continue cocaine use in his current pattern.

Desmond Devotee

A married man in his early 40s, Desmond earned over $40,000 annually in a demanding profession. He was highly successful in his career and had a stable home life with several children. His history of experience with illicit drugs went back over a decade and involved periods of heavy cocaine use, including freebasing, and distribution activities. Drug use tapered off as the demands of his career expanded. As he described the past few years, "You get busy and use less."

Currently, he used cocaine about twice a month, sometimes at home with his wife and friends and other times at parties. He never combined it with work, he stressed. The drug was often given to him, and he bought it two or three times a year. He still enjoyed the effects of cocaine: "the energy, the intensity and the mental activity" it provoked. He described himself as a person who "works hard and plays hard" and used cannabis almost daily, "to relax after work." Desmond did not feel that cocaine presented any problems of control for him. While his private life remained unconventional, his public persona was impeccable. Cocaine was a well-entrenched part of the private side but had no role in the public one.

Frances, a Former Devotee

This young actress was single and earned about $25,000 a year. About two years before being interviewed, she had started to use cocaine daily, buying nearly 2 grams a week. At first, she believed it helped her work. At the height of this period, she was spending $1,000 a month on cocaine. This went on for three months until she stopped on her own. As Frances described this time, the effects of cocaine she liked most, "the energy, the senses seem sharper," became the opposite: "Cocaine made me miserable, depressed; my personality changed." She reported that "it was easy to give up. I had taken myself to the limit, and spending all that money was incredibly foolish." She had continued to use occasionally, less often than once a month in the past year, but thought that she would use it even less, if at all, in the next year.

Fred, a Former Devotee

This successful writer in his late 30s reported an income in the $30,000-plus range. Despite using cocaine hundreds of times in his life, he had used it only once in the past year. At the peak of his use, about three years earlier, he had been doing runs lasting several days. He said he had used cocaine to enhance his ability to write for prolonged periods. His enthusiasm waned as he realized how self-centered and antisocial he was becoming. After becoming depressed and feeling helpless, he had sought psychiatric help, which was apparently successful. The interviewer sensed a desire in him to be able to continue the occasional use of cocaine without becoming compulsive again.

John and Mary, a Couple with a Problem

John and Mary's stories are intertwined, and both were interviewed. John was given a gram of cocaine for his birthday. After this first experience, he went out the next day and "bought $1,000 worth." John and Mary were living in a common-law relationship and had very little prior experience with drugs. They were both employed and in their mid-20s at the time of initiation to cocaine.

Their use soon escalated. John lost his job and took up dealing. He started injecting, up to several grams a day. Mary estimated they were going through an ounce every two weeks. John liked the nearly instantaneous effect: "I just push the button." Mary snorted it in the mornings: "It gives you something to get up for . . . it makes you feel great, on top of the world, and provides a never-ending source of energy." But "I couldn't stop using it when it was around the house," which was most of the time. Despite the dealing, they were heavily in debt.

John went to hospital emergency departments several times, thinking he was experiencing a heart attack. Mary had several severe crashes—headaches and depression—when they ran out of cocaine. Their use was brought to an end when John was arrested for trafficking. Interviewed while he was awaiting trial, neither of them had used cocaine for three months, nor did they intend to use again.

Summary

This chapter has provided some individual accounts of cocaine users' experiences. Cases were selected to indicate a broad range of experience with the drug. Clearly reactions can vary widely, from lack of interest to obsession. A community-based sample can uncover serious cases of compulsive use. These examples correspond with the negative image in the media. We also found individuals who experimented with cocaine without any resulting attraction to it. The social-recreational users—those who use cocaine in an apparently controlled way—also have been underrepresented in the media's sensational coverage of "ruined lives." Nevertheless, the latter cases do occur. The variety of responses illustrated here will provide a more reasonable and objective basis for the assessment of the conclusions of our study in the final two chapters.

Part III

Cocaine and Crack Users in the Community
The Second Study

9

Design and Comparative Findings

W hen we embarked on the second study of cocaine users in the community, we deliberately set out to recruit from a different part of the spectrum of use patterns. This time, we were interested in current users who had moved beyond the stage of experimentation to a more regular pattern of use. The principal criterion was use of cocaine at least ten times in the past twelve months. This study was also designed prospectively, with plans to reinterview respondents after one year. It was essential to retain identifying information about the sample, so confidentiality issues were an even more serious consideration than in the first study. Commencing in early 1989, we interviewed one hundred users in the community and reinterviewed fifty-four of them one year later. This chapter describes our method and some descriptive findings about this new group of participants.

Method

The challenges of recruiting the practitioners of a deviant and criminal activity from a noncaptive population such as illicit drug users were examined at length in chapter 4. The difficulties evident in 1983 remained in 1989, compounded by our lack of any key informants in cocaine-using circles and the not-unrelated factor of the increasing stigmatization of cocaine and crack use in the popular press. Nevertheless we were, though somewhat more slowly than in the first study, able to recruit a fairly typical sample of more experienced cocaine users from the community.

The sample of one hundred participants was recruited from adult cocaine users who lived in the metropolitan Toronto area. The major vehicle for publicizing the study was through advertisements inviting those with recent experience with cocaine, aged 18 years or older, to call a number at the Addiction Research Foundation (ARF). Advertisements were placed in mainstream, arts, and entertainment and community newspapers. Cable television and radio public service announcements were repeated many times, and posters were put up in numerous public locations around the city. A telephone number directly to our research office was provided and an answering machine activated for calls outside office hours. The telephone line was answered personally on weekends after major advertising campaigns in the leading daily newspapers. Whenever possible, the interviewer was also the person who made the initial telephone contact, in order to provide continuity and trust from the onset.

If the caller met the entry criteria of age and recent experience with cocaine, an interview was arranged as soon as possible, either at our offices or at a restaurant or coffee shop of the caller's choosing. Assurance of confidentiality and protection of identities was established before the interview began. Interviews took from one to one and a half hours to complete. The ratio of calls to successfully completed interviews was 8:1, reflecting ineligibility (due mainly to cessation of cocaine use) far more often than failure to show up for an arranged interview. Although payment was not mentioned, participants were paid $30 after the interview. The question of permission to recontact participants was broached at the end of the interview, and details were recorded then, if the participant agreed; twenty-five of them did not. After one year, recruitment ceased and follow-up efforts begun with those who consented and provided tracing information ($N = 75$).

Despite efforts to build snowball referral chains through those responding to the advertisements, this approach produced very few additional contacts with cocaine users. The great public and media attention paid to a perceived "crack menace" and the enhanced enforcement during the period of fieldwork was, we suspect, a disincentive for participants to direct other users to us from among their friends and acquaintances. On the more positive side, we believe that the trustworthy reputation of ARF and the nonjudgmental approach and experience of the interviewers promoted candor among participants in describing sensitive and illegal behavior. Many of those we interviewed professed a desire to share their experiences with cocaine and crack in order to benefit others, and some participants seemed genuinely interested in contributing their knowledge to a research project. Although it is not possible to ascertain precisely how volunteers for such a study may differ from the more reclusive majority who do not, the lesson of both our studies is that illicit drug users will risk their anonymity and come forward when the topic interests them and a secure research environment is available.

In the same year as that of sample recruitment, 1989, a random household survey of Ontario adults aged 18 years or over was also conducted by the ARF (Adlaf & Smart, 1989). The prevalence of cocaine use in the previous twelve months was 2.1 percent and for crack less than 1 percent. Since only 5.5 percent of these current (past-year) users reported a frequency of using cocaine once a month or more often, and rates of use in metropolitan Toronto are about double those of the rest of Ontario, we derived an estimate of a minimum of 10,000 monthly or more frequent users. If under-reporting of heavier use is also likely, then the upper limit may be two or even three times higher. We conclude that the sample of one hundred community users is drawn from a population of between 10,000 and 30,000 current, more frequent users of cocaine in metropolitan Toronto in 1989.

Sample Characteristics

Participants were, for the most part, young (mean age, 27.2 years), male (70 percent), and single (71 percent). Racial composition was almost exclusively white, and ethnic background was not solicited. The demographic characteristics of the participants are shown in table 9–1. The highest level of education attained was high school for 41 percent, other postsecondary for 32 percent, and some level of university for 26 percent. While 57 percent were employed full time, only 13 percent were actively seeking work. The balance were on social assistance, students, working parttime, or engaged in miscellaneous activities. Annual income was under $31,000 for nearly

TABLE 9-1

Demographic Characteristics of Two Samples of Cocaine Users (in percentages)

	Cocaine Users from the Community (N = 100)	Cocaine Users from Ontario[a] (N = 62)
Gender		
Male	70	66
Female	30	34
Age[b]		
18–20	13	4
21–25	39	28
26–30	22	40
31–35	17	16
36–40	4	10
41 +	5	1
Marital status		
Single (never married)	71	45
Common-law relationship	6	9
Married	9	38
Separated	9 ⎫	
Divorced	5 ⎭	8
Education		
Grade 9–11	16	16
Grade 12–13	25	24
Some postsecondary schooling	17	11
Postsecondary diploma/certificate	15	16
Some university	13	11
University degree	11 ⎫	
Graduate degree	2 ⎭	20
Gross personal annual income		
$10,000 or less	18	4
$11,000–$20,000	24	12
$21,000–$30,000	20	32
$31,000–$40,000	18	13
$41,000 +	17	31
No response	3	9
Employment status		
Employed full time	57	63
Looking for job	13	—
Employed part time	8	16
Student	8	8
Social assistance	7	—
Illegal activities	2	—
Other	5	14

TABLE 9–1 *(continued)*

	Cocaine Users from the Community (N = 100)	Cocaine Users from Ontario[a] (N = 62)
Living situation		
Own house/condominium	7	—
Rent house/apartment	36	—
Rent shared accommodation	26	—
Live with parents	17	—
Live in hostel/residence/looking		
for place to live	13	—
No response	1	—

[a] Based on a sample of cocaine users drawn from a Gallup probability sample of Ontario adults aged 18 and over (Adlaf & Smart 1989).

[b] Mean age 27.2 years.

two-thirds (62 percent) of respondents; less than one in five (17 percent) was earning more than $40,000 annually. Most rented accommodation (62 percent) or lived with their parents (17 percent).

Compared with cocaine users in the Ontario population survey, also shown in table 9–1, the community sample displays similar characteristics with respect to sex, education, employment, status, and living situation. Although none of the differences was statistically significant (on a chi-square test at $p < .05$) the community sample is somewhat younger, with a greater proportion of single persons and those in lower income brackets than cocaine users in the Ontario-wide random sample.

Since participants in the first community study had to be at least 21 years of age and employed, they of course differ from participants in the second study on these and age-related dimensions such as education and marital status. In gender and income, interestingly, they are very similar (see table 4–1). Socioeconomic status according to occupation was not assessed in the second study.

Cocaine Use Characteristics

The major difference in the self-selection process between the two studies was the appearance by 1989 of far more cocaine users with experience of crack. Of the one hundred participants, seventy-nine had used crack, twenty-two had injected cocaine at some time, and all but two had experience with snorting powder cocaine. While these two participants were exclusive crack users who said they had never snorted cocaine, three others who concentrated on crack had only one or two experiences with powder.[1] All of the injectors had used both powder and crack. Thus, it is evident that this sample can best be described as consisting of cocaine users with multimode experience.

A number of questions were asked about the participants' first experience with cocaine (table 9–2). The usual initiation to cocaine occurred in someone's home with the aid of a male friend. The average age of onset of use was 22.7 years, and nearly half the participants (47 percent) had their first cocaine experience before age 20 years. The sample was quite evenly divided between those with relatively brief histories of cocaine use—less than three years—and those who had used for longer. Most (82 percent) had started by the intranasal route, but smoking crack and injecting cocaine had also occurred. The most and least appealing aspects of their first experience were diverse and did not reflect unequivocal enthusiasm.

Their past histories of cocaine use are shown in table 9–3. Their current preference for mode of administration was smoking or snorting; fewer than a quarter of all participants used cocaine solely by the intranasal route. Most preferred to use both snorting and smoking, depending on the occasion and the type of high that was desired. Amount and frequency of use were elicited for their first year of use, the period of heaviest use, and the three months prior to the interview. The average dose of cocaine consumed per occasion of use was less than 1 gram initially for over half of participants, whereas the proportion taking 3 grams or more tripled in the heaviest use period (from 7 percent to 23 percent). By the last three months, only 4 percent were using 3 grams or more, and 36 percent had not used at all. The majority of those still using were reduced to less than 1 gram per occasion. Frequency of use also rose from the first year to the heaviest use period, and then dropped off in the past three months to lower than first-year levels. Binges—protracted periods of repeated cocaine administration during a single overall use occasion—were reported by most participants.

TABLE 9-2
First Cocaine Experience (N = 100) (in percentages)

Method of Administration		Age at first use[b]	
Snorted	82	15–20 years	47
Smoked	12	21–25 years	31
Injected	3	26–30 years	9
Other	3	31 and older	13
Relationship to and Gender of Introducer		Number of years since first experience	
Friend	69	Less than one	11
Co-worker/associate	12	One to less than three	42
Intimate friend (spouse,		Three to less than six	25
partner)	8	Six to less than nine	8
Relative	4	Nine or more	14
Dealer	3	Very or fairly important reasons for	
Other	4	trying cocaine	
Male	75	Interest/curiosity	79
Female	21	It was available	75
More than one person	4	For the adventure	60
Reactions experienced to some or a great		Heard good things about it	54
extent during first use		New experience/better high	47
More alert/aware	86	Wanting to fit in	13
Energy boost	82	Did cocaine meet expectations?	
Euphoria	82	Yes	48
A rush	65	No	42
More sociable	60	No expectations	10
Mellow	58	Most appealing aspects of first use[a]	
Anxiety/nervousness	54	Euphoria	18
Unpleasant taste	52	Increased sociability	16
Nasal irritation/burning	49	Energy boost	10
Overstimulated	41	Liked nothing	10
Sexually aroused	40	Rush	6
Felt nothing	32	Self-confidence	6
Depressed	22	Location of first use	
Nauseous	14	Friends'/acquaintances' home	41
Least appealing aspects of first use[a]		My home	7
Disliked nothing	17	Bar/club	7
Weak/lack of effect	13	At work	7
Coming down	12	Car	4
Financial cost	11	Family's home	4
Craving to use more	9	Party	4
Short high	9	At school	2
Nose/throat irritation	8	Stairwell	2
Psychological effects		Other	14
(e.g., paranoia)	8	Missing	2
Other physical effects	9		

[a] Multiple responses permitted.
[b] Average age 22.7 years.

TABLE 9-3

History of Cocaine Use: Mode of Administration, Frequency of Use, and Quantity Ingested (in percentages)

	Usual Method of Administration (N = 100)		
Number of Times per 10 occasions	Snort	Inject	Smoke
0 times	28	85	28
1–3 times	17	5	18
4–7 times	21	3	23
8–10 times	34	7	31

Usual Dose of Cocaine per Occasion[a]	First Year (N = 96)	Heaviest Use Period (N = 99)	Last 3 Months (N = 98)
0 gram (g)	0	0	36
less than ¼ g	35	16	20
¼ g to less than ½ g	15	15	10
½ g to less than ¾ g	19	10	11
¾ g to less than 1 g	1	5	1
1 g to less than 2 g	17	20	14
2 g to less than 3 g	6	9	3
3 or more grams	7	23	4
Median dose	.45 g	1.0 g	.13 g

Frequency of Use[a]	First Year (N = 97)	Heaviest Use Period (N = 99)	Last 3 Months (N = 100)
No use	0	0	36
Less than 1/month to 1/week	59	15	35
More than 1/week	41	85	29

Longest Interval of Use	(N = 100)
6 hours or less	6
7–12 hours	11
13 hours–1 day	11
More than 1–3 days	40
More than 4–5 days	18
6 or more days	14
Median duration	3.0 days

[a] Responses do not equal 100 because of nonresponse, because the respondent could not remember, or because the respondent did not know the answer to the question.

TABLE 9–4
Situation of Cocaine Use
(N = 100) (in percentages)

Usual time of day for use	
Morning	3
Noon	1
Afternoon	4
Night/evening	65
Any time/whenever possible	21
Varies	6
Situations ever used	
At friends' homes	95
At home with friends	84
At parties	79
At club/bar	74
At home alone	71
At home with others who live there	57
At work alone	41
At work with others	39
In a car	21
Most typical situation of use	
At friends' homes	26
At home with friends	17
At home with others who live there	12
At home alone	12
At clubs/bars	8
At parties	6
Other	14
Situation varies a lot	5
Ever stopped using for one month or more?	
Yes	91
No	9

The typical situation for cocaine to be used was a social event occurring in the evening at a friend's home (table 9–4). Being at home or at work alone was seldom the preferred venue for cocaine use, but rather high proportions acknowledged that they had ever done so: 71 percent at home and 41 percent at work. About 90 percent also reported that they had voluntarily stopped using cocaine for one month or more.

TABLE 9–5
Use of Other Drugs
(N = 100) (in percentages)

Drug	Ever in Lifetime	Ever in Past Year	Ever in Past Month
Alcohol	100	97	81
Cannabis	99	92	71
Cocaine[a]	98	90	44
Hallucinogens other than LSD/PCP	87	36	9
LSD	84	34	8
Stimulants/amphetamines	83	41	10
Crack	79	68	26
Tranquilizers	58	34	10
Narcotics other than heroin	53	19	5
Barbiturates	41	19	3
PCP	33	2	2
Heroin	21	9	1

[a]Two respondents had never used powder cocaine; their cocaine experience was exclusively with crack.

Other Drug Use

Most participants had an extensive history of multiple drug use (table 9–5). Besides current (past-year) alcohol, cannabis, and cocaine use by nearly all of those interviewed, over 80 percent also reported lifetime experience with LSD, other hallucinogens, amphetamines, and other stimulants. Past prescription drug use of tranquilizers and barbiturates was reported by 58 percent and 41 percent, respectively. One-third had tried PCP and one-fifth heroin. Yet despite this considerable exposure, relatively few—10 percent or less—had been using any drug other than alcohol, cannabis, and cocaine in the month before the interview. Tobacco also was widely used. The age of onset, or first use, of the array of drugs began with tobacco at a mean age of 13.2 years, followed by alcohol and cannabis in the early teens, then prescription drugs and hallucinogens in the later teen years, and rounded out with heroin (where applicable), cocaine, and finally crack at a mean age of 25.4 years (table 9–6).

TABLE 9-6

Mean Age in Years of First Use of Drugs (N = 100)

Drug	Age
Tobacco	13.2
Alcohol	13.4
Cannabis	14.8
Barbiturates	17.5
Stimulants/amphetamines	17.5
Hallucinogens	17.6
Narcotics other than heroin	18.8
Tranquilizers	19.0
Heroin	22.1
Cocaine[a]	22.5
Crack	25.4

[a]Two respondents had never used powder cocaine; their cocaine experience was exclusively with crack.

Characteristics of Follow-up Sample and User Characteristics

After one year, fifty-four of the one hundred participants were reinterviewed.[2] Table 9–7 compares their social demographic and drug use characteristics to those who were lost to follow-up. Chi-square tests of significance indicated that the two groups were not significantly different. The one exception was sex: males were disproportionately lost from the second interview group (61 percent male versus 80 percent at initial interview). Interestingly, despite the overrepresentation of females in our follow-up group, other factors were not affected. In other words, female demographics and patterns of drug use were very like male ones. Thus, we can conclude that nonresponse bias was minimal and does not affect the generalizability of the results of the second interviews to the sample as a whole.

The picture presented at the first interview was one of diminishing frequency and amount of use compared to initial and maximal periods of use. This pattern was evident one year later as well (table 9–8). Of the 30 percent (N = 16) of the fifty-four follow-up respondents who had not used either cocaine or crack in the past

TABLE 9-7

Nonresponse Bias in a Longitudinal Study of Cocaine Users (in percentages)

	t_1 Interview Only ($N = 46$)	t_2 Interview Completed ($N = 54$)
Age[a]		
30 +	26	35
25–29	41	29
18–24	33	37
Sex[b]		
Male	80	61
Female	20	39
Marital status[a]		
Never married	67	74
Married	17	13
Separated/divorced	15	13
Education[a]		
High school or less	13	19
Postsecondary	87	81
Income[a]		
$20,000 or less	46	39
More than $20,000	54	61
Months since first tried cocaine[a]		
36 or less	67	70
More than 36	33	30
Amount of cocaine consumed during heaviest use[a]		
Less than 1.5 gram	61	57
1.5 gram or more	39	43
Ever injected cocaine[a]		
No	76	80
Yes	24	20
Cocaine use in past year[a]		
0–9 times	33	19
10–99 times	39	48
100+ times	28	33
Crack use in past year[a]		
Never	30	33
1–39 times	30	39
40+ times	39	28
Cannabis use in past year[a]		
0–19 times	33	39
20–99 times	28	31
100+	39	30

[a] Not significant.
[b] $p \leq .05$

TABLE 9–8

Current Use of Cocaine Powder by Use of Crack
in Past Twelve Months (N = 54)

Current Use of Cocaine Powder	Current Crack Use					
	Some		Not in Past Year		Never	
	(N)	(%)	(N)	(%)	(N)	(%)
None	0	0	11	41	5	45
Some	16	100	16	59	6	55
Totals	16	100	27	100	11	100

year, those with and without crack experience were about equally likely to have quit. All of the sixteen current crack users also used powder in the past year, and sixteen respondents who were former crack users had continued to use powder cocaine in the past year. Of the thirty-eight respondents in total who were still using cocaine or crack, the patterns in the past year varied widely (figure 9–1).

FIGURE 9–1

Six Cocaine Use Patterns Displayed By the Thirty-eight Respondents Who Continued to Use Cocaine Between the First and Second Interviews (16 Had Quit)

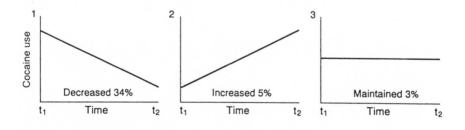

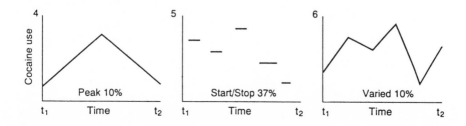

The most common patterns were either a steady decrease, characterizing 34 percent of this group, or an erratic start/stop graph describing 37 percent of continuing users. For the remaining one-third, use had peaked and declined (10 percent), fluctuated widely (10 percent), increased (5 percent), or remained the same as one year earlier (3 percent).

Summary

This chapter has described the characteristics of one hundred experienced cocaine users recruited from the community and the fifty-four respondents reinterviewed one year later. This study relied more than the first one on advertisements and attracted many more users with multimode experience.[3] The first study consisted of mainly social-recreational snorters who used infrequently, no crack users, and only seven with injection experience. This second study contained a majority of 79 participants with experience with crack and twenty-two with a history of injection, though snorting and smoking were the currently preferred modes. The two studies were similar in that nearly all respondents were current alcohol and cannabis users with a lifetime history of a variety of drugs.

10

Crack Use in Toronto

A Distant American Cousin

with Yuet W. Cheung

The drug habit in Toronto is on the increase, but the increase has not been very remarkable. It is not an alarming increase. Canadian do not take to the habit like their American cousins.[1]
Toronto Star, *June 3, 1905*

To many Canadians, their much larger American relative to the south is a crystal ball for forecasting forthcoming drug problems in Canada. When large American cities are reported to be plagued with a certain drug epidemic, Canadians expect a similar epidemic to strike them. This kind of convenient referencing is not totally illusory. Illicit drugs and their dealers recognize no geographical boundaries, and their tentacles tend to stretch far in all directions. The histories of illicit drug use and misuse in the two countries have also shown a more or less similar pattern: heroin increased in both countries in the 1950s, followed by cannabis in the 1960s and 1970s, and cocaine in the 1980s (Erickson 1992). However, what Canadians get from the American crystal ball are mainly caricatured images of crime and drug problems in the United States, and these images shape, or misshape, the perception of these social problems in Canada. Such a "misplacement" of images of social problems is often facilitated by the American media, especially television, to which Canadians are heavily exposed. Research has shown that Canadians tend to overestimate both the extent and seriousness of crime in Canada, perceiving that their problems are

177

similar to those in the United States (Griffiths and Verdun-Jones 1989:25), when actual crime rates and levels of violence in Canada are substantially lower than in the United States (Hagan 1991:46–54; Currie 1985).

The long tradition of harsh drug law and the influence of the U.S. media have been shaping Canada's reactions to drug problems facing the United States. It came as no surprise, therefore, that strong warning signals were hoisted by the Canadian police and media when the United States was reported to be devastated by crack in the mid-1980s. Beginning in 1987, when crack began to appear in Canada, the Canadian media and police reports quickly alerted Canadians to the arrival of a "crack epidemic."

The *Toronto Star* (1989a) told its readers that the "crack problem" was "the greatest threat to society in general, of any single development over the past 15 years." It also claimed (1989c) that crack was "a one-way ticket to hell for the user." The *Globe and Mail* (1989) reported that crack use had reached "crisis proportions," having its most devastating effects in poorer neighborhoods; it characterized users as "a very, very paranoid, psychotic group." Unlike the image of freebase smoking among the middle and upper classes, crack was depicted as "the poor man's cocaine" and the "T.V. dinner version of freebase cocaine" (*Toronto Star* 1989b). *Maclean's*, a popular Canadian weekly magazine, devoted a number of pages in 1989 to describing the "deadly plague of drugs" in Toronto and other Canadian cities. Even a municipal newspaper in metropolitan Toronto warned that the "nightmare" of epidemic crack use, like that found in poor enclaves in U.S. cities, is "now taking a foothold in Metro" (*Mirror* 1989).

Police reported that "much" of the 73.7 kilograms of cocaine seized in metropolitan Toronto in 1989 was crack (*Toronto Star* 1990). The Royal Canadian Mounted Police described crack as "the drug of choice of a new sector in the cocaine-user population, primarily in Toronto" and said crack was at least partly responsible for the threefold increase in cocaine-related deaths from 1986 to 1988 (RCMP 1988). The media linked crack use to crime, asserting that its extraordinary addictiveness led users to do "anything" for another hit (*Globe and Mail* 1989; RCMP 1989).

Despite the abundance of anecdotal accounts by the media and police about crack's powerful addictive properties and devastating

TABLE 10-1
Frequency of Crack Use (N = 79)

Frequency	Use in Lifetime (%)	(N)	Use in Past Year (%)	(N)	Use in Past Month (%)	(N)
Never	0.0	0	13.9	11	67.1	53
1–2 times	11.4	9	13.9	11	13.9	11
3–5 times	11.4	9	10.1	8	5.0	4
6–9 times	3.8	3	3.8	3	0.0	0
10–19 times	8.8	7	10.1	8	5.1	4
20–39 times	5.1	4	6.3	5	6.3	5
40–99 times	22.8	18	12.7	10	1.3	1
100 times or more	36.7	29	29.1	23	1.3	1

effects on individuals and society, such reportage provided little concrete information about the prevalence of crack use in Canada and about the many crack users who are not identified in the media or by law enforcement agencies. The low extent of crack use in Canada has already been described. In this chapter, our objective is to present findings from a community-based study of crack users in Toronto as a basis for empirically comparing real crack users with media images. This study offered the first findings about crack use in a community-based sample in Canada (Cheung, Erickson & Landau 1991). We interviewed seventy-nine participants who were 18 or older and had used crack. Results showed an infrequent pattern of use even among this group of crack users (table 10–1).

In the past month, 67 percent had not used crack, while 19 percent had used it fewer than ten times, 5 percent had used it between ten and nineteen times, 6 percent had used it twenty to thirty-nine times, and only 3 percent had used it forty times or more. If we treat twenty times or more in the past month as heavy use, then 9 percent (N = 7) of respondents were currently heavy users. Their use in the past year and in their lifetimes was lower. In the past year, 14 percent had not used crack at all, and 38 percent had used it fewer than twenty times. Half had not used crack twenty times or more. As to lifetime use, 40 percent had used it less than forty times or more, 23 percent had used it between forty and ninety-nine times, and 37 percent had used it one hundred times or more.

Because each type of study or source of information has its limitations, the exact extent of crack use is difficult to determine. However, on the basis of findings from surveys and a community-based study, there is no strong evidence for media and police claims that crack use had reached an epidemic level in Canada. Even if increases in police seizures of cocaine and crack and the deflation of price of street cocaine do indicate increased distribution of crack, there is little evidence of increased consumption in the general student and adult population. However, increases in the use of crack may have occurred among impoverished segments of the population, such as street youths and the economic underclass.

The Crack Experience

A core premise of media and law enforcement claims of an epidemic is that crack's quick and intense high quickly leads to compulsive use and then a powerful addiction. Once addicted, the user would soon ruin his or her life by draining income, destroying family relationships, suffering physical and psychological problems, and losing his or her job. By the same logic, crack addicts would then pose a threat to society as they would engage in whatever level of crime or violence was needed to obtain the money for maintaining uncontrollable use. Anecdotal accounts of this sort abound in the media, and they have gained support from studies of known addicts, usually in clinical samples, which generally show that crack abuse entails serious physical, psychological, and social consequences (Washton, Gold & Pottash 1986; Golbe & Merkin 1986; Kissner et al. 1987; see also Smart 1991). However, because the samples in most such studies were heavy users requiring treatment, the results cannot be generalized to the much larger number of low-level users in the community. Our goal was to capture the phenomenon of crack use within the broader spectrum of crack users that exist in the community and to test the popular image of crack as powerfully addicting.

The method of obtaining respondents was described in the previous chapter. Briefly, through advertisements in the media and in public places, we recruited for interviews one hundred subjects aged 18 or older who had used cocaine, crack, or both. Among these respondents, seventy-nine had used crack, and the remaining twenty-one had used only cocaine powder. Of the seventy-nine who had ever used crack, seventy-seven had also used powder, two had not used forms of cocaine other than crack, and twenty-two had injected cocaine. Most of the respondents had experience with a wide range of licit and illicit drugs.

Three-quarters of the seventy-nine crack users were male. Over half were between 21 and 30 years old, and 70 percent were never married. Forty percent had finished only grades 9–13. Over half were employed full time, mostly in semi-, low-, or unskilled jobs. About 40 percent were earning $20,000 (Canadian) or less a year, and another 38 percent were earning between $21,000 and $40,000. Thus, the majority of the crack users in the sample were young, single males with relatively low-level educations, occupations, and incomes. These crack users did not differ significantly from the twenty-one other respondents in the sample who only snorted powder cocaine with respect to sociodemographic characteristics or with respect to self-rated physical health and psychological well-being. Moreover, most of the crack users were current or past powder users as well. Thus, these crack users were not a distinct group of cocaine users. They used crack in addition to powder rather than as a substitute for it.

The respondents were asked a number of questions concerning various aspects of their crack use (table 10–2). Over three-quarters of the respondents had not tried crack until three years prior to our interviews (about 1986), when crack began to enter the Canadian scene. Most were introduced to crack by males, and over 60 percent of introducers were friends of the respondents. The most common situation for crack use was with friends in one's own home or a friend's home (67 percent). Thirty percent of respondents reported that "about half" or "almost all" of their friends sometimes used crack. Compared to peer use of cocaine and cannabis, this figure indicates low peer use of crack.[2] The majority of respondents (83 percent) reported that it was "easy" or "very easy" to get crack.

We asked respondents to name up to three things they liked most about crack. Almost half mentioned "the rapid, intense reaction" (the "rush") as one of their three. About one-fifth mentioned "the really good or euphoric feeling." Some other pleasurable effects were also reported, including "boost in energy," "sexual arousal," "improvement in sociability," "escape from worries or tensions," "new experience," and "the taste of it."

TABLE 10-2
Experience of Crack Use
(N = 78 unless otherwise stated)

	%	N
Years ago first used crack (N = 77)		
1 year	23.4	18
2 years	41.5	32
3 years	13.0	10
4 years	11.7	9
5 years	2.6	2
6 years	5.2	4
7 years	2.6	2
Sex of introducer		
Male	74.4	58
Female	19.2	15
More than one person	6.4	5
Introducer's relationship to respondent		
Spouse/common-law/intimate friend	10.3	8
Other friends	61.5	48
Co-worker	6.4	5
Dealer	11.5	9
Other	10.3	8
Most common situation for use (N = 73)		
Club/bar	2.7	2
Parties	5.5	4
Own home alone	9.6	7
Own home with others living there	9.6	7
Own home with friends	19.2	14
Friend's home	38.4	28
Other situation	10.9	8
Varies a lot	4.1	3
Availability of crack		
Very difficult	6.4	5
Difficult	1.3	1
Sometimes difficult	9.0	7
Easy	11.5	9
Very easy	71.8	56
Friends who sometimes use crack		
None	19.2	15
Only a few	48.7	38
About half	11.5	9
Almost all	19.2	15
Don't know	1.3	1
Effects of crack liked most (selected responses		
"Rush"	43.6	34
Euphoric feeling	16.7	13

TABLE 10–2 (*continued*)

	%	N
Effects of crack liked least (selected responses)		
"Coming down"	17.9	14
Short "high"	11.5	9
Craving to use more	21.8	17
Financial cost	15.4	12
Various adverse physical effects	43.6	34
Frequency of craving for crack		
Never	35.9	28
Rarely	17.9	14
Sometimes	15.4	12
Most times	14.1	11
Always	16.7	13
Perceived risk of harm in trying crack once or twice		
No risk	10.3	8
Slight risk	15.4	12
Moderate risk	19.2	15
Great risk	55.1	43
Perceived risk of harm in using crack regularly		
No risk	1.3	1
Slight risk	0.0	0
Moderate risk	7.7	6
Great risk	91.0	71
Perceived risk of harm in using crack occasionally		
No risk	2.6	2
Slight risk	12.8	10
Moderate risk	17.9	14
Great risk	66.7	52
Ever concerned about becoming addicted		
No	68.7	38
Yes	48.7	38
No answer	2.6	2
Preferred form of cocaine		
Powder	47.4	37
Crack	46.2	36
No preference/don't know	5.1	4
No answer	1.3	1

Note: *N* was reduced from seventy-nine to seventy-eight because of one missing case.

We also asked them to name up to three effects they liked least about crack. Over 40 percent disliked the adverse physical effects, such as "nausea," "faster heart rate," "sweating," and "burnt lungs." Eighteen percent mentioned "coming down," and 12 percent mentioned the related "short high" as things they liked least. Also, 15 percent complained about the "financial cost" of use, whereas a larger percentage (22 percent) considered "the urge/craving to use more" to be what they liked least. This craving problem became more apparent when nearly a third (31 percent) reported that they "always" or "most of the time" experienced this urge; another 15 percent admitted that they had "sometimes" experienced such an urge.

It is noteworthy that fewer than half of these subjects reported any problem with craving. This suggests that crack may not be as overwhelmingly reinforcing as one might guess from examining the minority of users who experience sufficient problems to end up in jail or treatment. However, based on their experience of negative effects and craving, our respondents showed a healthy respect for the risks; a majority thought that people would be at least in danger of harming themselves if they used crack. More than half said there would be great risk if people "try crack once or twice," two-thirds mentioned great risk if people "use crack occasionally," and nine-tenths perceived great risk if people "use crack regularly." But when asked about their own use, fewer than half our respondents felt concerned about becoming addicted to crack. In fact, fewer than half (46 percent) considered crack their preferred form of cocaine.

In sum, a crack user was likely to have first tried crack fewer than three years ago, be introduced to crack by a male friend, and to use crack at one's own or a friend's home. Although crack was easily available to these respondents, it was used less commonly in their circles of friends than powder cocaine or cannabis. The rush and euphoria were what users liked most about crack. The short high, the "coming down," adverse physical effects, and the craving to use more were what users like least. About half of the respondents had experienced the craving, felt concerned about becoming addicted, and preferred crack over other forms of cocaine. Most perceived that people in general would run real risks with regular and even occasional use of crack.

In order to capture individual differences in use between two recent time periods, we constructed a typology of users, based on crack use in the past year and the past month. We identified three types: *continuous users*, who had used crack in the past year *and* in the past month (32 percent of the sample); *inactive users*, who had used crack in the past year but *not* in the past month (54 percent); and *abstainers*, who had *stopped* use for one year (14 percent). The fact that only 32 percent of the sample were currently continuous users and that among them only 28 percent were heavy users (twenty times or more per month) suggests that crack use is not necessarily compulsive, even well after first use. Most people in the sample had refrained from use for either a month or a year at the time of the interview. Thus, it is not unreasonable to predict that in the future, many, perhaps most, of the inactive users and abstainers will continue to avoid at least compulsive or addictive use.

Did the three types of users differ in their experience of crack use? We compared them with respect to most of the experience items. Our statistical tests (not reported here) indicated that the three groups did not differ significantly in friends' use of crack, what was liked most and least about crack, frequency of craving, concern about addiction, and preferred form of cocaine. They also did not differ in their view that regular crack use generally entails serious risks (100 percent of abstainers, 93 percent of inactive users, and 84 percent of continuous users).

The three types of users differed significantly only in their perception of the risk of harm in "trying crack once or twice" and in "occasional use of crack." Many more abstainers and inactive users perceived great or moderate risks in trying crack (90 percent and 80 percent, respectively) than did continuous users (56 percent). Conversely, many more continuous users (44 percent) than inactive users (19 percent) or abstainers (9 percent) saw no risk or only slight risk in trying crack. Similarly, nearly a third (32 percent) of continuous users perceived no risk or only slight risks in occasional use, whereas only 10 percent of inactive users and none of the abstainers held the same view.[3] All three groups perceived great risk in regular use, which may be why not even the continuous users used crack daily or even regularly (table 10–1). This apparent capacity of users to recognize the risks of crack and to modulate their use is at variance with media and police accounts.

Summary

Like other drug problems, crack in Canada must be understood in the context of the great American influence in the formation of popular images about the crack problem in Canada and Canada's traditionally punitive, law enforcement-centered approach to dealing with drug problems. The anticipation of the "crack epidemic," the portrayal of its arrival by the media and police reports, and government responses to such an "epidemic" neatly resembled the typical U.S. "war on drugs" approach. Crack was presented to the public as extremely dangerous because its quick and intense high made it so powerfully addictive that serious health and financial consequences were inevitable. In a short span of time after its appearance in 1986–1987, crack use was said to have reached crisis levels in Canada. According to available evidence about the scope and nature of crack use, however, virtually all of these claims are seriously misleading.

A review of different sources of evidence about the extent of crack use in Canada could not demonstrate the presence of crisis levels of crack use. More representative surveys of students and adults have shown low prevalence rates of crack use between 1987 and 1989–1990 (see chapter 3). Low frequencies of use were also reported in this community-based study of crack users in Toronto in 1989. As earlier chapters have shown, it is thus likely that rapid increases in crack use have occurred largely in socially and economically devastated segments of the population. However, there is little evidence that serious levels of crack use exist in the general Canadian population.

Findings from the community-based study of crack users in Toronto allowed us to illustrate some of the major aspects of crack use among a self-selected group of crack users from the Canadian city said to be most seriously plagued with the drug. These results lend support to only a small part of the popular images of crack. The "rush" and euphoria from smoking crack were indeed what the respondents were attracted to. However, there was little evidence that the use of crack is necessarily compulsive. Over half of the respondents had rarely or never experienced a craving to take crack. Less than half preferred crack to powder cocaine. At time of interview, two-thirds of the respondents had not used crack for a month, and 14 percent had stopped use for a year. Only 30 percent had used it continuously in the past year, and daily users comprised only 9 percent of the sample. For a majority of respondents, crack was not the drug of choice. The data do not show whether a respondent's use of crack had been uncontrollable in the initial period. Still, it is clear that even if compulsive use had occurred before, reduction to infrequent use or abstinence was the pattern for the majority of crack users over time, a conclusion reinforced by the findings of the follow-up study (see table 9–8).

If crack use is not necessarily compulsive for an extended period of time, just what factors determine level of use? This Toronto study suggests that it was precisely the possible dangerous physical, social, and financial consequences of crack addiction that kept most users away from regular use. The more that users perceived risks of harm in crack use, the less they used it. Yet this user rationality is ignored in claims that crack's pharmacological powers are omnipotent.

Crack users in this study were not sociodemographically different from other cocaine users. For most, crack was used in addition to powder, not as a substitute. Therefore, crack use and its consequences should be understood within the context of cocaine use in general. In a detailed review of animal studies, clinical studies, population surveys, and studies of community samples of cocaine users, Erickson and Alexander (1989) have shown that the "addictive liability" of cocaine has been overstated; only 5 to 10 percent of those who try cocaine progress to more intensive use, such as weekly or more often. Data from the Toronto study revealed a similar pattern. At most, only 9 percent of the crack users in the sample were in the heavy use category (twenty times or more per month). Others either maintained a very low level of continuous use or abstained from use for various lengths of time.

We began this chapter by pointing out Canada's long habit of seeing its own drug problems through U.S. lenses and following closely the U.S. approach to solving drug problems. The recent crack scare in Canada is yet another, and the latest, version of Canada's fateful predilection for its American cousin.

11

Cocaine, Set, and Setting

In chapters 9 and 10, we briefly described the characteristics of cocaine users interviewed for the second study. In this chapter, we will take a detailed look at cocaine experiences of users in study one and study two within the drug-set-setting framework (Zinberg 1984).

Drug-Set-Setting Factors

The ingestion of any psychoactive drug has the potential to induce an array of feelings and other consequences experienced by the user. Although many drug-induced experiences are the result of pharmacological action, many, especially those subjectively experienced, are influenced by sociological factors as well. Indeed, as Goode has argued,

> Drugs are both chemical substances and social, cultural, and symbolic phenomena that are perceived, dealt with, and used in certain ways by the general society and by groups within it. We must therefore examine the social climate surrounding drug use in order to understand its causes, extent, and consequences. Sociological factors always affect a drug's pharmacology. (Goode 1984:27)

The effect a drug has on a given person is determined by the interaction of three general factors: the drug, the pharmacological action of the substance; the individual's set, intraindividual factors

189

such as personal characteristics and attitudes, beliefs, and personality; and the setting, interpersonal factors such as the influence of social relations and physical environment (Goode 1984; Westermeyer 1987; Zinberg 1984).

One prominent setting factor that influences the effects of a drug is social interaction with other drug users. Becker (1967) has argued that association in drug-using subcultures serves to reduce the likelihood of negative drug reactions (see also Fromberg 1993). By comparing the historical development of LSD and marijuana subcultures, Becker argued that drug-induced psychoses, which he interpreted as an anxiety reaction of naive users, is a function of participation in a drug-using subculture. When a new substance enters the drug scene, negative reactions are likely because a subculture of use has yet to develop. Thus, there is no means to transmit knowledge—that is, rituals of use that serve to reduce adverse reactions. With time, a subculture develops that reduces the extent of adverse reactions. This he correctly predicted would occur for LSD during the late 1960s and early 1970s.

Since Becker's seminal piece, few other studies have specifically examined the role of primary group associations on drug effects. Those studies that have addressed this issue have examined the dominant substances of the times (alcohol, Orcutt 1978; tobacco, Krohn et al. 1985; cannabis, Becker 1953, Orcutt 1978, Kaplan et al. 1986; and hallucinogens, Becker 1967).

Without doubt, the dominant drug now is cocaine, with its derivative crack. Whether interactional exposure in cocaine-using social networks reduces the likelihood of adverse reactions as Becker suggests is largely unknown. The generalizability of the buffering effect is important to examine since Becker has argued this effect may depend on the pharmacological properties of the substance:

> Where the effects are clear and unmistakable, as with opiates, the culture is limited in the possible interpretations it can provide. Where the cultural interpretation is so constrained . . . the spread of a drug-using culture will increase morbidity rates. (Becker 1967:175)

Thus, if social interaction with other cocaine users reduces the likelihood of negative drug effects, then future rates of cocaine-related morbidity should decline; however, if the reverse is true, then morbidity should increase with time.

Cocaine Experiences of Study 2 Users

Table 11–1, presents the frequency of twenty-six cocaine reactions experienced while using cocaine and thirteen reactions experienced as a result of cocaine use; note that these data are similar to those presented in table 6–1 for study 1. The reactions cited most frequently were increased heart rate (88 percent), followed by euphoria (81 percent), acute insomnia (76 percent), and energy and restlessness, both occurring frequently among 72 percent. The cocaine reactions occurring most of the time or always by 10 percent or less of the respondents were nausea (10 percent), aggression and lights in vision (9 percent), and hallucinations (7 percent).

A brief comparison to table 6–1 suggests that the extent of cocaine reactions differs between users in the two studies. First, most reactions were generally more frequently reported by study 2 than study 1 users. In table 11–2 we show selected comparisons of the percentage of users who reported experiencing a cocaine effect most times or always when using cocaine. The exception to the more frequent reports by study 2 users was for effects that we labeled as social-stimulatory in chapter 6: self-confidence, talkativeness, and energy. For these three effects, reports were less frequent among study 2 than among study 1 users. Among study 2 users, 56 percent frequently reported self-confidence, 58 percent frequently reported talkativeness, and 72 percent frequently reported increased energy. This compares to 67 percent, 75 percent, and 77 percent, respectively, for study 1 users.

Regarding cocaine effects experienced as a result of using cocaine, we see in table 11–1 that the most frequently cited reactions were chronic insomnia, which occurred most times or always after using cocaine for 67 percent of respondents. This was followed by being unable to relax (54 percent), having an uncontrollable craving to use cocaine (48 percent), experiencing physical or mental exhaustion (44 percent), and experiencing weight loss (42 percent).

Again, cocaine reactions were more frequent among study 2 users than among study 1 users. In table 11–3 we show the percentage of users who reported the cocaine effect most times or always.

In table 11–4, we show the percentage experiencing cocaine reactions most times or always by the frequency of cocaine use in the last three months. We classified frequency of cocaine use into three

TABLE 11-1

Frequency of Cocaine Reactions
(N = 100) (in percentages)

	Never	Rarely/ Sometimes	Most Times/ Always
Experienced while using			
Increased heart rate	2	9	88
Euphoria	0	19	81
Acute insomnia	4	19	76
Energy	2	26	72
Restlessness	2	26	72
Dry mouth/throat	3	33	63
Loss of inhibitions	8	34	58
Talkativeness	6	36	58
Self-confidence	8	36	56
Nervousness	7	52	41
Sweating	11	47	41
Buzzing in ears	31	38	31
Tremors/shaking	16	54	30
Decreased sexual arousal	31	41	28
Need to relax	23	51	26
Sexual arousal	27	48	25
Self-consciousness	21	56	23
Paranoia	37	44	19
Fuzzy vision	46	41	13
Headache	35	54	11
Nausea	33	57	10
Aggression	49	42	9
Lights in vision	49	42	9
Hallucinations	60	33	7
Convulsions	78	22	0
Experienced as a result of using			
Chronic insomnia	4	29	67
Unable to relax	5	40	54
Uncontrollable craving/urge to use cocaine	19	33	48
Physical/mental exhaustion	8	48	44
Weight loss	26	32	42
Congested nose	15	46	39
Depression	19	44	37
Chronic lack of sexual interest	30	43	26
Unable to think clearly	19	54	26
Sore/bleeding nose	30	52	18
Skin disorders or abscesses	77	20	3
Hepatitis/jaundice	95	4	1
Cocaine overdose	70	30	0

TABLE 11–2

Cocaine Effects Experienced While Using Cocaine.
Study 1 versus Study 2 (in percentages)

	Study 2	Study 1
Increased heart rate	88	66
Acute insomnia	76	39
Restlessness	72	50
Dry mouth, throat	63	38
Buzzing in ears	31	6
Paranoia	19	0
Nausea	10	4
Hallucinations	7	1

TABLE 11–3

Cocaine Effects Experienced After Using Cocaine.
Study 1 versus Study 2 (in percentages)

	Study 2	Study 1
Chronic insomnia	67	16
Unable to relax	54	15
Uncontrollable craving to use	48	20
Physical/mental exhaustion	44	14
Weight loss	42	12
Congested nose	39	32

groups: nonusers, those who did not use cocaine during the past three months; less frequent users, those who used cocaine at least once during the past three months but did not use more often than once a week; and more frequent users, those who used cocaine more often than once a week.

Frequency of cocaine use does not show a strong relationship to frequent reports of cocaine reactions. Of the twenty-four effects, only two show differences that are statistically significant: sweating, reported by 61 percent of nonusers compared to 29 percent of less frequent users and 32 percent of more frequent users, and paranoia, reported frequently by only 11 percent of less frequent users compared to 22 percent of nonusers and 24 percent of more frequent users. Two other cocaine reactions—uncontrollable crav-

TABLE 11–4

Percentage Reporting Experiencing Effects Most Times or
Always in the Past Three Months (N = 100)

	Nonusers (N = 36)	Less Frequent Users (N = 35)	More Frequent Users (N = 29)
Experienced while using			
Increased heart rate	94	79	93
Euphoria	89	74	79
Acute insomnia	78	77	75
Restlessness	75	69	72
Energetic	69	74	72
Dry mouth/throat	67	54	71
Sweating[a]	61	29	32
Loss of inhibitions	57	60	59
Talkativeness	54	66	48
Self-confidence	42	63	66
Nervousness	39	29	59
Tremors/shaking	39	20	31
Buzzing in ears	33	31	28
Decreased sexual arousal	33	29	21
Need to relax	31	29	17
Self-consciousness	28	23	17
Sexual arousal	25	20	31
Paranoia[a]	22	11	24
Nausea	14	6	10
Fuzzy vision	14	9	17
Headache	14	11	7
Lights in vision	14	6	7
Aggression	8	9	10
Convulsions	0	0	0
Experienced as a result of using			
Chronic insomnia	75	60	66
Uncontrollable craving/urge to use cocaine[b]	72	29	41
Unable to relax	64	49	52
Physical/mental exhaustion	58	31	41
Weight loss[b]	50	17	62
Congested nose	47	37	31
Depression	44	26	41
Chronic lack of sexual interest	29	27	24
Unable to think clearly	29	23	28
Sore/bleeding nose	25	11	17
Skin disorders/abscesses[a]	3	0	7
Hepatitis/jaundice[a]	3	0	0
Cocaine overdose	0	0	0

[a]p < .05.
[b]p < .01.

ing to use cocaine and weight loss—also showed statistically significant differences among the three groups of users. Uncontrollable craving to use cocaine was reported frequently by 72 percent of nonusers, 29 percent of less frequent users, and 41 percent of more frequent users. Weight loss was reported frequently by 50 percent of nonusers, 17 percent of less frequent users, and 62 percent of frequent users.

Paranoia and Hallucinations

Of all the possible effects attributable to cocaine, we have chosen to study paranoia and hallucinations, by which we mean a subjective state defined by the user, with the former indicating whether the user ever felt that "someone was out to get" him or her and the latter indicating whether the user ever sensed or became aware of things that did not actually exist. There are both conceptual and empirical reasons for this choice. Conceptually, the study of subjective internal states has been a distinguishing feature of the social sciences, and "although subjective effects tend to be more difficult to study, they are also a great deal more interesting to the sociologist" (Goode 1984:28). What is important regarding subjectively defined experiences is their ontological existence. To cite a prime methodological rule of the interactionist perspective, "if men define situations as real, they are real in their consequences" (Thomas & Thomas 1928:567).

Empirically, we have chosen paranoia and hallucinations for several reasons. First, pharmacologically, both experiences have been shown to be directly related to the amount of cocaine consumed. Indeed, in order to show that interacting with other cocaine users mitigates the experience of paranoia or hallucinations, we must first know that these effects are a pharmacological expectation of heavy cocaine consumption. The pharmacological evidence and reports of users are clear in this regard (Jacobs & Fehr 1987; Siegel 1978). Regarding paranoia:

> The most frequently mentioned mental health problem was paranoia: two-thirds of our respondents reported feeling paranoid at some point in their cocaine-using careers. . . . The most frequently mentioned form of paranoia was fear of police or of discovery by others. . . . Many peo-

ple suggested that cocaine exaggerated whatever other anxieties people already felt. (Waldorf, Reinarman & Murphy 1991:162–164)

The findings of these studies leave little doubt that chronic, high-dose cocaine use can produce both paranoia and temporary psychosis. Most intravenous users experienced intense anxiety, paranoia and hallucinations. . . . Among men who used more than one gram per day, paranoia and other psychotic symptoms occurred regularly: "You feel you can't trust anyone. You get afraid that something is going to happen. You're afraid people are out to get you. You're afraid people can read your mind. You're afraid the police are going to break in any minute." "Every time I do more than two grams I get paranoid as hell." (Spotts & Shontz 1980:476)

Regarding hallucinations:

Slightly more than one-quarter of our respondents reported experiencing some form of hallucination. . . . Hallucinations usually took the form of imagining for a moment that inanimate objects were moving or seeing human figures that were not there. . . . One in ten of our subjects reported this experience ["cocaine bugs," a sensory perception of feeling bugs on top or under the skin] at least once. . . . [One subject] reported that after such heavy use she regularly saw bugs or insects crawling on her skin which she would pick off and put into a glass of water beside her bed. Invariably she would wake up in the morning to find a glass with numerous pieces of skin off her arms and legs. (Waldorf, Reinarman & Murphy 1991:165)

I have had under my care two physicians addicted to cocaine in whom the most marked symptoms were hallucinations of animals both over and under the skin. These patients, who had previously abused morphine, were in the habit of injecting cocaine all over the body. Despite the fact that Vallon and Bessiere (1914), among others, have never seen this symptom among their patients, I have clearly observed it in at least a third of mine. (Maier [1926] 1987)

Second, we chose these two experiences because, compared to acute objective effects with a dominant physiological response (e.g., increased heart rate), they should be more likely influenced by social contextual factors.

Third, although both are subjective internal states of awareness, they differ in their quality and dimensionality. Hallucinogenic experiences tend to be perceived as neutral or benign by users (Waldorf, Reinarman & Murphy 1991), whereas paranoia is typically an unpleasant state. Moreover, we found that of twenty-three cocaine effects, paranoia and hallucinations loaded on different factors. Paranoia was associated with a factor that also included aggressiveness, whereas hallucinations was associated with a factor that included three other items indicative of auditory and visual hallucinations.

Finally, there is an element of myth debunking in our focus on paranoia and hallucinations. There is a popular perception that paranoid behavior invariably follows the ingestion of cocaine. Indeed, the following comment is commonplace in the media: "Cocaine almost always produces paranoid suspicion which gets worse over time" (Panzica 1990). Although the pharmacological literature indicates that acute paranoia can result from prolonged cocaine ingestion (Jacobs & Fehr 1987), such experiences are far from inevitable (Cohen 1989; Spotts & Shontz 1980). Thus, given the recognition that cultural and sociological factors can influence and modify the pharmacological effects of drug use, consequences such as paranoia and hallucinations are worthy of scrutiny.

Studies of cocaine users have found that experiences of paranoia and hallucinations are not uncommon (table 11–5). The 1991 NIDA household survey noted that 7 percent of those who used cocaine in the past year reported indications of paranoia, "feeling suspicious and mistrustful of others" (see chapter 3). Feelings of paranoia in user studies range between 41 and 68 percent, with hallucinations ranging between 15 and 28 percent. Waldorf, Reinarman, and Murphy (1991) compared hallucinations and paranoia between 122 current users and 106 quitters. They found that quitters were generally more likely than current users to report hallucinations (36.8 percent versus 19.7 percent), paranoia (70.8 percent versus 63.1 percent), and experiencing "cocaine bugs" (12.3 percent versus 8 percent). Few studies have examined the influence of social contextual factors on the risk of experiencing these disturbances.

TABLE 11–5

Prevalence of Paranoia and Hallucinations Among Cocaine Users

Authors	Sample	Paranoia	Hallucinations
Spotts & Shontz (1980)	Based on "representative case method" of nine males whose preferred drug was cocaine; participants were derived from the criminal justice system and drug treatment programs; emphasis given to intravenous users	Common among heavy users (3 grams or more per day)	Auditory common among heavy users; olfactory showed no relationship to use; visual and tactile uncommon at all levels of use
Washton, Gold & Pottash (1984)	Sample of 70 users with incomes in excess of $50,000 annually, who called the 1-800-COCAINE hotline in the United States	65% lifetime	Not reported
Cohen (1989)	160 users from Amsterdam; participants must have used cocaine at least 25 times in life; those with criminal or treatment indicators during the past two years were ineligible; sample was drawn from a randomized snowball method	41% lifetime experience	15% lifetime experience
Waldorf, Reinarman & Murphy (1991)	228 current and former heavy users from California; participants derived from ethnographic, snowball sample	68% experienced during lifetime	28% experienced during lifetime

The Data

The data reported in this chapter are derived from the sample of cocaine users interviewed in the first study (1983–1984) and from the sample of crack users interviewed in the second study (1989). For this analysis, we merged data for 103 intranasal users interviewed in 1983–1984 with 77 crack users interviewed in 1989 into a single data set.[1] For convenience, we will refer to these two samples as powder and crack users, respectively.

A comparison of characteristics between these two samples showed no differences in gender, age, marital status, education, or income; however, their cocaine use and other drug use differed substantially. Crack users used cocaine with greater frequency and regularity, alcohol and stimulants less frequently, and tranquilizers more frequently. The use of other drugs, including heroin and other narcotics, did not differ between the two samples. As well, the pattern of cocaine use among crack users suggested greater commitment to cocaine and less social-recreational use. Compared to powder users, crack users were less likely to use it with others and more likely to use cocaine whenever it was available, to purchase frequently, to intend to quit, to experience cravings to use, and to have sought medical attention because of cocaine use.

The Variables

Our analyses center on nine drug, set, and setting factors. Drug factors are represented by two variables, cocaine consumption[2] and a dichotomous variable representing sample differences (powder versus crack users). Set factors are represented by four variables: age and gender of participants, the perceived risk of using cocaine,[3] and whether the user was a novice.[4] Setting factors are represented by three variables: the relative number of friends in the users' social network who also use cocaine,[5] the absolute number of friends who also use cocaine,[6] and whether the user typically uses cocaine in the presence of others.[7]

The two outcome measures, probability of reported paranoia and hallucinations, are measured by responses to the following questions: (1) "How often, if ever, have you experienced the following effects or experiences *while using cocaine?*" followed by whether they ever "feel that someone was out to get you?" and (2) "During a cocaine high, how often, if ever, have you had the experience of sensing or becoming aware of things you knew at that time, or realized afterwards, did not really exist (that is, hallucinations)?"[8]

Data Analysis

Our interest was the influence of drug, set, and setting factors on the probability of paranoia and hallucinations. We chose logistic regression as the most appropriate statistical model. Our analytic strategy was twofold. First, we entered all nine main effects into the model, and then added two-way interaction terms.[9] Our particular interest was in sample-by-set and sample-by-setting interactions. These interactions formally test whether the relationship between the set and setting factors and cocaine-induced effects is similar for both powder and crack users. Preliminary data analysis showed that the variables cocaine use and the number of cocaine-using friends were not normally distributed, and because nonnormality can impair regression results, we log-transformed both factors.

Results

Results of the final models are shown in table 11–6. Before turning to interpretation of the interactions, let us first examine the interpretable main effects. For paranoia, we see that after controlling for other factors in the model, the number of cocaine-using friends is statistically significant at $p = .028$ and is inversely related to paranoia, as expected ($b = -1.73$). Thus, each additional cocaine-using friend decreases the logit (the log of the odds) by 1.7 and decreases the odds of paranoia by 18 percent ($e^{-1.73} = .18$). For hallucinations, the only significant main effect shows that females are significantly more likely than males to report hallucinations.

Figures 11–1 through 11–4 present the four significant two-way interactions. The relationship in figure 11–1 demonstrates that the pharmacological influence of drug consumption is mediated by social factors. In this case we see that at high consumption levels, there is little difference in hallucinations between social and nonsocial users (probabilities of .45 versus .42). However, at lower levels of consumption, there is a dramatic difference. Among those who typically do not use cocaine with others, the probability of experiencing hallucinations is .89 compared to .23 for social users. Such an interaction is clearly in line with that hypothesized by Becker.

Figure 11–2 shows the Sample x Use interaction in predicting paranoia. For both powder and crack users, increasing cocaine use

TABLE 11–6

Influence of Drug, Set, and Setting Factors on Paranoia and Hallucinations (Logistic Regression)

	Paranoia		Hallucinations	
	b	*p*	*b*	*p*
Drug factors				
Use (log)	−0.060	.882	−1.570	.061
Sample (Powder = 1)	−3.933	.002	−1.055	.073
Set factors				
Age	0.002	.948	0.057	.057
Gender (Male = 1)	0.357	.424	−0.11	.015
Risk	−0.384	.050[a]	0.075	.229[a]
Novice (= 1)	−3.146	.005[a]	0.8	.077[a]
Setting factors				
Number of Using Friends (log)	−1.727	.028[a]	0.505	.221[a]
Proportion of Using Friends	−2.352	.003[a]	−0.051	.432[a]
Social User (= 1)	−0.154	.338[a]	−4.374	.002[a]
Interactions				
Use × Social	—	—	2.237	.012
Sample × Use	3.116	.004	—	—
Risk × Proportion of Friends	0.316	.004	—	—
Novice × Use	2.770	.013	—	—
Constant	4.586	.067	0.585	.773
N	167		166	
Model chi-square	56.14		30.74	
	13 df		10 df	
	p < .001		*p* < .001	

[a]One-tail test.

increases the odds of paranoia. However, this relationship differs in strength between samples. For powder users, the probability of paranoia increases from .05 to .94, while for crack users the probability rises from .38 to .65. Thus, at lower consumption levels, crack users are more likely than powder users to experience paranoia, while at high consumption levels, crack users are less likely than powder users to experience paranoia.

Figure 11–3 depicts the interaction between risk and the relative number of cocaine-using friends in predicting paranoia. We see here that paranoia increases with higher perceived risk for those

FIGURE 11–1
Predicted Probability of Hallucinations by Cocaine Use and Social
User Category

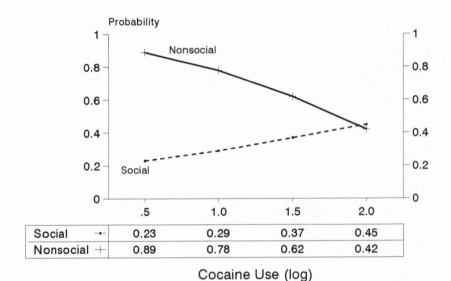

		.5	1.0	1.5	2.0
Social	–•–	0.23	0.29	0.37	0.45
Nonsocial	+	0.89	0.78	0.62	0.42

Cocaine Use (log)

FIGURE 11–2
Predicted Probability of Paranoia by Study and Cocaine Use

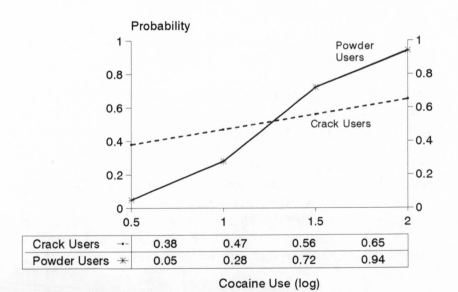

		0.5	1	1.5	2
Crack Users	–•–	0.38	0.47	0.56	0.65
Powder Users	–*–	0.05	0.28	0.72	0.94

Cocaine Use (log)

whose cocaine-using friends comprise about half of their friends (from .32 to .90) and among those whose friends all use cocaine (from .14 to .99). However, among those whose primary associations contain few cocaine-using members, risk shows a weak inverse relationship, dropping from .59 to .38. Thus, with the exception of cocaine users who have no or few cocaine-using friends, we find that paranoia increases with increasing perceptions of risk. The symmetric properties of the interaction also allow us to examine the buffering effect of the proportion of cocaine-using friends on paranoia. Among those with low risk scores (score of 4), more cocaine-using friends reduces the probability of paranoia, while among those with higher risk scores, more using friends increases paranoia.

Finally, figure 11–4 shows the Novice x Use interaction predicting paranoia. For both samples, we see a strong positive relationship between cocaine consumption and paranoia. However, it is also evident that the user's experience with cocaine modifies this relationship. For novice users (those having used fewer than twenty times in their lifetime) paranoia increases from .04 among light users to .97

FIGURE 11–3

Predicted Probability of Paranoia by Perceived Risk and Relative Number of Cocaine-Using Friends

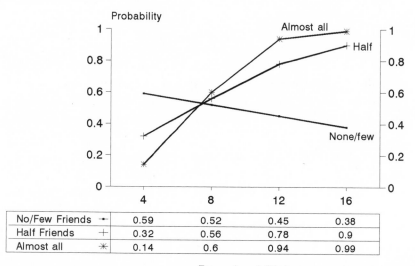

	4	8	12	16
No/Few Friends ▪	0.59	0.52	0.45	0.38
Half Friends +	0.32	0.56	0.78	0.9
Almost all ＊	0.14	0.6	0.94	0.99

Perceived Risk

FIGURE 11–4
Predicted Probability of Paranoia by Cocaine Use and Experience
of User

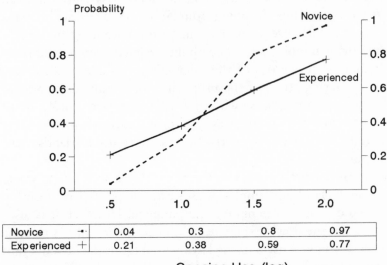

		.5	1.0	1.5	2.0
Novice	·-·	0.04	0.3	0.8	0.97
Experienced	+	0.21	0.38	0.59	0.77

Cocaine Use (log)

among heavy users. For experienced users, paranoia increases from
.21 to .77. What is important to note here is that at high levels of
consumption, experienced users are less likely to experience paranoia than are novice users (.77 versus .97, respectively).

Conclusions

Many researchers have commented on or have demonstrated empirically the complexity of relationships embodied in the drug-set-
setting framework (Jones 1971; Zinberg 1974; Sher 1985; Westermeyer 1987; Goode 1989). The results from this chapter add to
this literature.

We expected that the probability of paranoia and hallucinations
would decrease with increasing interactional exposure to cocaine-
using friends and that if this relationship is generalizable, it should
occur for both powder and crack users. Although we did not see a
significant interplay between interactional exposure and hallucinations, we did find evidence that this setting variable reduced the
probability of paranoia. We also found partial support for the re-

duction of the probability of hallucinations. This influence occurred in two respects. First, for both powder and crack users, the absolute number of cocaine-using friends was inversely related to paranoia. Second, there was further partial support of a buffering effect of the primary group association present in the interaction between risk and the proportion of using friends. Here we found that among those with low and moderate risk perceptions, the relative number of cocaine-using friends was inversely related to paranoia (while among those with high risk perceptions, the relationship between the relative number of cocaine-using friends and paranoia was positive).

We did not find an influential effect of the relative number of cocaine-using friends or the absolute number of cocaine-using friends on hallucinations. Why this is so is uncertain. Hallucinations often take the form of visual, tactile, or auditory hallucinations and may be more influenced by dose and sensory-system factors than by social interaction. On the other hand, feelings of paranoia tend to have a strong social component, since they are often based on fears of others and are highly correlated with social aggression (see chapter 6).

We also expected that the probability of paranoia and hallucinations would increase with greater perceived harm of cocaine use. We found partial support for the case of paranoia but not for hallucinations. For paranoia, on the other hand, we found a positive relationship with risk as expected, but only among those who stated that almost all their friends or about half of their friends also used cocaine.

Our third expectation was that the influence of interactional exposure and beliefs would weaken with increasing levels of cocaine consumption. The relationships between the absolute number and relative number of cocaine-using friends and perceived risk on the probability of paranoia and hallucinations were not mediated by the level of cocaine consumption. However, further analysis did provide support for a mediating effect of drug consumption on both paranoia and hallucinations. Cocaine consumption (as measured by frequency of use) was significantly and positively related to drug effect in the Novice x Use, Social x Use and Sample x Use interactions. The weakening of sociological factors with increased dose was especially prominent in the Use x Social interaction, where we found that although hallucinations were significantly more likely to occur among nonsocial users than among social users at low consumption levels, this difference disappeared as cocaine consumption increased.

Social factors influenced paranoia and hallucinations even at high consumption levels. In the Novice x Use interaction, we saw that among frequent users, the probability of paranoia was significantly higher among novices than among experienced users. Becker would probably attribute this finding to differences in learning between novice and experienced users. In this same relationship, we found that among low-frequency users, experienced users were significantly more likely to report paranoia than were novice users. This finding seems to confirm expectancy effects often noted in laboratory studies (e.g., Carlin et al. 1972). The Sample x Use interaction, which showed that the probability of paranoia increased at a greater rate with cocaine consumption among powder users than it did among crack users, should be treated cautiously. Two possibilities may account for this finding. First, there is something qualitatively different between powder and crack users that is not captured by the measures employed here. The other possibility is that the statistical control of cocaine use was not fully effective in partialing out its effect on paranoia.

Our findings cannot be generalized to all cocaine and crack users. Clearly, the self-selected, volunteer nature of the sample limits the findings in their application to cocaine users at large. Still, many agree that community-derived samples provide a better representation of drug users than do samples derived from clinical or criminal justice systems:

> Only about one-tenth of the number of regular users of illicit drugs or unauthorized users of licit drugs could be in prison or treatment at any one time. They could very well be less capable and adaptable than those users not in treatment or prison. Yet, because access to the treatment and prison population is so convenient for researchers, the picture of drug dependence that has emerged from studies of these populations may be incomplete. (Winick 1991:443)

Also, we cannot know whether unmeasured preexisting factors, such as psychopathologies, may account for or significantly alter some of the differences we found between powder and crack users.

Nor can we know to what extent differences between powder and crack users are due to differences in the societal climate existing between powder and crack. Clearly, compared to cocaine powder use, crack use was viewed societally as a demon (Reinarman 1989), and such a negative climate has been implicated in increasing negative drug-induced outcomes (Smith & Seymour 1985).

Despite some limitations of our data and analysis, we believe that this research contributes to the understanding of drug, set, and setting factors on drug effects. Clearly the drug-set-setting framework in accounting for drug effects, either implicitly or explicitly, has a broad interdisciplinary acceptance (Goode 1989; Jacobs & Fehr 1987; Zinberg 1984), yet few researchers have attempted to study specifically the role of setting factors on negative drug outcomes. Becker's seminal work on marijuana and LSD users was an analytical piece, his goal being to account for the role of subculture in buffering the negative effects of drug experiences. Given his methodological orientation, however, he did not provide quantitative data to support his propositions.

Orcutt, on the other hand, has been a central figure in empirically verifying Becker's propositions. Indeed, Orcutt's (1978, 1987) studies are among the few sociological works specifically examining such matters. Orcutt's work, however, was based on samples of college students and restricted to alcohol and marijuana, and the outcomes variable of interest was expectations of negative effects. This chapter extends Orcutt's work in several ways. First, it is based on samples of adults, many in the conventional world of work, marriage, or both. Therefore, the findings of an inverse relationship between primary group associations and drug effects have greater generalizability and robustness. Second, we focused on drug-induced reactions experienced by users, not on the expectations of reactions, as did Orcutt. Third, we studied the influence of primary group associations and drug effects for cocaine, a powerful stimulant. Other research in this area has been restricted typically to hallucinogenic substances, namely, marijuana and LSD. Little recent research on cocaine users has examined the influence of primary group associations on drug effects. Waldorf, Reinarman, and Murphy's (1991) revealing ethnographic account of cocaine use also noted the role of peer associations and negative effects: "Friends not only taught each other how to use cocaine, they also taught each other about the risks of doing so. The lessons learned by many of our respondents seem to have become part of the user lore" (p. 264).

We also demonstrated the complexity of the relationship between primary group associations and drug-induced effects. Indeed, as Goode (1993) has commented, "anyone peddling a simplistic theory of drug use cannot be taken seriously" (p. 86). The expected inverse relationship between interactional exposure and drug-induced outcomes does not hold among all groups of users.

This chapter also bears indirectly on the growing trend toward polices of harm reduction with respect to drug use. There is a growing consensus among sociologists who study the drug scene that current policies attempting to eliminate drug use are naive and fruitless at best, and hazardous at worst (Goode 1993; Winick 1991; Waldorf, Reinarman & Murphy 1991). In contrast to current policies, these observers seem to call for optimal levels of social control—optimal in the sense that formal and informal sanctions should be strong enough to deter the initiation of drug use and encourage cessation among uncommitted users, yet, given a population of heavy drug users in society, not too severe that sanctions fail to minimize the harm to both the users and society. These sociologists and others argue that unless society is willing to consider significant structural change, it must accept a certain level of drug use and that policies should be in place in order to reduce the harm caused by drug use (see also O'Hare et al. 1992; Heather et al. 1993).

One significant factor in reducing drug-induced outcomes is the influence of social contextual factors. In this context, we summarize some underlying commonalities found for both powder and crack users in table 11–7. First, the probability of paranoia declined with increasing absolute number of cocaine-using friends. This was an unqualified effect occurring among both powder and crack users. (The relationship did not hold for hallucinations.) Second, a social-contextual configuration that reduced paranoia (among both powder and crack users) was having a low perceived risk of harm in using cocaine and having a high proportion of cocaine-using friends. Again, this configuration was restricted to paranoia. Third, hallucinations were reduced among those who used cocaine in the presence of others and used cocaine infrequently. This configuration occurred for both powder and crack users but was unrelated to

TABLE 11-7

*Social Contextual Configurations That Serve to Reduce
Paranoia and Hallucinations*

	Paranoia	Hallucinations
Having a greater number of cocaine-using friends	X	
Having low perceived risk plus a high proportion of cocaine-using friends	X	
Using cocaine in the presence of others and infrequent cocaine consumption		X

paranoia. The critical point is that this study carried forward the investigation of relationships that serve to reduce the harm caused by drug use. To be effective, harm reduction policies must be based on a sound body of knowledge.

12

Case Studies

Three-Year Follow-up

The detailed case histories described in this chapter are the product of a second follow-up interview, occurring in 1992, about two years after the first follow-up interview with the participants. We had decided that the time and other resources required to pursue all fifty-four participants we had successfully reinterviewed then could not be justified, given the already high rate of attrition of 46 percent. Nevertheless, we knew that some of the participants would be easy to locate; indeed, some had called us asking us when they would be interviewed again. We recontacted a handful of participants who had still been using cocaine at the second contact and conducted a third interview with five of them.

This small group cannot be said to be representative of the follow-up sample of fifty-four, much less the original one hundred participants; nevertheless, important new information was gained from these interviews. Almost no studies have tracked cocaine users for as long a time as three years.[1] Because the picture of cocaine use depends very much on the point of contact in the user's cocaine use career (see Faupel 1991 for a similar observation about heroin use), longitudinal research is important for revealing the natural history of drug use within the life course of individuals.

A final caution is that we did not attempt to reinterview any abstainers, who had been the least enthusiastic group about the second interview; although they had obliged us, their experience with cocaine was behind them, and they were not interested in revisiting it. It is possible that some had reverted to cocaine use, but we did not wish to intrude further into their lives. Given the consistency between recent quitters at the first interview and nonuse at the second, we did not think it likely that we would unearth a regressor and preferred instead to focus on the continuous users.

Of the five cases, two were continuing to use and three had stopped by the last interview in 1992. Their experiences further emphasize the sheer diversity of experiences with cocaine. Names and specific details have been altered for protection of identities.

Jane

When we first met Jane, she was a 22-year-old single woman, a community college graduate, who was working as an office manager. She had first tried powder cocaine at age 19, and her typical pattern was to use about 1/4 gram less than once per month. She had never smoked crack or injected cocaine. Her own assessment was that she was in very good health but somewhat up and down emotionally.

By the second interview, Jane still had the same full-time job and was working in the evenings as well as a bartender. She had begun to use crack in the interim and described herself as "getting into it heavily for a month," using 1/2 gram more than once a week. Then she had stopped using crack and gone back to lower levels of snorting cocaine. She thought her health was still very good and that she was in better spirits.

By our third encounter, Jane's use of cocaine intranasally had increased to between 1/2 and 1 gram once a week, although she had not resumed crack use. She described this upswing as a steady, gradual one that was a result of increased cocaine availability in the evenings. She had changed her bartending job, and this had introduced her to a steadier supply. She had become involved in small-time dealing by acting as a liaison between some of her friends and the supplier but found all the telephone calls bothersome and bowed out by linking her friends directly with the source. Jane admitted that there were times when she grew concerned about her level of use but felt that it was still under her control. She thought she would continue to use cocaine, by snorting, in the near future.

She used alcohol about three times a week and cannabis infrequently, less than once a month.

She was still working as an office manager in the same firm and had been dating a man for eight months who was unaware of her cocaine use. She had not encountered any legal problems due to her drug use. In all, Jane appeared to be a stable, well-functioning individual, with a wide circle of friends (both users and nonusers), who was enjoying life. Despite her past brief involvement in crack use and currently escalating use of cocaine by snorting, she reported few adverse consequences and considered herself to be in control but not unaware of the risks. It is clear that her cocaine career, with its rises, falls, and rises, was not yet over.

Ted

This 35-year-old single man first tried cocaine at age 15. His early use period included an intense phase of injecting cocaine, 2 grams or more weekly, about fifteen years ago. This had tapered off, but he still injected about 1/2 gram once a week. He had had a period of rehabilitation and considered himself in good health, with no problems. He was also a regular, weekly cannabis user.

At the second interview, Ted was injecting less frequently, using 1 gram of cocaine less than once per month, and was no longer buying cocaine. He described his reasons as "needing to concentrate" because he was in school. Now he snorted almost as often as he injected cocaine, but he did not like to use crack because "there is no good buzz and I don't get high."

By our third meeting, Ted remained an infrequent but regular user, both injecting and snorting. He said that he could not afford to use cocaine more often, but even if he could, he would be worried about becoming addicted. He found that cocaine enhanced sexual experiences, if used occasionally for that purpose. He was on disability insurance due to an automobile accident some time ago and took a variety of medications. He still smoked marijuana and drank about once or twice a month. He had not moved, had no contact with the legal system, and had no other health problems that he was aware of. His pattern of cocaine use, extending over more than twenty years, has been one of early escalation, then decline, and stabilization at a low but regular level of use.

Lisa

When first interviewed, this 20-year-old woman still lived at home with her parents and was in school full time. She had first tried cocaine two years previously and was using 1/2 gram once a week by snorting. She had never used crack or injected cocaine.

A year later, Lisa was using crack almost exclusively. The level was 1 and 1/2 grams more than once per week. She had left the university, still lived at home, and was working full time. She expressed concern about addiction.

By the third interview, Lisa's drug use history had become much more complex. In the intervening two years, her crack use had escalated to daily use of 1 gram. She also sometimes injected cocaine or snorted it. This phase had peaked about one year earlier. Then her cocaine use slowly decreased while her heroin use increased. The switch to heroin was a conscious decision since she felt that cocaine was "driving her crazy." She had experienced hallucinations and was "looking for a downer," to slow herself down. When she was introduced to heroin, this use escalated too, until she entered treatment.

At this last meeting with us, Lisa had been "clean" for several months and had even stopped smoking cigarettes six weeks earlier. She was attending NarcAnon meetings weekly. Despite her difficulties, she had been promoted at work and had bought a house. She appeared hopeful and confident about her future.

Jody and Jim

In this study, we also interviewed a couple who shared their experiences with cocaine. At one time, it was part of their bond; later it contributed to their separation. Both were regular (at least weekly) crack users when we first met them. Since they worked at the same company, they sometimes snorted cocaine at lunchtime but saved crack for leisure time. They maintained separate domiciles but spent a lot of time together. Neither harbored any doubts about their ability to control their crack use, but Jody seemed more solid in her job and less interested in drug use than Jim. He also supplemented his income by dealing drugs, mainly cannabis.

At the second interview, they were still seeing each other but not seriously considering a future together. They were still friends but were soon to go their separate ways. Both had increased their use of crack. Jim had been charged with cannabis possession as a result of a car stop and search.

At the third interview, Jody said she had quit her job about two years ago. She began spending all her unemployment insurance money on crack. For about a year, she was smoking 1 gram of crack every day, usually with another unemployed friend. Until her truck was repossessed, they would drive about 60 kilometers most days into the city to buy drugs. Then she cut back to monthly crack use, due to lack of money and a desire to get her life together. She started working again. Then she became pregnant and stopped cocaine use completely, but continued to use tobacco and alcohol. She had broken up with the father of the baby, and they were in the process of selling her house. She planned to live out of the city, not close to crack locales, and felt that pregnancy had given her a chance to redirect her life.

Jim had also experienced an increase in crack use, followed by quitting using and dealing several months earlier. He felt that his relationship with Jody had to be terminated in order for him to stay away from cocaine. He thought that cocaine was controlling him, turning him into a different person he did not like, and making him depressed. Quitting was difficult, but he was glad that he no longer used. He was currently living with someone else in a stable relationship, and working irregularly.

Summary

This series of vignettes indicates the complexity of the interactions among users, other users, their life situations, and this appealing drug. Clearly the perceptions and experiences of users change over time, and it is thus imperative not to make generalizations about cocaine use solely on data derived from one point in time. For many, the romance with cocaine is short lived and easily swept aside; for others, there is a more persistent involvement that is not easily discarded.

Part IV

Conclusions and Implications

13

In the Balance

The First Study

C ocaine use has posed perplexing problems for modern society.
A drug whose potency and appeal had seemingly been eclipsed
early in this century, cocaine reemerged on the coattails of the drug
revolution of the 1960s. Tales of this glamor drug, embraced by the
rich and famous, assumed a more sinister air with the passage of
time. As the list of charges grew—lives ruined by bankruptcy, criminal careers to support a cocaine habit, lost jobs, family dissolution,
overdose deaths, medical complications—so did cocaine's popularity extend and become democratized in the population overall. In
the midst of claims and counterclaims about the threat posed by cocaine, it has often been difficult to obtain reliable, objective evidence.

This book has endeavored to inject a sense of proportion into
the cocaine issue. We did this by looking at cocaine historically, by
placing it in a cultural context, and by reviewing the available studies of use patterns. In embarking on a study of 111 cocaine users,
we intentionally avoided a focus on the worst cases. It seemed important to tap the experiences and perceptions of the more typical
users, not those whose medical problems have been well documented in the treatment literature or whose criminal status in society
made them already marginal. In this chapter, we shall summarize
the major findings and insights of the earlier chapters, with particular attention to the results garnered from interviews with users in

the first study. The policy implications will be discussed and some directions for future research suggested.

Chapter Summaries

In chapter 1, we learned that the use of cocaine constituted a social problem in Canada at the turn of the century. Concern was expressed in health professional journals, the news media, and the parliamentary debates of the times. The unregulated supply of patent medicines containing cocaine was available at drugstores, through the mail, and from door-to-door salesmen. Cocaine use was widespread, cutting across boundaries of age, gender, and social class. When legislative controls were eventually placed on the sale and possession of cocaine, through the 1908 Proprietary and Patent Medicine Act and the 1911 Opium and Drug Act, the problem was effectively eclipsed for the next sixty years or so. The resurgence of cocaine use was traced to a growing demand coupled with new sources of illicit distribution. Efforts to stem the sources of supply in South America have been markedly ineffective to date.

Chapter 2 examined the presence and image of cocaine in popular culture. Descriptions of cocaine were found in song lyrics, novels, biography, comics, newspapers, magazines, movies, and television. References to cocaine have become more numerous in these media; this process both reflects and shapes cocaine's status as a topic of contemporary interest and concern. The image of the drug has been portrayed in a progressively more negative fashion. The extremes of dependence and its various costs are typical themes of media emanating from the United States. Canadian perceptions of many issues, including the risks posed by cocaine, are influenced undoubtedly by American media sources. It is therefore likely that fears about the actual threat posed by cocaine in Canada are inflated to an unrealistic degree by the image of cocaine in popular, mainly American, culture.[1]

In chapter 3 a large body of literature on recent trends and current use of cocaine as of 1987 was reviewed. Our synopsis from the first edition was as follows. Despite the variety of sources, several generalizations are possible. One is that the recent increases in cocaine use are largely restricted to North America, as well as some parts of South America and Western Europe. The majority of the population has no experience with cocaine, and of those who do, most use infrequently. Users of cocaine are likely to be male, young (25 to 35 is the peak age range), and well educated. A low income is no barrier to experimentation and fairly infrequent use of the drug; heavier levels of use can require considerable financial outlay. Most persons who try cocaine have prior experience with other illicit drugs, notably cannabis. In the United States, use levels peaked about 1979 and appear to have leveled off. Because of the absence of national surveys, use trends in Canada are less clear; however, available data indicate that use is much lower than in the United States. The current reality of cocaine in Canada is less fearsome than its popular image.

Chapter 4 described the design of the first interview study with cocaine users in the community. The principal criteria for sample selection were that respondents have some experience with cocaine in the past three years, be aged 21 or over, and be employed at least six of the twelve months prior to the interview. A total of 111 participants were obtained from a network of personal contacts and an advertising campaign. Participants were predominantly male, single, and of medium socioeconomic status. They were classified mainly as social-recreational cocaine users who also used cannabis and alcohol regularly. Although some had histories of more extensive use than had occurred in the past year, only a small minority could be considered current, heavy users of cocaine.

The subjective appeal of cocaine to users was explored in chapter 5. Some respondents acknowledged that the "champagne of drugs" label was part of the attraction of cocaine. The stimulating properties of the drug—the "lift" it produces—were mentioned by many in conjunction with the notion of a controlled high that did not interfere with normal activities. Users were primed by favorable expectations of cocaine use before their first experience, and most were not disappointed. Cocaine was shared in social gatherings—sometimes in small, intimate groups and other times in larger partying groups. Cocaine was thought to facilitate interaction with others. Women's likes and dislikes about cocaine were similar to men's, but women were somewhat more likely to identify the enhancement of social relationships as a plus.

One concern of our study was to determine whether, in a community-based sample of cocaine users, any effects of cocaine use

were serious enough to be deemed problems. The findings presented in chapter 6 showed that the stimulating properties of cocaine
frequently led to relatively benign reactions, including increased
energy, talkativeness, self-confidence, and restlessness. More serious reactions of paranoia (23 percent) and violent or aggressive behavior (17 percent) did occur at least once among these proportions of users; moreover, 51 percent had an uncontrollable craving
for cocaine on at least one occasion. The most important factor related to experiencing problems with cocaine was frequency of use;
the tendency for more frequent users to report more problems was
maintained even when controlling for several other possible influences. For most in this sample, the attractions of cocaine outweighed the risks. A few past heavy users had reduced or forsworn
further use of the drug, some on their own initiative and others
with professional help.

Chapter 7 provided an overview of Canada's cocaine laws and
the extent of their enforcement. Cocaine convictions have risen
steadily since 1970, reaching over 8,000 in 1990. Maximum penalties for possession and trafficking are rarely imposed, however.
Users' perceptions of the legal barrier were generally inaccurate
with respect to the details of the law but more informed about actual sentencing practices. The cocaine prohibition appeared to present few difficulties in obtaining the drug, provided that one had
the money. The average price paid for a gram of cocaine by respondents in our study was from $100 to $150. One-quarter of the sample had never bought it; other ways of getting cocaine were by
barter, as a gift, or as part of the party refreshments. Respondents
felt that as long as they were discreet in their use and purchase of
cocaine, the risk of detection was virtually negligible. This low perceived risk renders the deterrent threat of the law impotent.

Chapter 8 consisted of selected case studies from the 111 interviews. A variety of experiences with cocaine were illustrated—dab-
blers, party goers and givers, current devotees, and former users
who had experienced problems. These portrayals fleshed out the
statistical material presented in earlier chapters and demonstrate
the richness of data available in a community study. Above all, we
were reminded that each of the 111 respondents is a unique individual. Let us now turn to some of the policy considerations that
are of concern.

Legal Policy and Deterrence

Policy decisions regarding cocaine must, of necessity, take into account a broader range of considerations than have been dealt with in this book. The limited social-recreational use of most of the people we interviewed was conducted in a climate of prohibitionary restraints on cocaine. Other issues relevant to cocaine policy include the control of availability, deterrence of use, dependence liability and other potentially harmful effects to the user, and some sense of the risks posed by cocaine in relation to those associated with other drugs.

When demand for an illicit commodity exists, it is very difficult to eliminate the source of supply. This has been the lesson of alcohol prohibition and of several decades of experience with heroin and cannabis. Cocaine was more readily available and less expensive in the mid-1980s than it was a decade previously (Kozel & Adams 1985). It is not our purpose to go into all the reasons why curtailment of a lucrative black market is ineffective. This has been done generally by Le Dain (1973) and with specific reference to cocaine by Wisotsky (1983, 1986) for the American market and by the Royal Canadian Mounted Police (1985) for the Canadian one. Indirect efforts to reduce the supply through elimination of the ether used in the manufacture of cocaine hydrochloride have been similarly unsuccessful. This strategy has apparently had the untoward effect of posing a cancer risk to cocaine users from benzene, the ether substitute next employed by the South American manufacturers.[2] Accepting the premise that enforcement efforts directed at availability have had very limited effectiveness and unsuccessful prohibition of supply will continue in the same manner in the immediate future, we are left to consider the problem of demand reduction. Essentially this issue boils down to coercion or persuasion.

Deterrence of use requires a threat of legal punishment that is real and credible. The existence of severe penalties does not, in and of itself, discourage use. Clearly, the law has not prevented the initial experimentation with cocaine and its spread throughout a cross-section of the population. The prohibition may have contained use to some degree by keeping prices high. As we know from experience with other illegal drugs such as cannabis, adult users who are cautious in their buying practices and have access to privacy are rarely subject to detection and prosecution. The interviews with 111 users underline this conclusion: for nearly all, the law was a remote and irrelevant force. This perception was reflected by the numerically small tally of annual convictions for the simple possession of cocaine compared to the number of occasions of use.

A further and equally compelling reason for reevaluating the current emphasis on coercive approaches to reduce demand for cocaine concerns the social costs and adverse individual consequences associated with attempts to reduce demand. The goal of illicit-drug policy is twofold: to minimize the health and safety hazards associated with use of the proscribed drug and to minimize the social costs involved in the control of use. Coercive strategies such as the reliance on the threat and imposition of criminal sanctions to reduce the health and safety risks associated with cocaine escalate these social costs. The criminalization of users and the associated stigma, the financial costs of operating the criminal justice machinery, and the interference with personal rights and freedoms mount up under a system of total prohibition. Education strategies aimed at reducing demand for cocaine, on the other hand, involve much lower social costs and fewer adverse individual consequences to users.

Education

Persuasion to avoid the use of potentially harmful substances rests on accurate evidence and a willingness to respect the informed judgment of the would-be consumer. With cocaine, the health indictments are harsh: it can be lethal, even if snorted in relatively small quantities. This unpredictability should urge caution; however, a fatal outcome is infrequent. Cocaine's powerful reinforcing effects give it a high dependence liability. Indeed the very Faustian nature of this drug—its seductive appeal in conjunction with a progressive loss of control over the compulsion to use—is what underlies much public concern. Nevertheless, it would not be wise to assign an "all-powerful" label to this drug. The interviews forming the substance of this book serve as a reminder that any drug is capable of being used moderately by some people and excessively by others. Some do not like cocaine at all and stop use after brief experimentation. The size of the risk posed depends both on the base population exposed to the drug and the proportion of triers who experience adverse consequences.

At this point, we will apply a risk assessment, at least briefly, to society's experience with other drugs. It is indisputable that the greatest health costs, and related loss of productivity, are engendered by the favorite legal drugs, tobacco and alcohol. For tobacco, the dependence liability is high, and users typically have difficulty limiting their consumption; most are addicted. The health risks, though potent, are of long-term nature. In addition, increasing evidence of the risks of second-hand smoke has fueled the movement to restrict public smoking. This increasing cultural unacceptability has no doubt contributed to the decline in smoking rates and provides some support for a combination of persuasive and coercive tactics.

Alcohol, on the other hand, is used by a greater proportion of the population than tobacco, at least occasionally, and has a fairly low dependence liability. The damage caused by alcohol is chiefly related to the substantial base population it can affect adversely. And considerable research supports the proposition that alcohol problems are directly related to the mean level of alcohol consumption in the population. The consequences can be deadly and debilitating in middle and old age and socially destructive at all ages. Nevertheless, society tolerates alcohol because it is enjoyed by many without problems, and it has a high level of cultural acceptability. Exceptions focus on specific alcohol-related behaviors, such as drinking while driving and violence. With both tobacco and alcohol, considerable effort from a health-oriented educational perspective is directed at preventing early experimentation and habit formation with these drugs.

Cannabis is North America's third most popular drug that raises questions of concern. (Caffeine is also in the top four as far as use, but of little known risk to date.) The long-term effects of cannabis use are less well understood and established than those of alcohol and tobacco but in our view are sufficient to urge a policy of restraint, if not total prohibition. Like use of tobacco and alcohol, use of cannabis is widespread enough that even relatively rare effects may be of considerable significance. Again, much concern is directed at young users, as well as workplace safety and driving. The dependence liability of cannabis, at least in less potent forms, also is low. Despite its illicit status, it has gained a degree of acceptability among some of the more youthful segments of society and older users who have grown up with the practice.

Cocaine, when used moderately for socializing, appears to share many of the attributes of alcohol and cannabis. Like them, the "enormous difference between the consequences of very light and very heavy use" (Kalant 1974:80) must be considered when assessing the overall impact of a drug. Moreover, cocaine's more destructive and widely publicized social impacts—lost jobs, broken families, ruined careers—can be matched by innumerable cases in the literature of alcoholism. Cocaine's long-term physical effects are rarely life threatening; excessive alcohol use is associated with high morbidity and mortality. Alcohol withdrawal can be fatal; no comparable risk exists for cocaine cessation after prolonged, heavy use. Overdose deaths can occur with cocaine but are rare with alcohol since unconsciousness usually intervenes. An injectable drug always has the potential for lethal irreversible effects. The appeal of cocaine can likely be telescoped very rapidly to dependence for those at risk. The proportion of those who do try cocaine who are seriously at risk for significant problems has been conservatively estimated at 2.5 percent by Clayton (1985). Smith (1986) accepts the figure of 10 percent, analogous to the prevalence of alcoholism. If cocaine use becomes more widespread—and this would require quite a marked increase in social acceptability—the number of people adversely affected could reach significant proportions. On the other hand, Musto (1986) suggested that vigorous public rejection may be the next step in the cycle, leading to a decline in use.

Future Research

Devising an appropriate societal response to the problems posed by cocaine requires a sound, up-to-date knowledge base. There are many questions to be considered. It is important to monitor trends in youthful and adult cocaine use, as well as other precursor drugs such as cannabis. The natural history of cocaine use requires longitudinal studies of users from initiation through to problem use. Such research can also address questions regarding reasons for stopping, reducing, and even refusing to start cocaine use. What is the relative role of formal and informal controls on the use of cocaine? Treatment needs and effectiveness are important areas to consider, as are the identification of groups that may be at special risk, for example, upper-income professionals, certain occupational groups, and career women.

Policy Directions

The basic premise of this study is that the actual risks of infrequent cocaine use have been exaggerated in the media and consequently in the public's perception of the problem. This is even more true for Canada than the United States, as the survey data indicated. But the potential risks are serious enough to justify concern without resorting to hyperbole. Our community-based sample revealed many individuals whose occasional use of cocaine had not disrupted their lives. We interviewed others, fewer in number, who had gotten into serious difficulties. There is no way of knowing, without a follow-up of our sample, how many more might eventually experience problems.

Clearly the safest course is never to try the drug, but people do not always choose safety over adventure. The allure of cocaine will ensure that some will try the drug, and some of these will develop problems. Society's responsibility is to provide reasonable information about risks, avoid criminal punishments and stigmatization for users, and provide treatment resources for those who need help. The successful repression of supply that occurred at the turn of the century does not appear to be a realistic option now, so efforts must be directed at primary prevention of demand and a humane response to casualties of this very dangerous drug.

Let us consider some more specific policies that might help to meet these objectives. First, with respect to the legal model, which relies on deterrence, it is necessary to separate sale from possession. The importation of cocaine presents an intractable problem for enforcement authorities. They have described the impossibility of effectively limiting production and distribution from source countries in South America. Nevertheless, we believe that efforts to restrict availability should not be relaxed; the high price of cocaine, artificially inflated by the policy of prohibition, helps to restrain consumption of the drug. We recognize that in many ways this has been a futile and self-defeating approach, since the high prices—

and profits—enhance incentives for traffickers. But until demand reduction policies can have some impact or international efforts to seize the assets of the kingpin cocaine traffickers can be successful, thus reducing the profitability of the trade, or both, it is essential that prices for cocaine be kept as high as possible.[3]

Can deterrence be effective in reducing or eliminating the demand for cocaine? The response to this question turns on perceptions of the harshness of penalties and likelihood of detection by the would-be user. Under the status quo—severe potential penalties and a very remote chance of apprehension—deterrent effects on the user are minimal. The effectiveness of deterrence, at least hypothetically, could be increased by imposing the maximum sentence for possession (seven years) on those convicted and by dramatically increasing enforcement efforts so that greater numbers are arrested (e.g., raids on private dwellings and public places where cocaine is thought to be used). Society is unlikely to be willing to pay these high prices in terms of the harm to individual offenders, the system that processes them, or the encroachment on personal rights and freedoms. The token enforcement that now occurs against cocaine users, as has been demonstrated with cannabis, is a high cost–low benefit policy for restricting demand. Therefore, we favor the decriminalization of simple possession of cocaine by adults in private surroundings; we would retain offenses for public possession and for possession of amounts greater than 1 gram. (This amount is somewhat arbitrary and intended to reflect a reasonable amount for a social occasion of use.) Such a measure as decriminalization should not occur in isolation but rather should be part of a more general policy initiative that would encompass a move away from reliance on criminal sanctions for possession of any illicit drug and the introduction of alternative, less coercive means of control over demand.

Education is another means of influencing demand for cocaine. In countries, such as Canada, where cocaine users are few in number and mainly adults, a well-aimed educational program is likely the most feasible and financially defensible approach. The objective would be to increase awareness of the real risks of cocaine and thus counter its safe and glamorous image. Such a presentation should be fairly sophisticated and directed to adults. A particular focus on those deemed to be at risk, such as upper-income professionals and certain occupational groups, might be warranted. Education of children and young people about cocaine should not be over-looked; however, there is the danger of singling it out for too much attention and creating a boomerang effect. Programs that take a more integrated approach to drug problems might be better suited to the youthful audience.

Even if education efforts were quite successful in reducing the use of cocaine, some users inevitably would require treatment for cocaine dependence. Whether these compulsive users benefit more from specialized programs for cocaine or from general programs for alcohol and other drug dependence remains unclear. It may well be that both approaches should be available in order to reach the greatest number of those in need. The decriminalization of pos-session would help to overcome the criminal stigma associated with cocaine use and encourage problem users to seek treatment early. Currently, the demand for treatment in Canada does not appear be-yond that available, although some have modified or expanded their programs for cocaine users. Needs may increase in the future, and careful monitoring is required.

We have presented the two sides of this "steel drug." Many of those we interviewed concurred with Dr. Freud in his assessment of its pleasurable, invigorating effects. Others, like Mr. Bones (see ap-pendix A) took a harsher view of its potential for harm, especially its corrupting influence.[4] For some individuals, cocaine is an instant love affair; for others, dependence is built link by link, until like Marley's ghost, they wear a ponderous chain. In the years since we initiated this project, we have talked with many colleagues about cocaine. We have yet to find anyone who is complacent about the potential risks attached to this drug. Our impression is that feelings of concern have heightened rather than diminished in response to the new knowledge that has become available. We consider it essen-tial that the problems posed by cocaine and other drugs, legal or il-legal, be kept in perspective in order for society to devise an in-formed and effective response.

14

Epilogue

The Second Study

with Yuet W. Cheung

I n this final chapter, we consider how the new evidence presented in parts I and III of this second edition may temper our previous conclusions. We continue to be guided by the view that objective appraisal of research findings from a variety of sources, including our own original studies, will aid in the achievement of a more balanced societal response to the difficult issues posed by the use of this potent, alluring, and dangerous drug.

The focus of the new portion of this book has been on the period from 1986 onward, designated as the "crack era" in chapter 1. Images of cocaine and crack have remained highly visible in the popular culture, as described in chapter 2. The recent literature on current use trends reviewed in chapter 3 indicated that the epidemic phase of cocaine and crack use has abated in the United States, and levels of use have remained low in Canada. Convictions for cocaine offenses have risen steadily in the 1980s. Cocaine use has also emerged in many more countries than in the mid-1980s, but levels remain low and crack use has been almost exclusively an American problem.

The designation of a crack crisis in Canada was largely a media creation engendered by extensive exposure to American sources and misperceptions of the threat posed by crack. This image was countered both by Ontario and Canada survey results and the community study in Toronto described in chapters 9 and 10. One hundred cocaine users, of whom seventy-nine had also used crack, were interviewed intensively about their experiences, and fifty-four of them were reinterviewed one year later. These results were consistent with a number of studies elsewhere indicating that cocaine and crack use is predominantly a self-limiting phenomenon of relatively short duration (Waldorf, Reinarman & Murphy 1991; Bieleman et al. 1993; Cohen & Sas 1993). Chapter 11 showed that even acute cocaine-induced reactions such as paranoia and hallucinations were buffered by set and setting. The popular view that pharmacology is somehow an instantly addicting destiny is clearly an oversimplification, given the many complex patterns of use and outcomes that occur. Chapter 12, which presented several case histories of ongoing users who were followed up for two additional years, further illustrated this point. The implications of the analysis of Toronto crack users led us to formulate the following explanation for what we consider the overreaction to the dangers posed by crack.

The discrepancy between popular beliefs about crack and the findings of the Toronto study is due to a fundamental difference in perspective. The popular perspective, derived from media images and police claims, is a mechanistic one. It focuses only on the pharmacological properties of a drug and assumes that users are vulnerable biological organisms who can only passively and mechanically behave according to what the drug dictates. Such a view is supported by cases of addicts who have become victims of compulsive use. Some users do become compulsive users. Many more users do not. Research showed that even most of those whose maximal period of use was intense and compulsive were later able to regain control, usually without therapeutic intervention. Thus, the power of this mechanistic perspective to help us understand the nature of the crack problem and what to do about it is quite limited.

The second perspective, a voluntaristic one, views the user as an active human subject capable of making choices. This approach does not downplay the pharmacological powers of drugs, but it does not consider them the only important factor. Drug use does not occur in a social vacuum; psychological, social, economic, and cultural factors all play important roles in shaping a person's drug use behavior. For example, social policies that reduce inequality, ensure that basic human needs like health care are met and do not marginalize racial or ethnic groups, all help to shape a social context in which the harms that drugs can do are reduced. In such a context, more users of potentially highly addictive drugs are able to weigh the pleasure derived from the use of the drug with perceived risk and undesirable consequences. Many of them maintain a level of ongoing use that their physical, social, and financial conditions allow. Others may simply quit; either the risk is too high for continuous use, or the excitement of experimentation with the drug has faded. Data from the Toronto crack users study suggest that this perspective is a more accurate description of actual crack use patterns.

These different perspectives paint different pictures of the drug problem and have radically different implications for treatment, prevention, and drug policy. First, a mechanistic approach predicts a strong, positive association between the addictiveness of a particular drug and the level of destructive use in society. The cocaine scare during the 1980s greatly inflated the estimate of cocaine users requiring treatment and related services (Erickson & Alexander 1989:264). The "crack menace," which was depicted as even more catastrophic than cocaine, may lead to unrealistic predictions of treatment needs.

Second, as studies in the United States have shown, a crucial part of why politicians and police perceived a crack epidemic was crack's association with subordinate groups who were already seen as threatening or in need of social control, such as, inner-city minorities and the poor (Reinarman & Levine 1989). One result has been increasingly punitive measures that made U.S. crack users face stiffer penalties than similar drug offenders in court, which in turn has put additional burdens on the criminal justice system (Belenko & Fagan 1987, 1988; Belenko, Fagan & Chin 1991). A pilot study of Toronto courts has suggested that a similar process may have also been operating in Canada (Erickson & Cohen 1994). Such intensive enforcement may discourage crack users with problems from seeking treatment for fear of exposing themselves to officialdom.

Third, overemphasis on the extraordinary pharmacological powers of crack could dilute the effects of prevention efforts. The worst-case scenario of crack addiction that the media have depicted as typical is not likely to match the experience of most current users. For potential users, the credibility of prevention information could be drastically eroded once they learn from current users that the worst-case scenario is an exception rather than a rule. The real risks of crack addiction are grim enough and should be spelled out so that the potential users and the public can have an accurate perception of the risks involved if they, or those they know, start use. The importance of accurate information about risks in prevention efforts has been noted in recent studies showing that users' perceived health risks of illicit drug use have contributed to reductions in use (Bachman, Johnston & O'Malley 1990; Erickson & Murray 1989).

Moreover, since use leads inexorably to addiction in the mechanistic approach, the prevention effort is directed at stopping initiation of use, and success is indicated by fewer users overall (regardless of level or pattern of use). Any measure that might increase availability is therefore suspect. But the evidence from both cocaine and alcohol is that the relationship is not that simple. Price of cocaine dropped dramatically and purity increased in the 1980s, despite increased law enforcement; nevertheless, overall prevalence declined while heavy use and problems increased (Caulkins, Crawford & Reuter 1993; DiNardo 1993; Kennedy, Reuter & Riley 1993; Erickson 1993). Even for a legally available drug like alcohol, declines in alcohol consumption and alcohol-related problems have been observed in Ontario while price has remained stable and availability of alcohol has increased (Smart & Mann forthcoming). It would appear that alternative measures such as health promotion and concerns about harmful effects can influence choices about drug taking.

The voluntaristic approach to prevention does not stop at providing accurate information about risks. It also points to the need to understand the psychological, social, and economic factors that affect a person's decisions to use or to continue using a drug. As Waldorf, Reinarman & Murphy (1991) have shown in their book on heavy cocaine users, the user's "stake in conventional life"—job, career, family, community responsibilities—is a crucial determinant of his or her capacity for controlling use. While they show that this may well be more difficult with crack than with powder cocaine, the principle still holds. People with jobs, homes, and families to protect and who have the life chances that make this protection possible are less likely to be overwhelmed by their drug use. Again, this is why social and economic policies that shape the distribution of such stakes and life chances are crucial parts of the context of drug use.

There is a need for prevention work to move beyond imploring people to "just say no"—an approach predicated on the pharmacology-based mechanistic perspective. A prevention policy rooted in the more accurate, voluntarist perspective on drug problems would focus on the social sources of vulnerability and the social support programs that could raise people's capacities for resisting crack and other drugs. Existing data do not allow us to prove it, but we suspect that Canada has less of a crack problem than the United States precisely because its social welfare and race relations policies do a better job of reducing the social sources of vulnerability and increasing citizens' capacities for controlling their drug use.

What Canada should have learned from the American "wars" on drugs in the twentieth century and from its own "wars" is that they are not only very costly but ineffective in solving drug problems (Trebach 1987; Alexander 1990; Mitchell 1990). In order to find a "way out of the War on Drugs" (Alexander 1990), Canada should rely less on criminal sanctions and consider other options. These alternatives must replace the conventional mechanistic view of drug use with a voluntaristic one and shift the pendulum from interdiction and other supply-side measures to health-directed approaches. We no longer believe that keeping cocaine prices as high as possible (as we said in the first edition) is a viable option.

Both Canadian and American drug researchers have suggested that a promising framework for policy development is the harm reduction approach, which incorporates prevention and health promotion as proactive strategies and mobilizes informal social controls among families, peers, social groups, and communities to reduce demand and risky practices for illicit drugs (Erickson 1989, 1990a, 1990b; Erickson & Ottaway 1993; Alexander 1990; Jonas 1990; Morgan, Wallack & Buchanan 1988; Goodstadt 1990). Australia and some European countries have made strides in articulating and testing this approach (O'Hare et al. 1992; Heather et al. 1993). The commitment to testing and developing a harm reduction approach is Canada's greatest challenge in drug policy in the 1990s. Canada's relatively good record on social welfare and social justice makes this feasible. That such a challenge may be more difficult in the United States does not make it any less important there.

There are complex interrelationships among the use of drugs such as cocaine, their benefits and adverse consequences, and the effectiveness of various control systems. All of these must affect the aims and strategies of social policy. In order to take harm reduction seriously for cocaine, it is essential to acknowledge that use is controllable and that harm can be prevented or minimized by means other than total abstinence and complete suppression of availability. The present climate of aggressive prohibition and its associated mythology regarding drug addiction have largely precluded, until recently, any comprehensive application of the public health-based concept of harm reduction to any of the illicit drugs, including cocaine (Erickson 1993). Much remains to be learned about the various forms and expressions of harm reduction and what impact they may have on health, social, economic, and legal aspects of substance use and misuse (Cheung 1994).

Research on the most recent wave of cocaine and crack use has demonstrated a number of important features:

1. Most use is infrequent and self-limiting.
2. The most adverse effects are associated with chronic, heavy use and the most intensive forms of administration.
3. Users display awareness of risks and spontaneously take action to lessen them.
4. Personal and informal social controls operating in user networks are a potent source of endogenous influence for potential harm reduction.

These features have important implications for the reduction of morbidity, mortality, compulsive use, and any other adverse consequences of cocaine use. We need to shed the blinkers imposed by the legacy of prohibition and consider multiple approaches that characterize public health efforts. These could include primary prevention to discourage new users, controlled availability for the most hardcore, poly drug users as an incentive both to receive primary care and to facilitate treatment entry, honest eduction and instruction in safer use practices, low-risk products, and an assortment of harm-reducing practices for the most active users (Erickson, 1993). In order to capitalize on the informal controls that keep most cocaine use infrequent and under control, it is important to relate harm minimization strategies to different levels and experiences with cocaine all along the use continuum.

Finally, although we retain our concern about the potential risks attached to the use of cocaine and crack, we feel even more unease about the policies that have been promulgated worldwide in an effort to eradicate coca growing and cocaine use. We prefer instead to recognize the global challenge posed by the spread of cocaine distribution networks (Flynn 1993) and the need to develop new, cooperative, international responses that deal with the actual harm done by cocaine (Bieleman et al. 1993; World Health Organization 1993). Coca growers in developing countries and cocaine and crack users at the lower end of the socioeconomic scale in the developed countries have borne the brunt of coercive, punitive interventions. Meanwhile, institutions of law enforcement and criminal justice have received seemingly endless infusions of resources in the face of mounting evidence about the impossibility of seriously interfering with supply (Christie 1993). We are hopeful that keeping cocaine and crack in perspective will encourage a major policy shift by the end of the 1990s.

Appendix A
Jah Bones Letter

Of Rastas, Ital,

real and Godly*

Rastafarians have been blamed for causing the riot in Handsworth which, we are told, is a consequence of the bad relationship between police and drug-pushers, who are Rastas. It would seem that Rastas are a weak link in the social scheme of things, therefore, it is easy to blame I and I because we are defenseless.

No evidence has been put forward to show the supposed link between Rastas and drugs. It is widely assumed that the ganja plant which Rastas use is a drug in the same class as heroin, cocaine, opium and other steel-hard drugs. To the Rastas ganja is not even a drug; it is just another plant which is potent with medicinal values and properties.

Rastas believe in the goodness of ganja and our constant use of it has helped to popularise the plant. Now ganja is international because it is in great demand by people of all nationalities. But there are those who are bitterly opposed to Rastas and ganja and will do anything in order to discredit I and I.

The middle class users of steel drugs like cocaine and heroin, who can't stand Rasta and dismiss ganja as "soft" enter the ghetto with their devilish concoction, identify those who are greedy and unscrupulous and, soon after, the wicked drugs are distributed amongst the people for the sake of making a fortune.

Still, the true Rastafarians refuse to deal with steel drugs. They ardently stick to ganja for that is Ital, real and godly. The true

---

*Reprinted with permission from the *Manchester Guardian Weekly*, October 6, 1985.

Rastafarian has no inherent desire to break society's laws, not even those of Babylon. But when the law is unfair then not only forced to break it. As far as I see it the struggle for justice, rights and liberty means a fight to get Rastafari accepted as a real culture for real people and the freeing-up of ganja amongst other things, for only a people can know what is best for them.

Jah Bones
London N4

Appendix B
Cocaine Reactions: Some Statistical Results

Mean Reaction Scores by Frequency of Use

Reaction[a]	Frequent (N = 38)	Intermediate (N = 46)	Infrequent (N = 19)	F[b]	p
Nasal sores/bleeding	2.52	1.79	1.26	14.21	.000
Uncontrollable urge to use	2.93	1.89	1.39	13.39	.000
Weight loss	2.45	1.83	1.04	12.16	.000
Acute insomnia	3.62	3.02	2.09	11.62	.000
Inability to relax	2.92	2.29	1.82	8.45	.000
Self-consciousness	2.32	1.82	1.41	8.82	.001
Nervousness	3.32	2.81	2.13	7.33	.001
Nausea	1.95	1.66	1.17	6.99	.001
Physical/mental exhaustion	2.62	2.31	1.65	6.63	.002
Chronic insomnia	2.77	2.17	2.00	4.71	.011
Energy	4.07	4.17	3.43	4.52	.013
Paranoia	1.47	1.29	1.04	4.01	.021
Self-confidence	3.95	3.71	3.17	3.43	.040
Increased heart rate	4.13	3.89	3.32	3.37	.038
Restlessness	3.60	3.69	2.96	3.26	.042
Dry mouth/throat	3.42	3.25	2.77	2.72	.071
Sexual arousal	3.57	3.14	3.00	2.11	.126
Buzzing in ears	2.00	1.58	1.63	1.99	.142
Talkativeness	3.90	4.06	3.61	1.93	.150
Aggressiveness	1.30	1.14	1.13	1.53	.221
Fuzzy vision	1.65	1.50	1.30	1.25	.290
Hallucinations	1.17	1.29	1.09	1.03	.362
Lights in vision	1.70	1.58	1.43	0.66	.514
Congested nose	3.12	3.08	3.04	0.04	.954

Note: For a description of the frequency-of-use groups, see pp. 96–97 and note 1, Chap. 4.
[a]*Codes for reaction scale:* never = 1; rarely = 2; sometimes = 3; most times = 4; always = 5.
[b]F distributed with approximately 2 and 108 degrees of freedom.

TABLE B-2

Acute Insomnia–Nasal Disorder (Factor 1) Regressed on Demographic, Use, Social, and Psychological Variables

	B	(SE)	B*	Variable Statistics (N = 93) Mean	SD
Demographics					
Gender	−.014	(.212)	.006	.720	.451
Age	−.034	(.023)	−.197	29.376	5.521
Marital status[a]					
Married/common law	.097	(.221)	—	.269	.446
Separated/divorced	.291	(.304)	—	.151	.360
Blishen score	.001	(.000)	.085	43.656	12.843
Use					
Frequency[b]					
Frequent	.879	(.317)**	—	.344	.478
Intermediate	.578	(.272)**	—	.462	.501
Years of use	.019	(.027)	.089	7.183	4.453
Alcpoly	−.045	(.239)	−.021	.247	.434
Canpoly	.306	(.354)	.096	.097	.297
Poly2	.121	(.236)	.058	.290	.456
Social					
Others present	−.228	(.147)	−.183	4.355	.761
Percent of users	.026	(.121)	.020	2.882	.870
Number who use	−.011	(.001)**	−.261	19.097	23.258
Psychological					
Perceived risk	.000	(.023)	.034	12.785	2.972
Perceived high	.242	(.145)	.177	3.075	.695
Constant	.189	(1.101)			

$R^2 = .338$

$F[16,76] = 2, 42; p = .005$

Notes: B* standardized regression coefficient; not presented for dummy variable sets. For discussion of Factor 1, see p. 131.

**Significant at $p < .05$.

[a]Versus single.

[b]Versus infrequent.

TABLE B-3

Sensory–Perceptual Distortions (Factor 2) Regressed on Demographic, Use, Social, and Psychological Variables

	B	(SE)	B*
Demographics			
Gender	−.252	(.221)	.115
Age	1.070	(.024)	.000
Marital status[a]			
Married/common law	−.136	(.230)	—
Separated/divorced	−.000	(.318)	—
Blishen score	−.014	(.000)	−.186
Use			
Frequency[b]			
Frequent	−.053	(.330)	—
Intermediate	−.054	(.284)	—
Years of use	.081	(.028)**	.363
Alcpoly	.221	(.249)	.097
Canpoly	−.015	(.369)	.000
Poly2	.430	(.246)	.199
Social			
Others present	−.256	(.154)	−.197
Percent of users	−.270	(.126)**	−.238
Number who use	−.000	(.000)	.000
Psychological			
Perceived risk	.000	(.024)	.035
Perceived high	.320	(.151)**	.225
Constant	.924	(1.157)	
R^2 = .338			
$F[16,76]$ = 2.43; p = .005			

Notes: B* standardized regression coefficient; not presented for dummy variable sets. For discussion of Factor 2, see pp. 131–133.

**Significant at $p < .05$.

[a]Versus single.

[b]Versus infrequent.

TABLE B-4

Stimulatory Effects (Factor 3) Regressed on Demographic, Use, Social, and Psychological Variables

	B	(SE)	B*
Demographics			
Gender	−.236	(.218)	−.110
Age	.043	(.024)	.245
Marital status[a]			
Married/common law	.062	(.227)	—
Separated/divorced	−.404	(.313)	—
Blishen score	−.014	(.000)	−.187
Use			
Frequency[b]			
Frequent	.952	(.326)**	—
Intermediate	.460	(.280)	—
Years of use	−.026	(.028)	−.118
Alcpoly	−.100	(.246)	−.045
Canpoly	−.488	(.364)	−.150
Poly2	−.125	(.243)	−.059
Social			
Others present	−.297	(.151)	−.234
Percent of users	−.118	(.124)	−.106
Number who use	−.000	(.000)	−.092
Psychological			
Perceived risk	.064	(.024)**	.263
Perceived high	.077	(.149)	.055
Constant	−5.132	(1.141)	
$R^2 = .330$			
$F[16,76] = 2.34; p = .007$			

Notes: B* standardized regression coefficient; not presented for dummy variable sets. For discussion of Factor 3, see p. 133.

**Significant at $p < .05$.

[a]Versus single.

[b]Versus infrequent.

TABLE B-5

Aggressive–Paranoiac Reactions (Factor 4) Regressed on Demographic, Use, Social, and Psychological Variables

	B	(SE)	B*
Demographics			
Gender	.227	(.198)	.110
Age	.014	(.021)	.086
Marital status[a]			
Married/common law	−.158	(.207)	—
Separated/divorced	−.061	(.285)	—
Blishen score	−.015	(.000)**	−.206
Use			
Frequency[b]			
Frequent	.395	(.296)	—
Intermediate	.065	(.225)	—
Years of use	.014	(.026)	.065
Alcpoly	.452	(.223)**	.211
Canpoly	−.526	(.331)	−.168
Poly2	.049	(.221)	.024
Social			
Others present	−.383	(.138)**	−.314
Percent of users	−.213	(.113)	−.199
Number who use	.000	(.000)	.197
Psychological			
Perceived risk	.028	(.022)	.121
Perceived high	.207	(.136)	.155
Constant	.948	(1.038)	

$R^2 = .397$

$F[16,76] = 3.13; p = .001$

Notes: B* standardized regression coefficient; not presented for dummy variable sets. For discussion of Factor 4, see p. 134.

**Significant at $p < .05$.

[a]Versus single.

[b]Versus infrequent.

TABLE B-6

Social Effects (Factor 5) Regressed on Demographic, Use, Social, and Psychological Variables

	B	(SE)	B*
Demographics			
Gender	−.323	(.216)	−.162
Age	.009	(.024)	.058
Marital status[a]			
Married/common law	−.151	(.226)	—
Separated/divorced	.094	(.311)	—
Blishen score	.007	(.008)	.198
Use			
Frequency[b]			
Frequent	.230	(.324)	—
Intermediate	−.002	(.278)	—
Years of use	.023	(.028)	.115
Alcpoly	.266	(.244)	.128
Canpoly	.275	(.362)	.091
Poly2	−.229	(.241)	−.116
Social			
Others present	.060	(.150)	.051
Percent of users	.002	(.123)	.002
Number who use	−.004	(.004)	−.114
Psychological			
Perceived risk	.013	(.024)	.056
Perceived high	.389	(.148)**	.300
Constant	−2.137	(1.133)	
R^2 = .234			
$F[16,76]$ = 1.45; p = .142			

Notes: B* standardized regression coefficient; not presented for dummy variable sets. For discussion of Factor 5, see p. 134.

**Significant at $p < .05$.

[a]Versus single.

[b]Versus infrequent.

TABLE B-7

Acute Physiological Reactions (Factor 6) Regressed on Demographic, Use, Social, and Psychological Variables

	B	(SE)	B*
Demographics			
Gender	−.130	(.197)	−.068
Age	−.016	(.021)	−.101
Marital status[a]			
Married/common law	.121	(.205)	—
Separated/divorced	.294	(.283)	—
Blishen score	.016	(.007)	.232
Use			
Frequency[b]			
Frequent	−.787	(.294)**	—
Intermediate	−.702	(.253)**	—
Years of use	−.013	(.025)	−.068
Alcpoly	.013	(.222)	.006
Canpoly	−.088	(.329)	−.030
Poly2	.144	(.219)	.076
Social			
Others present	−.032	(.137)	−.028
Percent of users	.103	(.112)	−.104
Number who use			−.114
Psychological			
Perceived risk	−.034	(.022)	−.158
Perceived high	−.232	(.135)	−.187
Constant	1.531	(1.031)	
$R^2 = .312$			
$F[16,76] = 2.155; p = .014$			

Notes: B* standardized regression coefficient; not presented for dummy variable sets. For discussion of Factor 6, see p. 135.

**Significant at $p < .05$.

[a]Versus single.

[b]Versus infrequent.

TABLE B-8

Chronic—Problematic Reactions (Factor 7) Regressed on Demographic, Use, Social, and Psychological Variables

	B	(SE)	B*
Demographics			
Gender	−.264	(.170)	−.133
Age	−.036	(.018)	−.222
Marital status[a]			
Married/common law	−.144	(.178)	—
Separated/divorced	−.048	(.245)	—
Blishen score	−.004	(.006)	.059
Use			
Frequency[b]			
Frequent	.748	(.255)**	—
Intermediate	.152	(.219)	—
Years of use	.044	(.022)**	.218
Alcpoly	.016	(.192)	.008
Canpoly	−.377	(.285)	.125
Poly2	−.108	(.190)	.055
Social			
Others present	−.157	(.118)	−.134
Percent of users	−.150	(.097)	−.146
Number who use	−.005	(.004)	−.145
Psychological			
Perceived risk	.033	(.019)	.146
Perceived high	.429	(.117)**	.333
Constant	.409	(.892)	
$R^2 = .519$			
$F[16,76] = 5.14; p < .001$			

Notes: B* standardized regression coefficient; not presented for dummy variable sets. For discussion of Factor 7, see p. 135.

**Significant at $p < .05$.

[a]Versus single.

[b]Versus infrequent.

Notes

Chapter 1

1.   See the annotated bibliography by Anglin (1985) and overview by Kalant (1978) for accounts of cocaine's history and effects.

2.   For interesting and informative accounts of the early uses of coca and cocaine, see Aldrich and Barker (1976), Ashley (1975), and Siegel (1985).

3.   Quoted in Aldrich and Barker (1976).

4.   These statements were abstracted from the following reports, respectively: House of Commons Debates, Canada (November 25, 1910), 1910–11a:260; *Canadian Pharmaceutical Journal*, December 1910:213–214, quoting from a recent issue of the *Montreal Star*; House of Commons Debates, Canada (January 26, 1911), 1910–11b:2527, quoting correspondence from Professor Welsh of the Presbyterian College of Montreal; *Canadian Pharmaceutical Journal*, March 1909:396; House of Commons Debates, Canada (January 26, 1911), 1910–11b:2525, quoting from the *Montreal Witness*, November 23, 1910; House of Commons Debates, Canada (January 26, 1911), 1910–11b:2524–5, quoting from the *Montreal Witness*, November 23, 1910.

Chapter 2

1.   Blau (1964) makes essentially the same point: "The media of communication serve in part as media of repositories of information that is transmitted to people and helps shape their opinions, as illustrated by newspapers" (p. 265).

2.   Riesman (1961) argues that popular music is largely an adolescent phenomenon. Johnsson–Smaragdi (1983), conducting a longitudinal study among a sample of Swedish adolescents aged 11 to 15, found that use of family-oriented media (e.g., television, books) declined with age, while peer-oriented media (e.g., popular music and movies) increased in frequency.

3.   Other reference to Holmes' cocaine use are the following: "Save for the occasional use of cocaine he had no vices and he only turned to the drug as a

249

protest against the monotony of existence when cases were scanty and the paper uninteresting" (*The Yellow Face*, c. 1894). "For years I had gradually weaned him from that drug mania which had threatened once to check his remarkable career. Now I know that under ordinary conditions he no longer craved for this artificial stimulus; but I was well aware that the fiend was not dead, but sleeping" (*The Missing Three Quarter*, c. 1904). ". . . buried among his old books, and alternating from week to week between cocaine and ambition" (*A Scandal in Bohemia*, c. 1892).

4.　　*Toronto Sun*, February 15, 1985, pp. 1, 2.

5.　　Also see *People*, November 8, 1982.

6.　　The Canadian News Index indexes about thirty major Canadian newspapers and popular magazines. All periodicals are indexed cover to cover. For newspapers, twenty to sixty articles are indexed in each daily paper. Articles are selected by indexers trained in reference library studies. Data are derived from volumes 4–14.

7.　　The Canadian Periodical Index covers over 375 periodicals with an emphasis on mainstream and academic titles. Data are derived from volumes 33–43.

8.　　The estimates of the number of cocaine users are based on the National Health Promotion Surveys of 1985 and 1990 and the National Alcohol and Other Drug Use Survey of 1989. Estimates refer to the number of Canadians aged 15 and over who reported using cocaine at least once during the twelve months before the interview.

9.　　Indeed, Porter (1965) felt that influence of the American media was deeply embedded in Canadians' perceptions: "Anyone familiar with the reading habits of Canadians knows that the handful of magazines and periodicals published in Canada does not represent the ideological exposure of the general population. Publications from the United States circulate far more widely than do those of Canadian origin. . . . There can be little doubt that these foreign publications contribute substantially to 'Canadian' values and to the view of the world held by Canadians" (p. 465).

10.　　For example: *The Mystery of the Leaping Fish* (1916); *A Scandal in Bohemia* (1921); *Sisters of Eve* (1928); *The Pace That Kills* (1928); *El Cocaine* (1930); *Down River* (1931); *The Mad Genius* (1931); *Der Weisse Daemon* (1932); *Modern Times* (1933); *The Invisible Man* (1933).

11.　　References are included in such films as *Paris Blues* (1961), *Easy Rider* (1969), *Two Mules for Sister Sara* (1970), *The French Connection* (1971), *Dealing* (1972), *Go Ask Alice* (1972), *Superfly* (1972), *The Discreet Charm of the Bourgeoisie* (1972), *Harry in Your Pocket* (1973), *A Star is Born* (1975), *Sensations* (1977), *The Rubber Gun* (1977), *Cocaine Cowboys* (1978), *Pretty Baby* (1978), *Up in Smoke* (1978), *Wolfen* (1981), *Annie Hall* (1977), *Looking for Mr. Goodbar* (1977), *Atlantic City* (1981), *Scarface* (1983), *The Big Chill* (1983), *St. Elmo's Fire* (1985), *Angel Heart* (1987), *Less Than Zero* (1987), *Bright Lights, Big City* (1988), *Colors* (1988), *City of Hope* (1990), *Postcards from the Edge* (1990), *Boyz N the Hood* (1991), *Jungle Fever* (1991), *New Jack City* (1991), *Juice* (1992), *My Own Private Idaho* (1992), and *Mad Dog and Glory* (1993).

Chapter 3

1.   Bear in mind some of the inherent problems in comparing findings from different sample surveys. It is not uncommon to find surveys differing in sample design, method of administration, and question format, to name a few. Thus, the use of identical methods and impact of identical influences is rarely achieved. Consequently, caution should be exercised when interpreting differences.

2.   In Ontario, students who intend to proceed into university are required to complete five years of secondary education (i.e., grades 7 through 13). Thus, Ontario grade 13 students (aged approximately 18 years) leave high school one year later than their American counterparts.

3.   The purpose of the Epidemiological Catchment Area Program, a project funded by the National Institute of Mental Health, is to assess psychiatric conditions among the general population of adults in five sites (Baltimore, St. Louis, Durham, Los Angeles, and New Haven). The survey consists of interviews with 13,538 respondents interviewed between 1981 and 1984.

Chapter 4

1.   The clustering solution employed was based on an agglomerative hierarchical cluster analysis executed in SPSSX. Everitt (1980) and Lorr (1983) are excellent works reviewing this technique. Essentially, this method begins by treating each observation as a unique cluster and, by employing some measure of similarity (in our case, squared Euclidean distance), then successively combines and recombines similar observations into larger and larger cluster groupings. The procedure employed to determine the combination of observations is based on Ward's minimum-variance method. Like dimensional analyses, such as factor analysis, more than one meaningful cluster solution may exist. Although the analysis on the three frequency-of-use measures suggested that both the three- and four-cluster solutions adequately represented the data, the three-cluster solution was chosen since it resulted in group sample sizes appropriate to use with further multivariate analyses and also was easily conceptualized within an infrequent, intermediate, and frequent use framework. The mean scores for each group are in the table shown here.

Mean Scores for Frequency-of-Use Variable

	Infrequent	Intermediate	Frequent
Lifetime	3.1	6.0	7.4
Prior year	2.0	3.4	6.9
Prior month	1.0	1.3	2.9

Frequency-of-use codes:				*Size of group:*
Never	1	10–19 times	5	Infrequent = 23
1–2 times	2	20–39 times	6	Intermediate = 48
3–5 times	3	40–99 times	7	Frequent = 40
6–9 times	4	100+ times	8	

Chapter 6

1.   Hepatitis and skin disorders at injection site, which were included in the original list, are not presented since these reactions are irrelevant for intranasal users and were almost nonexistent in our sample.

2.   The means and F-ratios were as follows: for talkativeness, 4.17 for females and 3.79 for males ($F[1,109] = 4.27, p = .041$); for dry mouth and throat, 3.58 among females and 3.04 among males ($F[1,108] = 6.44, p = .01$); for weight loss, 2.13 among females and 1.69 among males ($F[1,109] = 6.64, p = .011$); for violence and aggression, 1.28 among males and 1.03 among females ($F[1,109] = 7.63, p = .007$); for heart rate, 4.03 among males and 3.50 among females ($F[1,109] = 4.63, p = .034$).

3.   The F-ratio associated with nonlinear component was $F = 3.01, p = .086$. Generally, the test for linearity represents the explained increment due to nonlinearity and takes the form $(BSS/TSS - r^2)^{\Sigma}y^2$.

4.   Bartlett's test of sphericity ($1007.54; p < .001$), which tests the null hypothesis that the observed correlation matrix is an identity matrix (i.e., entries of ones in the main diagonal and zero in the remaining ones), was significant, indicating the appropriateness of the factor-analytic model. Maximum-likelihood factor analysis was employed; in addition to its desirable properties for estimation, its use in factor analysis affords the opportunity to examine the factor structure empirically. Incremental chi-square tests indicated that a seven-factor solution best fit these data. Also, employing the eigenvalue-of-unity rule, two other factoring methods, principle components and principle axis factoring, also extracted seven-factor solutions. The rotation method employed was oblique, which obtained a more satisfactory and simpler structure than did the orthogonal varimax rotation.

5.   Since the factor analysis employed oblique rotation, the factor loadings presented refer to the factor pattern matrix.

6.   For descriptive purposes, one-way analysis of variance was performed on these data. The reaction scores of factors 2 and 5 did not differ significantly across groups ($F = 1.53$ and $F = .66$, respectively). Scores for all remaining dimensions differed well beyond the .05 level of significance.

7.   The final regression model was fit as a single equation; all variables entered simultaneously as a single block. Prior to fitting the final model, the data were examined for problems that may violate or retard estimates (nonnormality, nonlinearity, heteroscedasity, and collinearity). Examination of residuals and their associated plots did not reveal serious violations of ordinary least squares assumptions. An examination of one degree of freedom regressors failed to indicate serious collinearity determined by the condition number (the square root of the ratio of the largest eigenvalue to the smallest one) of 2.81. Missing values due to item nonresponse were deleted casewise, resulting in a final sample size of ninety-three cases.

8.   The use of quantitative variables in regression is straightforward. Qualitative variables, those indicating difference in kind, however, are usually repre-

sented by dummy variables, which in the simplest case indicate presence (usually coded 1) or absence (usually coded 0) of a given condition. The reader unfamiliar with the application of dummy variable regression can refer to one of several sources (e.g., Blalock 1972; Fox 1984).

9. The omnibus F tests the null hypothesis that all regression coefficients are zero.

10. In the most general sense, suppression effects occur when the partialed effect of a given variable exceeds its zero-order effect. See Cohen and Cohen (1975:85–91) for an elucidation of suppression effects.

11. There are inherent limitations in the results of our study, and extrapolation to other populations and sample sizes must be done with caution.

Chapter 7

1. The Opium Act of 1908 was concerned only with opium. The Opium and Drug Act, which was discussed in more detail in chapter 1, was enacted in 1911.

2. Heckathorn and Lucas (1982:443) observed that the literature on drug use is fragmented because of the practice of "concentrating exclusively upon the use of a single substance."

3. The most convictions were awarded for cannabis, and the sentencing dispositions for it are the most lenient. At the other extreme, heroin convictions are the least common, and they earn the most severe dispositions. If convictions for cocaine continue to increase, will the judiciary respond with a progressively more lenient sentencing response?

4. Our discussion of sentencing patterns is limited to the offense of simple possession. As Erickson (1992) showed, this offense category accounts for most of the drug convictions in Canada.

5. In the second study, participants interviewed in 1989 reported no difficulty obtaining cocaine, and the average price paid per gram had decreased to between $75 and $125. In the past year, over half of these users (58 percent) bought cocaine at least once a month or more often, usually in small amounts (less than 3 grams), and total expenditures on cocaine had exceeded $5,000 for 43 percent of the sample. Yet despite this more frequent and expensive procurement of cocaine compared to the first study, participants in the second study also reported very little criminal involvement in order to obtain cocaine (see Erickson & Weber 1994).

6. Murray and Erickson (1987) found, in a longitudinal study, that a prospective measure of marijuana use serves as a good proxy for actual subsequent use.

7. Since our dependent variable is a dichotomy, a log-linear framework is most appropriate. Logistic regression, in particular, allows us to take advantage of continuous variables (see Feinberg 1977).

Chapter 9

1.   The two respondents whose cocaine experience was solely crack and the three who were almost exclusively crack users led us initially to group them together and report them this way in earlier publications (Erickson, Watson & Weber 1992; Erickson 1993).

2.   Of the seventy-five participants who had consented to follow-up, nearly all of those who were not reinterviewed could not be contacted due to change of address and/or telephone number; one had died and one was in prison.

3.   Additional findings of this study relating to the impact of cocaine use on health, social relationships, criminality, and other factors have been reported elsewhere (Erickson, Watson & Weber 1992; Erickson & Weber 1994).

Chapter 10

1.   Reprinted in the *Toronto Star*, February 24, 1992, p. A2.

2.   For example, in a separate analysis of the results of the first study of 111 cocaine users in 1983–1984, it was found that about 50 percent of the subjects had half or more of their friends using cocaine, and about 90 percent had at least half of their friends using cannabis (Erickson & Murray 1989).

3.   The associations between level of use (user type) and perceived risk of harm in trying and occasional use do not by themselves suggest any causality between use and risk perception. However, there is reason to believe that perceived risk influenced level of use rather than vice versa. If increases in use could reduce perceptions of risk, then the percentage of continuous users perceiving great risk in regular crack use should have been much smaller than percentages for the other two groups. However, as reported earlier, as many as 84 percent of continuous users perceived great risk, which is not substantially smaller than the 93 percent for inactive users.

Chapter 11

1.   These data differ slightly from earlier chapters because for the 1983–1984 samples our analyses are based on 103 intranasal users and the 1989 sample is based on 77 users who reported using both crack and cocaine powder.

2.   For powder users, cocaine use is measured by the frequency of cocaine powder use during the prior twelve months, and for crack users cocaine use is as a function of (1) frequency of cocaine powder use during the past twelve months, (2) frequency of crack use during the past twelve months, (3) the proportion of times crack is used out of all cocaine uses, and (4) a crack purity factor. The computation is as follows: Use = $CokeFQ + (CrackFQ \times \%Crack \times 1.8)$, where, $CokeFQ$ = number of times cocaine powder was used during the prior twelve months to the interview; $CrackFQ$ = number of times crack was used during the prior twelve months to the interview; and $\%Crack$ = the number of times, out of ten cocaine uses, that crack was used. It is important not to ignore that crack users

typically consume greater doses of cocaine than powder users in two respects. First, most crack users consume both cocaine powder and crack. In addition, crack typically has greater purity than does street-level cocaine powder. While purity of crack averages 80 to 90 percent, the typical purity of cocaine powder is 45 percent (Fagan & Chin 1989; Metro Toronto Research Group on Drug Use 1993). Thus, on average, crack is 1.8 times more potent than is cocaine powder.

3. Risk, a summated three-item scale, measures the perception of risk in using cocaine. Each item is measured on a four-point scale from no risk = 1 to great risk = 4, in (1) trying cocaine once or twice, (2) using cocaine occasionally, and (3) using cocaine regularly. The summated measure results in values from 3 to 16, with higher values representing greater perceived risk. The reliability coefficient of the summated measure shows reasonable internal consistency for the total sample (α = .84), for crack users (α = .77) and for powder users (α = .75).

4. Becker argues that novice drug users should be more likely to experience negative subjective experiences than would seasoned drug users, since the latter has had the time and experience to assimilate the cultural understanding regarding drug use consequences. A crude indicator of cocaine experience is the number of times participants used cocaine in their lifetime. We computed an indicator variable (NOVICE) having a value of 1 for those who used cocaine fewer than twenty times in their lifetime (N = 47) and a value of zero otherwise (N = 102).

5. The relative number of cocaine-using friends is measured by the following question: "Of the people you usually socialize with, would you say that none, only a few, about half, or almost all use cocaine sometimes?" This question varies slightly for crack users: "Of the people you usually socialize with, how many would you say use cocaine sometimes?" Response categories for both questions are identical (1 = none; 2 = only a few; 3 = about half; 4 = almost all). Unlike powder users, all crack users reported having cocaine-using friends. To reduce the likelihood of heteroscedasticity (unequal variances) we recoded the relative number of cocaine-using friends into three values (1 = none or a few friends, 2 = about half, 3 = almost all). Although this factor takes on only three discrete values, it is treated as a continuous variable on both conceptual and statistical grounds.

6. The absolute number of cocaine-using friends consists of a continuous measure ranging between 0 and 97. The value 97 represents 97 or more cocaine-using associates. This upper limit was reported by 7 percent of powder users and 9 percent of crack users.

7. Central to Becker's perspective is the importance of interaction occurring in intimate group settings. Thus, those who restrict their cocaine use to settings that promote interaction and learning should experience fewer negative consequences of cocaine use (Zinberg 1984; Becker 1967). We computed an indicator variable (SOCIAL) derived from a question measuring how frequently the participant used cocaine in the presence of others. The question read as follows: "When you use cocaine are there other people present"? Response categories were (1) never, (2) rarely, (3) sometimes, (4) most times, and (5) always.

8. Originally, response categories were (1) never, (2) rarely, (3) sometimes, (4) most times, and (5) always; however, since our interest is in the probability of

ever experiencing such cocaine-induced effects, the responses were recoded as 0, representing never, and 1, representing rarely through always.

9. In total, twenty-one two-way interactions, which measured sample-by-set and sample-by-setting factors, were tested for statistical significance. Only significant interactions were retained in the final model.

Chapter 12

1. Exceptions are Siegel (1985), Waldorf, Reinarman & Murphy (1991), and Cohen and Sas (1993). This most recent book reports on the follow-up study of 64 cocaine users in Amsterdam, four years after the original sample of 160 users was interviewed in 1987 (Cohen 1989).

Chapter 13

1. For a recent example, consider the manifestation of cocaine use in the form of crack. This is an inexpensive, potent variant on freebase that is quickly absorbed by smoking (see Jacobs & Fehr, 1987). Despite alarmist stories in the American and Canadian press, the availability and use of crack in Canada appears to be minimal and is not considered a threat by local experts (*The Journal*, August 1, 1986, p. 1).

2. See the *Montreal Gazette*, March 3, 1986.

3. Wisotsky (1986) presented a full account of the likely repercussions of various strategies to control cocaine. He argued that seizing the assets of drug traffickers would serve to make the drug enforcement industry self-financing and lead to the escalation of the war on drugs. By 1994, events have proven him correct.

References

Adams, E. H., & Gfroerer, J. (1991). Risk of cocaine abuse and dependence. In S. Schober & C. Schade (eds.), *The Epidemiology of Cocaine Use and Abuse*. Research Monograph 110. Rockville, MD: National Institute on Drug Abuse.

Adelaken, M. I., & Odejide, O. A. (1989). The reliability and validity of the WHO student drug use questionnaire among Nigerian students. *Drug and Alcohol Dependence* 24:245–249.

Adlaf, E. M. (1986). Self-reported cocaine reactions among social-recreational users: A factor-analytic study. *Drug & Alcohol Dependence* 18:203–212.

Adlaf, E. M. (1993). Alcohol and other drug use. In T. Stephens & D. Fowler Graham (eds.), *Canada's Health Promotion Survey 1990: Technical Report* (pp. 103–123). Ottawa: Health and Welfare Canada.

Adlaf, E. M. (forthcoming). The nature and stability of provincial differences in drug use. In N. Giesbreicht & J. Ferris (eds.), *Alcohol, Tobacco and Other Drug Use in Canada: Profiles, Consequences and Responses*. Victoria: University of British Columbia Press.

Adlaf, E. M., & Smart, R. G. (1989). *The Ontario Adult Alcohol and Other Drug Survey, 1977–1989*. Toronto: Addiction Research Foundation.

Adlaf, E. M., Smart, R. G., & Canale, M. D. (1991). *Drug Use Among Ontario Adults: 1977–1991*. Toronto: Addiction Research Foundation.

Adlaf, E. M., Smart, R. G., & Walsh, G. W. (1993). *The Ontario Student Drug Use Survey: 1977–1993*. Toronto: Addiction Research Foundation.

Aguilar, E. (1990). Prevalence of improper use of alcohol, tobacco and drugs in the Ecuadorian population. *Bulletin of the Pan American Health Organization* 24(11):35–38.

Alcoholism & Drug Dependency Commission of New Brunswick (1990). *1989 Provincial School Drug Survey*.

Aldrich, M. R., & Barker, R. W. (1976). Historical aspects of cocaine use and abuse. In S. J. Mule (ed.), *Cocaine, Chemical, Biological, Clinical, Social and Treatment Aspects* (pp. 2–11). New York: CRC Press.

Alexander, B. K. (1990). *Peaceful Measures: Canada's Way Out of the "War on Drugs."* Toronto: University of Toronto Press.

Anderson, P. (1981). *High in America: The True Story Behind NORML and the Politics of Marijuana*. New York: Viking Press.

257

Anglin, L. (1985). *Cocaine: A Selection of Annotated Papers from 1880 to 1984 Concerning Health Effects*. Toronto: ARF Books.

Anta, G. B. (1991). The spread of cocaine in Europe. In F. Bruno (ed.), *Cocaine Today: Its Effects on the Individual and Society*. Rome: United Nations Interregional Crime and Justice Research Institute.

Anthony, J. C., & Petronis, K. R. (1989). Cocaine and heroin dependence compared: Evidence from an epidemiologic field survey. *American Journal of Public Health* 79:1409–1410.

Ashley, R. (1975). *Cocaine: Its History, Uses and Effects*. New York: Warner Books.

Bachman, J. G., Johnston, L. D., & O'Malley, P. M. (1990). Explaining the recent decline in cocaine use among young adults: Further evidence that perceived risks and disapproval lead to reduced drug use. *Journal of Health and Social Behavior* 31:173–184.

Baker, W., Homel, P., Flaherty, B., & Trebilco, P. (1987). *The 1986 Survey of Drug Use by Secondary Students in New South Wales, Sydney*. Sydney, Australia: New South Wales Drug and Alcohol Authority.

Becker, H. S. (1953). Becoming a marijuana user. *American Journal of Sociology* 54:235–242.

Becker, H. S. (1963). *Outsiders*. New York: Free Press.

Becker, H. S. (1967). History, culture and subjective experience: An exploration of the social bases of drug-induced experiences. *Journal of Health & Social Behavior* 8:163–176.

Behr, R. L., & Iyengar, S. (1985). Television news, real-world cues, and changes in public agenda. *Public Opinion Quarterly* 49:38–57.

Belenko, S., & Fagan, J. (1987). *Crack and the Criminal Justice System*. New York: New York City Criminal Justice Agency.

Belenko, S., & Fagan, J. (1988). The System "Gets Tough": The Adjudication of Crack Arrestees in New York City. Paper presented at the annual meeting of the American Society of Criminology, Chicago, November.

Belenko, S., Fagan, J., & Chin, K. L. (1991). Criminal justice responses to crack. *Journal of Research in Crime and Delinquency* 28(1):55–74.

Beniger, J. R. (1984). Mass media, contraceptive behavior, and attitudes on abortion: Toward a comprehensive model of subjective social change. In C. F. Turner & E. Martin (eds.), *Surveying Subjective Phenomena* 2:475–545. New York: Russell Sage.

Bieleman, B., Diaz, A., Merlo, G., & Kaplan, C. D. (eds.). (1993). *Lines Across Europe*. Amsterdam: Swets & Seitlinger.

Biernacki, P., & Waldorf, D. (1981). Snowball sampling: Problems and techniques in chain referral sampling. *Sociological Methods and Research* 10:141–163.

Bishop, D. M. (1984). Legal and extralegal barriers to delinquency: A panel analysis. *Criminology* 22(3):403–419.

Blackwell, J. (1983). Drifting, controlling and overcoming: Opiate users who avoid becoming chronically dependent. *Journal of Drug Issues* 13(2):219–235.

Blalock, H. M. (1972). *Social Statistics*. 2nd ed. New York: McGraw-Hill.

Blau, P. M. (1964). *Exchange and Power in Social Life*. New York: Wiley.

Blishen, B. R. (1967). A socio-economic index for occupations in Canada. *Canadian Review of Sociology and Anthropology* 4(1):41–53.

British Columbia Ministry of Health (1991). *1990 British Columbia Student Drug Use Survey: Summary Report*. Victoria: British Columbia Ministry of Health & Ministry Responsible for Seniors.

Bureau of Dangerous Drugs (1984). *Narcotic, Controlled and Restricted Statistics, 1984*. Ottawa: Health Protection Branch, Health and Welfare Canada.

Canadian Medical Association Journal (1913). Cocain[e] in Canada. *Canadian Medical Association Journal* 3(4):300–304.

Canadian Pharmaceutical Journal (1874). Patent medicines. *Canadian Pharmaceutical Journal* 7(10):367–371.

Canadian Pharmaceutical Journal (1905). Drug habits. *Canadian Pharmaceutical Journal* 39(2):67.

Canadian Pharmaceutical Journal (1907). G. A. Burbidge, President, Nova Scotia Pharmaceutical Association, "Patent medicine legislation and Canadian Pharmaceutical Association." *Canadian Pharmaceutical Journal* 40(10):475.

Canadian Pharmaceutical Journal (1908a). The sale of cocaine. *Canadian Pharmaceutical Journal* 41(8):357.

Canadian Pharmaceutical Journal (1908b). Anti-cocaine bill. *Canadian Pharmaceutical Journal* 41(9):401–402.

Canadian Pharmaceutical Journal (1908c). Cocaine restriction. *Canadian Pharmaceutical Journal* 41(9):404–405.

Canadian Pharmaceutical Journal (1908d). Cocaine pilfering. *Canadian Pharmaceutical Journal* 41(10):456.

Canadian Pharmaceutical Journal (1908e). The sale of cocaine. *Canadian Pharmaceutical Journal* 42(4):176–177.

Canadian Pharmaceutical Journal (1909). Cocaine selling. *Canadian Pharmaceutical Journal* 42(8):396.

Canadian Pharmaceutical Journal (1910). Cocaine selling in Quebec. *Canadian Pharmaceutical Journal* 44(5):212–214.

Canadian Pharmaceutical Journal (1911). Illegal cocaine selling. *Canadian Pharmaceutical Journal* 44(7):306.

Carlin, A. S., Bakker, C. B., Halpern, L., & Post, R. D. (1972). Social facilitation of marijuana intoxication: Impact of social set and pharmacological activity. *Journal of Abnormal Psychology* 80:132–140.

Carlini-Cotrin, B., & Carlini, E. A. (1988). The use of solvents and other drugs among children and adolescents from a low socio-economic background: A study in Sao Paulo, Brazil. *International Journal of Addictions* 23(11):1145–1156.

Caulkins, J. P., Crawford, G. C., & Reuter, P. (1993). *Simulation of Adaptive Response: A Model of Drug Interdiction*. RAND/RP-193. Santa Monica, CA:RAND.

Cheung, Y. W. (1994). In search of harm reduction: A book review of two harm reduction conferences. To be published in *Contemporary Drug Problems*.

Cheung, Y. W., Erickson, P. G., & Landau, T. C. (1991). Experience of crack use: Findings from a community-based sample in Toronto. *Journal of Drug Issues* 21(1):121–141.

Chitwood, D. D. (1985). The Acquisition of Cocaine for Personal Use: Legal and Illegal Sources of (Funds to Purchase) Cocaine. Paper presented at the American Society of Criminology Annual Meeting, San Diego, California, November 13–17.

Chitwood, D. D., & Morningstar, P. J. (1985). Factors which differentiate cocaine users in treatment from non-treatment users. *International Journal of the Addictions* 20:449–460.

Christie, N. (1993). *Crime Control as Industry*. New York: Routledge.

Clark, R. J. (1983). The Nether World of Professionalization: Druggists in Nineteenth-Century Ontario. Paper presented to the History Workshop on Education in Modern Societies, University of Waterloo, Waterloo, Ontario, March 11–13.

Clark, S. C. and McKiernan, W. (1981). Contacts with a Canadian 'street level' drug and crisis centre. 1975–1978. *Bulletin on Narcotics XXXIII: 23–31*.

Clayton, R. R. (1985). Cocaine use in the United States: In a blizzard or just being snowed? In N. J. Kozel & E. H. Adams (eds.), *Cocaine Use in America: Epidemiologic and Clinical Perspectives* (pp. 8–34). Rockville, MD: National Institute on Drug Abuse.

Climent, C. E., & de Aragon, L. V. (1984). Clinical aspects of coca-paste smoking ("basuco") in Columbia. Paper presented at the WHO Advisory Group Meeting on the Adverse Health Consequences of Cocaine and Coca Paste Smoking, Bogotá, September 10–14.

Cohen, J., & Cohen, P. C. (1975). *Applied Multiple Regression/Correlation Analysis for the Behavioral Sciences*. Hillsdale, NJ: Erlbaum.

Cohen, P. (1989). *Cocaine Use in Amsterdam in Non Deviant Subcultures*. Amsterdam: University of Amsterdam.

Cohen, P., & Sas, A. (1993). *Ten Years of Cocaine: A Follow-up Study of 64 Cocaine Users in Amsterdam*. Amsterdam: University of Amsterdam.

Coleman, J., Katz, E., & Menzel, H. (1966). *Medical Innovation—A Diffusion Study*. Indianapolis: Bobbs-Merrill.

Colliver, J. D., & Kopstein, A. N. (1991). Trends in cocaine abuse reflected in emergency room episodes reported to DAWN. *Public Health Reports* 106(1):59–68.

Currie, E. (1985). *Confronting Crime: An American Challenge*. New York: Pantheon.

De Pabon, E. (1984). Epidemiology of Cocaine and Coca Paste in Columbia. Paper presented at the WHO Advisory Group Meeting on Adverse Health Consequences of Cocaine and Coca Paste Smoking, Bogotá, September 10–14.

Desranleau, C. (1984). *La Consommation de Drogues Chez les Jeunes du Secondaire en 1984*. Montreal: La Commission des Ecoles Catholiques de Montreal.

DiNardo, J. (1993). *Law Enforcement, the Price of Cocaine and Cocaine Use.* RAND/RP-192. Santa Monica, CA: RAND.

Dominick, J. R. (1978). Crime and law enforcement in the mass media. In C. Winick (ed.), *Deviance in the Mass Media* (pp. 105–128). Beverly Hills: Sage Publications.

Drug Abuse Warning Network (1991a). *Annual Emergency Room Data 1990: Data from the Drug Abuse Warning Network (DAWN).* Rockville, MD: National Institute on Drug Abuse.

Drug Abuse Warning Network (1991b). *Annual Medical Examiner Data 1990: Data from the Drug Abuse Warning Network (DAWN).* Rockville, MD: National Institute on Drug Abuse.

Drug Enforcement Administration (1985). *The Illicit Drug Situation in the United States and Canada.* Washington, DC: U.S. Department of Justice.

Duster, T. (1970). *The Legislation of Morality: Law, Drugs and Moral Judgement.* New York: Free Press.

Eliany, M., Giesbrecht, N., & Nelson, M. (eds.) (1990). *National Alcohol and Other Drugs Survey: Highlights Report.* Ottawa: Minister of Supply and Services Canada.

Erickson, P. G. (1989). The Law in Addictions: Principles, Practicalities and Prospects. Prepared for the 40th Anniversary Scientific Lecture Series, Addiction Research Foundation, Toronto, Ontario, November 8.

Erickson, P. G. (1990a). A public health approach to demand reduction. *Journal of Drug Issues* 20:563–575.

Erickson, P. G. (1990b). Past, current and future directions in Canadian drug policy. *International Journal of the Addictions* 25:981–1000.

Erickson, P. G. (1992). Recent trends in Canadian drug policy: The decline and resurgence of prohibitionism. *Daedalus* 121(3):239–267.

Erickson, P. G. (1993). Prospects of harm reduction for psychostimulants. In N. Heather, A. Wodak, E. A. Nadelmann, & P. O'Hare (eds.), *Psychoactive Drugs and Harm Reduction: From Faith to Science* (pp. 184–210). London: Whurr Publishers.

Erickson, P. G., & Alexander, B. K. (1989). Cocaine and addictive liability. *Social Pharmacology* 3:249–270.

Erickson, P. G., & Cohen, J. (1994). Preliminary report of "Alcohol and Other Drugs in the Criminal Justice System." Unpublished manuscript, Addiction Research Foundation, Toronto, Ontario.

Erickson, P. G., & Moreau, J. A. E. (1990). A Tale of Two Stimulants: A Content Analysis of Cocaine and Tobacco in Toronto Newspapers. Unpublished manuscript, Addiction Research Foundation, Toronto, Ontario.

Erickson, P. G., & Murray, G. F. (1989). The undeterred cocaine user: Intention to quit and its relationship to perceived legal and health threats. *Contemporary Drug Problems* 16:141–156.

Erickson, P. G., & Ottaway, C. A. (1993). Drugs and social policy. In P. Nathan, J. Langenbucher, B. McCrady, & W. Frankenstein (eds.), *Annual Review of Addictions Research and Treatment.* Volume 3. New York: Pergamon Press.

Erickson, P. G., Watson, V., & Weber, T. (1992). Cocaine users' perception of their health status and the risks of drug use. In P. A. O'Hare, R. Newcombe, A. Matthews, E. C. Buning, & E. Drucker (eds.), *The Reduction of Drug Related Harm* (pp. 82–89). London: Routledge.

Erickson, P. G., & Weber, T. (1994). Cocaine careers, control and consequences: Results from a Canadian study. To be published in *Addiction Research*, 2.

Everitt, B. S. (1980). *Cluster Analysis*. 2nd ed. London: Heineman Educational Books.

Fagan, J., & Chin, K. (1989). Initiation into crack and cocaine: A tale of two epidemics. *Contemporary Drug Problems* 16:579–617.

Faupel, C. E. (1991). *Shooting Dope: Career Patterns of Hard-Core Heroin Users*. Gainesville: University of Florida Press.

Feinberg, S. E. (1977). *The Analysis of Cross-Classified Categorical Data*. Cambridge: MIT Press.

Fischer, B. (1994). Contemporary Canadian drug policy: The blurred line between "maps" and "moves." *International Journal of Drug Policy* 5(2).

Fischman, M. W. and Foltin, R. W. (1992). Self-administration of cocaine by humans: A laboratory perspective. In Ciba Foundation, *Cocaine: Scientific and Social Dimensions* (pp. 165–172). Chichester: Wiley.

Florenzano, R. (1990). Alcoholism and other substance abuse: Preventive programs in Santiago, Chile. *Bulletin of the Pan American Health Organization* 24(11): 86–96.

Flynn, S. E. (1993). *The Transnational Drug Challenge and the New World Order. The Report of the CSIS Project on the Global Drug Trade in the Post–Cold War Era*. Washington, DC: Center for Strategic and International Studies.

Fox, J. (1984). *Linear Statistical Models and Related Methods: With Applications to Social Research*. New York: Wiley.

Freud, S. (1974[1884]). Uber coca. In R. Byck (ed.), *Cocaine Papers* (pp. 49–73). New York: Stonehill Publishing.

Fromberg, E. (1993). Prohibition as a necessary stage in the acculturation of foreign drugs. In N. Heather, A. Wodak, E. A. Nadelmannm & P. O'Hare (eds.), Psychoactive Drugs and Harm Reduction: From Faith to Science (pp. 127–136). London: Whurr Publishers.

Gawin, F. H. and Kleber, H. D. (1985). Cocaine use in a treatment population: Patterns and Diagnostic Distinctions, pp. 182–192. In N. J. Kozel and E. H. Adams (eds.), *Cocaine Use in America: Epidemiologic and Clinical Perspectives. Rockville, MD: National Institute on Drug Abuse*.

Giffen, P. J., Endicott, S., & Lambert, S. (1991). *Panic and Indifference: The Politics of Canada's Drug Laws*. Ottawa: Canadian Centre on Substance Abuse.

Gillies, M. (1978). *The Durham Region Survey: A Preliminary Report. Substudy No. 996*. Toronto: Addiction Research Foundation.

Globe and Mail [Toronto] (1989). Crack use near epidemic, Toronto police warn. February 11.

Golbe, L. I., & Merkin, M. D. (1986). Cerebral infarction in a user of free-base cocaine (crack). *Neurology* 36:1602–1604.

Gold, M. S. (1984). *800-COCAINE*. New York: Bantam Books.

Goldstein, P. J. (1979). *Prostitution and Drugs*. Lexington, MA: Lexington Books.

Goode, E. (1970). *The Marihuana Smokers*. New York: Basic Books.

Goode, E. (1989). *Drugs in American Society*. 3rd ed. New York: Alfred A. Knopf.

Goode, E. (1993). *Drugs in American Society*. 4th ed. New York: McGraw-Hill.

Goodstadt, M. S. (1990). The Future of Substance Abuse Prevention: Etiology, Public Health, and Health Promotion. Unpublished manuscript, Center of Alcohol Studies, Rutgers University, New Brunswick, NJ.

Goodstadt, M. S., Sheppard, M. A., & Chan, G. C. (1984). Non-use and cessation of cannabis use: Neglected foci of drug education. *Addictive Behaviors* 9:21–31.

Griffiths, C. T., & Verdun-Jones, S. N. (1989). *Canadian Criminal Justice*. Toronto: Butterworths.

Grinspoon, L., & Bakalar, J. B. (1976). *Cocaine: A Drug and Its Social Evolution*. New York: Basic Books.

Guest, R. G. (1966). The development of patent medicine legislation. *Applied Therapeutics* 8:786–789.

Hagan, J. L. (1991). *The Disreputable Pleasures*. 3rd ed. Toronto: McGraw-Hill.

Hall, W., Carless, J. M., Homel, P. J., Flaherty, B. J., & Reilly, C. J. (1991). The characteristics of cocaine users among young adults in Sydney. *Medical Journal of Australia* 155:11–14.

Hartgers, C., Van den Hoek, J., Krijnen, P., Van Brussel, G. H., & Coutinho, R. O. (1991). Changes over time in heroin and cocaine use among injecting drug users in Amsterdam, The Netherlands, 1985–1989. *British Journal of Addiction* 86:1091–1097.

Health and Welfare Canada [HWC]. (1985). *Health Promotion Survey: Prepublication Results*. Ottawa: Health Promotion Studies Unit.

Heather, N., Wodak, A., Nadelmann, E., & O'Hare, P. (eds.). (1993). *Psychoactive Drugs and Harm Reduction: From Faith to Science*. London: Whurr Publishers.

Heckathorn, D. D., & Lucas, W. L. (1982). Bridging consensus and conflict theory in drug use research: A unified theoretical perspective. *Journal of Drug Issues* 12:445–455.

Hill, D. B. (1985). Viewer characteristics and agenda setting by television news. *Public Opinion Quarterly* 49:340–350.

Hollander, M. J. and Davis, B. L. (1983). *Trends in Adolescent Alcohol and Drug Use in Vancouver*. Vancouver: Ministry of Health.

House of Commons Debates, Canada (1910–1911a). November 25, 1910.

House of Commons Debates, Canada (1910–1911b). January 26, 1911.

Hunt, D. E., Strug, D. L., Goldsmith, D. S., Lipton, D. S., Spunt, B., Truitt, L., & Robertson, K. A. (1984). An instant shot of "Aah": Cocaine use among methadone clients. *Journal of Psychoactive Drugs* 16:217–227.

Inciardi, J. A. (1988). *Crack Cocaine in Miami*. NIDA Technical Review Meeting on the Epidemiology of Cocaine Use and Abuse, May 3–4. Rockville, MD: National Institute on Drug Abuse.

Jacobs, M. R., & Fehr, K. O. (1987). *Drugs and Drug Abuse: A Reference Text*. 2nd ed. Toronto: Addiction Research Foundation.

Javaid, J. I., Fischman, M. W., Schuster, C. R., Dekirmenjian, H., & Davis, M.

(1978). Cocaine plasma concentration: Relation to physiological and subjective effects in humans. *Science* 202:227–228.

Jeri, F. R. (1984). Coca paste smoking in Latin America: A review of a severe and unabated form of addiction. *Bulletin on Narcotics* 36:15–32.

Johnsson-Smaragdi, U. (1983). *TV Use and Social Interaction in Adolescence.* Stockholm: Almquist and Wiksell International.

Johnston, L. D., O'Malley, P. M., & Bachman, J. G. (1984). *Drugs and American High School Students, 1975–1983.* Rockville, MD: National Institute on Drug Abuse.

Johnston, L. D., O'Malley, P. M., & Bachman, J. G. (1993a). *National Survey Results on Drug Use from the Monitoring the Future Study, 1975–1992.* Vol. 1: *Secondary School Students.* Rockville, MD: National Institute on Drug Abuse.

Johnston, L. D., O'Malley, P. M., & Bachman, J. G. (1993b). *National Survey Results on Drug Use from the Monitoring the Future Study, 1975–1992.* Vol. 2: *College Students and Young Adults.* Rockville, MD: National Institute on Drug Abuse.

Jonas, S. (1990). Solving the drug problem: A public health approach to the reduction of the use and abuse of both the legal and the illegal recreational drugs. *Hofstra Law Review* (Spring).

Jones, R. T. (1971). Marihuana-induced "high": Influence of expectation, setting and previous drug experience. Pharmacological Reviews, 23:359–369.

Kalant, O. J. (1974). The vagaries of drugs. *Addictions* 21:75–80.

Kalant, O. J. (1978). Cocaine. *The Journal* 7(4).

Kaplan, H. B., Martin, S. S., Johnson, R. J., & Robbins, C. A. (1986). Escalation of marijuana use: Application of a general theory of deviant behavior. *Journal of Health and Social Behavior* 27:44–61.

Katz, E., & Lazarsfeld, P. F. (1955). *Personal Influence.* New York: Free Press.

Kennedy, M., Reuter, P., & Riley, K. J. (1993). *A Simple Economic Model of Cocaine Production.* RAND/RP-191. Santa Monica, CA: RAND.

Killorn, J. (1982). *Chemical Use Among P.E.I. Students.* Charlottetown, P.E.I.: Alcohol and Drug Problems Institute.

Kirsh, M. M. (1986). *Designer Drugs.* New York: Free Press.

Kissner, D. G., Lawrence, W. D., Selis, J. E., & Flint, A. (1987). Crack lung: Pulmonary disease caused by cocaine abuse. *American Review of Respiratory Disease* 136:1250–1252.

Kolar, A. F., Brown, B. S., Weddington, W. W., & Ball, J. (1990). A treatment crisis: Cocaine use by clients in methadone maintenance programs. *Journal of Substance Abuse Treatment* 7:101–107.

Kozel, N. J. (1993). *Epidemiologic Trends in Drug Abuse: Community Epidemiological Working Group 1992.* Rockville, MD: National Institute on Drug Abuse.

Kozel, N. J., & Adams, E. H. (eds.). (1985). *Cocaine Use in America: Epidemiologic and Clinical Perspectives.* Rockville, MD: National Institute on Drug Abuse.

Krohn, M. D., Skinner, W. F., Massey, J. L., & Akers, R. L. (1985). Social learning theory and adolescent cigarette smoking: A longitudinal study. *Social Problems* 32:455–473.

Lamarche, P., and Rootman, I. (1988). Drug Use. In I. Rootman, R. Warren, T. Stephens, & L. Peters (eds.), *Canada's Health Promotion Survey: Technical Report*. Ottawa: Health and Welfare Canada.

Lanza-Kaduce, L., Akers, R. L., Krohn, M. D., & Radosvich, M. (1984). Cessation of alcohol and drug use among adolescents: A social learning model. *Deviant Behavior* 5:79–96.

Lazarsfeld, P. F., & Merton, K. (1948). Mass communication, popular taste and organized social action. In L. Bryson (ed.), *Communication of Ideas* (pp. 95–118). New York: Harper and Brothers.

LeCavalier, J. G. (1983). Evaluation of the single convention on narcotic drugs: The Canadian experience. In R. G. Smart, G. F. Murray, & H. D. Archibald (eds.), *International Control of Narcotic Drugs*. Internal Document No. 29(a). Toronto: Addiction Research Foundation.

Le Dain, G. (1973). *Final Report of the Commission of Inquiry into the Non-Medical Use of Drugs*. Ottawa: Information Canada.

Lidz, C. W., & Walker, A. L. (1980). *Heroin, Deviance and Morality*. Beverly Hills: Sage.

Life (1984). Cocaine: America's 100 years of euphoria and despair. *Life*, pp. 57–68.

Lillie-Blanton, M., Anthony, J. C., & Schuster, C. R. (1993). Probing the meaning of racial/ethnic group comparisons in crack cocaine smoking. *Journal of the American Medical Association* 269:993–997.

Lorr, M. (1983). *Cluster Analysis for Social Scientists: Techniques for Analysing and Simplifying Complex Blocks of Data*. San Francisco: Jossey-Bass.

MacKuen, M. B. (1983). Reality, the press, and citizens' political agendas. In C. F. Turner & E. Martin (eds.), *Surveying Subjective Phenomena* (pp. 443–473). New York: Russell Sage Foundation.

Maclean's (1989). A deadly plague of drugs. April 3.

MacNeil, P., Shaffelburg, S., Poulin, C., & Mitic, W. (1991). *Student Drug Use 1991: Technical Report*. Halifax: Nova Scotia Commission on Drug Dependency.

Maier, H. W. (1987 [1926]). *Cocaine Addiction*. (Trans. Oriana J. Kalant.) Toronto: Addiction Research Foundation of Ontario.

Means, L. B., Small, M., Capone, D. M., Condren, R., Peterson, M., & Hayward, B. (1989). Client demographics and outcome in outpatient cocaine treatment. *International Journal of the Addictions* 24(8):765–783.

Medina-Mora, M. E., Tapia, C. R., Rascone, M. L., Solache, G., Otero, B. R., Lazcano, F., & Marino, M. D. (1990). Epidemiological status of drug abuse in Mexico. *Bulletin of the Pan American Health Organization* 24(1):1–11.

Meier, R. F., & Johnson, W. T. (1977). Deterrence as social control: The legal and extralegal production of conformity. *American Sociological Review* 42:292–304.

Metro Toronto Research Group on Drug Use (1992). *Drug Use in Metropolitan Toronto*. Toronto: Metro Toronto Research Group on Drug Use.

Metro Toronto Research Group on Drug Use (1993). *Drug Use in Metropolitan Toronto, February, 1993*. Toronto: Metro Toronto Research Group on Drug Use.

Meyer, N. (1974). *The Seven-Per-Cent Solution*. New York: Ballantine Books.

Miller, J. D., Cisin, I. H., Gardner-Keaton, J., Harrell, A. V., Wirtz, P. W., Abelson, H. I., & Fishburne, P. M. (1982). *National Survey on Drug Abuse: Main Findings 1982*. Rockville, MD: National Institute on Drug Abuse.

Miller, N. S., Gold, M. S., Belkin, B. M., & Klahr, A. L. (1989). The diagnosis of alcohol and cannabis dependence in cocaine dependents and alcohol dependence in their families. *British Journal of Addiction 84*:1491–1498.

Minor, W. W., & Harry, J. (1982). Deterrent and experiential effects in perceptual deterrence research: A replication and extension. *Journal of Research in Crime and Delinquency 19*(2):190–203.

Mirror (1989). Creating a social nightmare. March 15.

Mitchell, C. N. (1990). *The Drug Solution: Regulating Drugs According to Principles of Justice, Efficiency and Democracy*. Ottawa: Carlton University Press.

Mofenson, N. C., Copeland, P., & Carraccio, T. R. (1987). Cocaine and crack: The latest menace. *Contemporary Pediatrics 3*:25–29.

Montreal Medical Journal (1904). Patent medicines. *Montreal Medical Journal 33*(9):656.

Montreal Medical Journal (1906). Patent medicines. *Montreal Medical Journal 35*(4):274–275.

Morgan, P., Wallack, L., & Buchanan, D. (1988). Waging drug wars: Prevention strategy or politics as usual. *Drugs and Society 3*:99–124.

Murillo, E. A. (1990). Drug abuse in Costa Rica: A review of several studies. *Bulletin of the Pan American Health Organization 24*(11):30–34.

Murray, G. F. (1984). The cannabis-cocaine connection: A comparative study of use and users. *Journal of Drug Issues 14*(4):665–675.

Murray, G. F., & Erickson, P. G. (1987). Cross-sectional versus longitudinal research: An empirical test of projected criminality. *Social Science Research 16*:107–118.

Musto, D. F. (1968). A study in cocaine: Sherlock Holmes and Sigmund Freud. *Journal of the American Medical Association 204*(1):125–130.

Musto, D. F. (1986). Lessons of the first cocaine epidemic. *Wall Street Journal*, June 11.

Nasmith, G. G. (1904). Patent medicines and drug foods. *Annual Report of the Ontario Provincial Board of Health 23*(36):113–117.

National Institute on Drug Abuse (1992). *Epidemiological Trends in Drug Abuse: Community Epidemiology Work Group, December 1992*. Rockville, MD: National Institutes on Health.

National Institute on Drug Abuse (1993). *Epidemiologic Trends in Drug Abuse: Community Epidemiology Work Group, June 1993*. Rockville, MD: National Institutes of Health.

Noya Tapia, N. (1984). Coca Paste Effects. Paper presented at the WHO Advisory Group Meeting on Adverse Health Consequences of Cocaine and Coca Paste Smoking, Bogota, September 10–14.

O'Hare, P., Newcombe, R., Matthews, A., Buning, E. D., & Drucker, E. (eds.). (1992). *The Reduction of Drug-Related Harm*. New York: Routledge.

Ontario Provincial Board of Health (1904). *Annual Report.*

Orcutt, J. D. (1978). Normative definitions of intoxicated states: A test of several sociological theories. *Social Problems* 25:385–396.

Orcutt, J. D. (1987). Differential association and marijuana use: A closer look at Sutherland (with a little help from Becker). *Criminology* 25:385–396.

Orcutt, J. D., & Turner, J. B. (1993). Shocking numbers and graphic accounts: Quantified images of drug problems in the print media. *Social Problems* 40:190–206.

Ortiz, A. (1990). Development of a system for registry of information on drug use in Mexico. In *Drug Abuse* (pp. 60–69). Washington, DC: Pan American Health Organization.

Panzica, N. (1990). Legalization no solution to drug problem. *Toronto Star*, August 29, p. A25.

Parke, Davis and Company (1974 [1885]). Coca erythroxylon and its derivatives. In R. Byck (ed.), *Cocaine Papers* (pp. 127–150). New York: Stonehill Publishing.

Peyrot, M. (1984). Cycles of social problem development: The case of drug abuse. *The Sociological Quarterly* 25: 83–96.

Phillips, J. L., & Wynne, R. D. (1980). *Cocaine: The Mystique and the Reality.* New York: Avon Books.

Piazza, M. (1993). Regional patterns of coca and cocaine consumption in Peru. In N. J. Kozel (ed.), *Epidemiologic Trends in Drug Abuse: Community Epidemiological Working Group, 1992.* Rockville, MD: National Institute on Drug Abuse.

Plant, M. A. (1975). *Drug Takers in an English Town.* London: Tavistock.

Pompidou Group: Council of Europe (1990). 13th Meeting of Experts in the Epidemiology of Drug Problems. November 27–30, Strasbourg, Germany.

Porter, J. (1965). *The Vertical Mosaic.* Toronto: University of Toronto Press.

Powell, D. H. (1983). A pilot study of occasional heroin users. *Archives of General Psychiatry* 28:586–594.

Price, R. (1992). *Clockers.* New York: Avon Books.

Raison, A. V. (1967). *A Brief History of Pharmacy in Canada.* Mimeographed. Toronto: Canadian Pharmaceutical Association.

Reinarman, C. (1980). Crack in context: Politics and media in the making of a drug scare. *Contemporary Drug Problems,* 16:535–577.

Reinarman, C., & Levine, H. G. (1989). The crack attack: Media and politics in America's latest drug scare. In J. Best (ed.), *Images of Issues: Current Perspectives on Social Problems.* New York: Aldine deGruyter.

Riesman, D. (1961). *The Lonely Crowd: A Study of the Changing American Character.* New Haven: Yale University Press.

Rose, M. R., Brown, B. S., & Haertzen, C. A. (1989). Comparison of the characteristics and functioning of cocaine treatment and cocaine research subjects. *American Journal of Drug and Alcohol Abuse* 15(3):251–260.

Royal Canadian Mounted Police (1985). *National Drug Intelligence Estimate, 1984–1985.* Ottawa: Supply and Services Canada.

Royal Canadian Mounted Police (1988). *National Drug Intelligence Estimate, 1987/1988*. Ottawa: Minister of Supply and Services Canada.

Royal Canadian Mounted Police (1989). *National Drug Intelligence Estimates, 1988/1989*. Ottawa: Minister of Supply and Services Canada.

Rutherford, P. (1974). Introduction. In P. Rutherford (ed.), *Saving the Canadian City: The First Phase, 1880–1920* (pp. ix–xxiii). Toronto: University of Toronto Press.

Rutherford, P. (1982). *A Victorian Authority: The Daily Press in Late Nineteenth-Century Canada*. Toronto: University of Toronto Press.

Saltzman, L., Paternoster, R., Waldo, G. P., & Chiricos, T. G. (1982). Deterrent and experiential effects: the problem of causal order in perceptual deterrence research. *Journal of Research in Crime and Delinquency* 19(2): 172–189.

Sarinana, M.E., Maya, M., and Aguitar, M.A. (1982). Consum de sustancios tobacos y tabaco en la pablacion estudiants de 14 a 18 anos del Distute Federal y Zona Metropolitana: Medicion Transversal, 1980. Unpublished paper. Mexico City: The Mexico Institute of Psychiatry.

Schnoll, S.J., Karrigan, J., Kitchen, S.B., Daghestani, A., & Hansen, T. (1985). Characteristics of cocaine abusers presenting for treatment. In N.J. Kozel & E.H. Adams (eds.), *Cocaine Use in America: Epidemiologic and Clinical Perspectives* (pp. 171–181). Rockville, MD: National Institute on Drug Abuse.

Schuster, C.R., & Fischman, M.W. (1985). Characteristics of humans volunteering for a cocaine research project, In N.J. Kozel & E.H. Adams (eds.), *Cocaine Use in America: Epidemiologic and Clinical Perspectives* (pp. 158–170). Rockville, MD: National Institute on Drug Abuse.

Schwartz, E. S., Feinglass, S. J., & Drucker, C. (1973). Popular music and drug lyrics: Analysis of a scapegoat. In *Drug Use in America: Problem and Perspective* (pp. 718–746). Washington, DC: U.S. Government Printing Office.

Seiden, M. H. (1974). *Who Controls the Mass Media? Popular Myths and Economic Realities*. New York: Basic Books.

Sessional Papers: Canada (1906). To an order of the House of Commons, dated April 23, 1906, for a copy of the Report of A.E. DuBerger on the Drug and Proprietary Medicine Trade of Canada. *Sessional Papers* 40(14):No. 125.

Sher, K. J. (1985). Subjective effects of alcohol: The influence of setting and individual differences in alcohol expectancies. *Journal of Studies on Alcohol* 46:137–146.

Siegel, R. K. (1978). Cocaine hallucinations. *American Journal of Psychiatry* 135(3):309–314.

Siegel, R. K. (1980). Long term effects of recreational cocaine use: A four year study. In F. R. Jeri (ed.), *Cocaine 1980* (pp. 11–16). Lima: Pacific Press.

Siegel, R. K. (1982a). History of cocaine smoking. *Journal of Psychoactive Drugs* 14(4):277–299.

Siegel, R.K. (1982b). Cocaine free base abuse: A new smoking disorder. *Journal of Psychoactive Drugs* 14(4): 321–337.

Siegel, R. K. (1984). Cocaine and the privileged class: A review of historical and contemporary images. *Advances in Alcohol and Substance Abuse* 4:37–49.

Siegel, R. K. (1985). New patterns of cocaine use: Changing doses and routes. In

N. J. Kozel & E. H. Adams (eds.), *Cocaine Use in America: Epidemiologic and Clinical Perspectives* (pp. 204–220). Rockville, MD: National Institute on Drug Abuse.

Singh, B. K. (1978). Deterrence from drug offenses. In J. Cramer (ed.), *Preventing Crime* (pp. 163–183). Beverly Hills: Sage Publications.

Smart, R.G., & Adlaf, E.M. (1984). *Alcohol and Drug Use Among Ontario Adults in 1984 and Changes Since 1982*. Toronto: Addiction Research Foundation.

Smart, R. G. (1988). "Crack" cocaine use in Canada: A new epidemic? *American Journal of Epidemiology*, 127(6):1315—1317

Smart, R. G. (1991). Crack cocaine use: A review of prevalence and adverse effects. *American Journal of Drug and Alcohol Abuse* 17:13–26.

Smart, R. G., & Adlaf, E. M. (1990). Trends in treatment admissions for cocaine and other drug abusers. *Canadian Journal of Psychiatry* 35(7):621–623.

Smart, R. G., Adlaf, E. M., Walsh, G. W., & Zdanowicz, Y. M. (1992). *Drifting and Doing: Changes in Drug Use Among Toronto Street Youth, 1990–1992*. Toronto: Addiction Research Foundation.

Smart, R.G., Liban, C., and Brown, G. (1981). Cocaine use among adults and students. *Canadian Journal of Public Health* 72:433–438.

Smart, R. G., & Mann, R. E. (1994). The relative importance of treatment, health promotion and alcohol controls in the decrease of alcohol consumption problems in Ontario 1975–1993. Unpublished manuscript, Addiction Research Foundation, Toronto, Ontario.

Smart, R. G., Ogborne, A. C., & Newton-Taylor, B. (1990). Drug abuse and alcohol problems among cocaine abusers in an assessment/referral service. *British Journal of Addiction* 85:1595–1598.

Smart, R. G., & Patterson, S. D. (1990). Comparison of alcohol, tobacco and drug use among students and delinquents in the Bahamas. *Bulletin of the Pan American Health Organization* 24(11):39–45.

Smith, D. (1986). Cocaine-alcohol abuse: Epidemiological, diagnostic and treatment considerations. *Journal of Psychoactive Drugs* 18(2):117–129.

Smith, D. E., & Seymour, R. B. (1985). Dream becomes nightmare: Adverse reactions to LSD. *Journal of Psychoactive Drugs* 17:297–303.

Snyder, C. A., Wood, R. W., Graefe, J. F., Bowers, A., & Magar, K. (1988). Crack smoke is a respirable aerosol of cocaine base. *Pharmacology, Biochemistry and Behavior* 29:93–95.

Solomon, E., Hammond, T., & Langdon, S. (1985). *Drug and Alcohol Law for Canadians*. 2nd ed. Toronto: Addiction Research Foundation.

Soucy, P. (1953). The proprietary or Patent Medicine Act of Canada. *Food Drug Cosmetic Law Journal* 8:706–716.

Spotts, J. V., & Shontz, F. C. (1980). *Cocaine Users: A Representative Case Approach*. New York: Free Press.

Stamler, R. T., Fahlman, R. C., & Keele, S. A. (1984). Illicit traffic and abuse of cocaine. *United Nations Bulletin on Narcotic Drugs* 36(2):45–55.

Stephens, T., & Fowler Graham, D. (1993). *Canada's Health Promotion Survey 1990: Technical Report*. Ottawa: Minister of Supply and Services Canada.

Stone, N., Fromme, M., and Kagan, D. (1984). *Cocaine: Seduction and Solution.* New York: Crown.

Strang, J., Griffiths, P., & Gossop, M. (1990). Crack and cocaine use in South London drug addicts: 1987–1989. *British Journal of Addiction* 85:193–196.

Substance Abuse & Mental Health Services Administration [SAMHSA] (1993). *National Household Survey on Drug Abuse: Main Findings 1991.* Rockville: National Institute on Drug Abuse.

Swainson, D. (1972). *Oliver Mowat's Ontario.* Toronto: Macmillan.

The Journal of the American Medical Association (1897). Chronic cocainism from catarrh snuff. *Journal of the American Medical Association* 28:1092.

The Journal (1982). RCMP watching drug patterns as U.S. puts squeeze on Florida. *The Journal* 11(7):1.

The Journal (1985). Most Canadian users are social sniffers: Cocaine use delineated. *The Journal* 14(5):1.

The Journal (1986). "Crack": Threat to Canada being overplayed. *The Journal* 15(8):1.

Therapeutic Gazette (1880). Coca in the opium habit. (Excerpt from Louisville Medical News). *Therapeutic Gazette* 1(7):215.

Therapeutic Gazette (1881). Coca in the opium habit. *Therapeutic Gazette* 2(2):79.

Thomas, W. I., & Thomas, D. S. (1928). *The Child in America.* New York: Knopf.

Toronto Star (1989a). New group joins fight to curb cocaine trade. February 24.

Toronto Star (1989b). Metro drug trade wide open. May 7.

Toronto Star (1989c). "Aroused" public needed to fight drugs, mayor says. June 16.

Toronto Star (1990). Drug seizures double as charges jump 36%. February 1.

Toronto Star (1992). Quotation excerpted from *Toronto Star*, June 3, 1905, and reprinted. February 24, p. A2.

Toronto Sun (1985). We're cocaine city. Cocaine epidemic in Metro. February 15, pp. 1, 2.

Toronto Sun (1986). Editorial. September 21.

Trebach, A. S. (1987). *The Great Drug War.* New York: Macmillan.

Trinkoff, A. M., Ritter, C., & Anthony, J. C. (1990). The prevalence of self-reported consequences of cocaine use: An exploratory and descriptive analysis. *Drug and Alcohol Dependence* 26:217–225.

Uchtenhagen, A. (1984). Global Assessment and Epidemiology of Cocaine in Europe. Paper presented at the WHO Advisory Group Meeting on Adverse Health Consequences of Cocaine and Coca Paste Smoking, Bogota, September 10–14, 1984.

Usprich, S. J., & Solomon, R. M. (1993). A critique of the proposed Psychoactive Substance Control Act. *Criminal Law Quarterly* 35:211–240.

Waldorf, D., Murphy, S., Reinarman, C., & Joyce, B. (1977). *Doing Coke: An Ethnography of Cocaine Users and Sellers.* Washington, DC: Drug Abuse Council.

Waldorf, D., Reinarman, C., & Murphy, S. (1991). *Cocaine Changes.* Philadelphia: Temple University Press.

Wallace, B. C. (1990a). Crack cocaine smokers as adult children of alcoholics: The dysfunctional family link. *Journal of Substance Abuse Treatment* 7:89–100.

Wallace, B. C. (1990b). Crack addiction: Treatment and recovery issues. *Contemporary Drug Problems* 17:79–119.

Washton, A. M., Gold, M., & Pottash, A. C. (1984). Upper-income cocaine abusers. *Advances in Alcohol and Substance Abuse* 4:51–57.

Westermeyer, J. (1987). Cultural patterns of drug and alcohol use: An analysis of host and agent in the cultural environment. *Bulletin on Narcotics* 39:11–27.

Williams, T. (1989). *The Cocaine Kids: The Inside Story of a Teenage Drug Ring.* Reading, MA: Addison-Wesley.

Winick, C. (1959). The use of drugs by jazz musicians. *Social Problems* 7:240–253.

Winick, C. (1978). *Deviance and Mass Media.* Beverly Hills: Sage Publications.

Winick, C. (1991). Social behavior, public policy, and nonharmful drug use. *Milbank Quarterly* 69:437–459.

Wisotsky, S. (1983). Exposing the war on cocaine: The futility and destructiveness of prohibition. *Wisconsin Law Review* 6:1305–1426.

Wisotsky, S. (1986). *Breaking the Impasse in the War on Drugs.* Westport, CT: Greenwood Press.

World Health Organization (1984). Report of Advisory Group Meeting on Adverse Health Consequences of Cocaine and Coca Paste Smoking, Bogotá, September 10–14.

World Health Organization (1993). *Report of the WHO Expert Committee on Drug Dependence.* Twenty-eighth Report. Geneva: World Health Organization.

Wright, C. R. (1975). *Mass Communication: A Sociological Perspective.* New York: Random House.

Zinberg, N. E. (1984). *Drug, Set and Setting: The Basis for Controlled Intoxicant Use.* New Haven: Yale University Press.

Index

About the Authors

Patricia G. Erickson is a senior scientist with the Addiction Research Foundation in Toronto, Canada, where she has been conducting criminological research since 1973. She received her Ph.D. from Glasgow University, Scotland in Criminology/Social Administration in 1983. She has published several books and many articles in the field of addictions, and has acted as an adviser to the World Health Organization Project on Cocaine. Dr. Erickson is also Adjunct Professor in the Department of Sociology, University of Toronto, and is just beginning a term there as the Director of the Collaborative Program on Alcohol, Tobacco, and other Psychoactive Substances.

Edward M. Adlaf has recently completed his work toward a Ph.D. in Sociology at York University. He is a scientist in the Social & Evaluation Research Department of the Addiction Research Foundation. His research interests include survey methodology, with particular emphasis on drug use epidemiology. Along with Reginald Smart, he is Co-Director of the Ontario Student Drug Use Survey. He has published widely in the areas of alcohol and drug use, and has served as a consultant to the World Health Organization, Pan American Health Organization, and the governments of Canada and Mexico.

Reginald G. Smart got his Ph.D. in Psychology from the University of Toronto in 1963. He has been with the Addiction Research Foundation in various roles since that time. His main field is the epidemiology of drug and alcohol use. He has published many papers and books on drug abuse, and much of his work has an international flavour. He has been involved in many projects on drug abuse with the World Health Organization, other international agencies, and research institutions in other countries. His most recent book is *The Smart Report: Substance Abuse and Canadian Youth*.

Glenn F. Murray has an M.A. in criminology from the University of Toronto and has several publications in law, criminology and drug journals. He was a research associate in the Prevention Studies Department of the Addiction Research Foundation from 1979 to 1986, when he joined the provincial government of Ontario as a policy analyst. Glenn Murray has a long standing interest in the social history of Canadian drug laws.

Contributing Author

Yuet W. Cheung received his Ph.D. from the University of Toronto in 1982. After teaching sociology at The Chinese University of Hong Kong, in 1988 he joined the Addiction Research Foundation as a Research Scientist. He is the author of *Missionary Medicine in China* and some 30 journal articles or book chapters. In 1992 he rejoined the faculty of The Chinese University of Hong Kong and is continuing his research interest in the use of alcohol and other drugs in the Hong Kong community.